Improving Quality in Outpatient Services

Improving Quality in Outpatient Services

Carole Guinane, RN, MBA
Noreen Davis, RN, MPH

Foreword by Kevin M. Fickenscher, MD

CRC Press
Taylor & Francis Group
Boca Raton   London   New York

CRC Press is an imprint of the
Taylor & Francis Group, an **informa** business

A PRODUCTIVITY PRESS BOOK

CRC Press
Taylor & Francis Group
6000 Broken Sound Parkway NW, Suite 300
Boca Raton, FL 33487-2742

Printed in the United States of America on acid-free paper
Version Date: 20110511

International Standard Book Number: 978-1-4398-5060-2 (Hardback)

Visit the Taylor & Francis Web site at
http://www.taylorandfrancis.com

and the CRC Press Web site at
http://www.crcpress.com

Contents

Foreword

Improving Quality in the Outpatient Setting

As a student of the healthcare management literature and a physician executive involved in leading healthcare organizations, I'm always searching for pragmatic materials that provide a roadmap for the path forward in our complex and changing healthcare environment. I'm also interested in "thought leadership" pieces that help all of us to frame our approach on the three critical issues of our time: increasing quality, enhancing service, and reducing the cost of healthcare. These are the prime objectives that face our industry now and into the foreseeable future. Unfortunately, too much of the literature provides a conceptual framework without the practical elements. *Improving Quality in Outpatient Services* hits the mark as both a roadmap and practical guide.

First and foremost, Carole Guinane and Noreen Davis bring a wealth of practical experience to the table which is amply displayed in each chapter. Their nursing backgrounds coupled with their strong business and public health experiences in ambulatory care provide a foundation for understanding critical segments of the industry where change is sweeping through the care delivery model.

As we all know, the advent of comprehensive, coordinated care (C3) models are becoming the norm, primarily because of the efficiency and effectiveness of the approach in providing healthcare services. The major component of all such models is an effective ambulatory care model, which has been woefully underestimated and underinvested under traditional approaches. We should all anticipate that ambulatory care will become the primary focus for care delivery extending from chronic congestive heart failure patients to the usual acute care problem. Guinane and Davis bring us a wealth of pragmatic advice on how to traverse the complexities of ambulatory care in the new environment of healthcare reform.

Whether you are pursuing an accountable care organization (ACO), primary care medical home (PCMH), bundled payments, or other similar model, the clear challenge in the future will be on how to best organize and deliver quality ambulatory care services. It is the diligent attention to standards, guidelines, and protocols in the outpatient setting that will provide the roadmap forward, and *Improving Quality in Outpatient Services* provides the foundation for moving from rhetoric into reality.

From the opening chapter, where the authors describe the fact that "the quality canvas is changing," to the Appendices, where detailed information is provided on where and how to apply for certification, the authors have provided a credible overview of the elements of ambulatory care management.

Improving Quality in Outpatient Services provides not only a broad visionary direction for where we need to go in outpatient care management, but also provides the details that must be considered as part of our efforts to lead the future of healthcare delivery. Ambulatory and outpatient care are the fastest growing segments of the healthcare industry, and it's not just about healthcare reform. As leaders in healthcare, we increasingly recognize that the provision of care on a more efficient and effective basis is the norm to which we must aspire. Simply admitting people to institutions does not meet that standard. As a result, we must consider alternative delivery models—most of which are ambulatory in nature.

Guinane and Davis provide the path for moving forward. The ambulatory environment has been captive to a cottage industry model which is no longer sustainable. We need standards. We need models. We need to embrace care delivery requirements. *Improving Quality in Outpatient Services* establishes the critical foundation for how we—as leaders in healthcare—can carry forward an approach to care delivery that meets and exceeds the requirements of consumers across the nation.

There are ample checklists and "to do" items included in this pragmatic book on outpatient care and management. We need to accept their challenge that ambulatory care is *the future* and requires our *involvement*. We have a significant distance to go in our quest for increasing the quality of care, let alone enhancing service and decreasing cost. Starting with ambulatory care would be a good place to begin. Guinane and Davis provide the roadmap. We need to implement their ideas and embrace the changes they suggest.

Kevin Fickenscher, MD
Washington, DC
December 2010

Preface

Apprehension, uncertainty, waiting, expectation, fear of surprise, do a patient more harm than any exertion.

—Florence Nightingale

Overview

Two bigger-than-life myths exist—that outpatient care is easy and safe and that anyone can do it.

In all fairness, if an outpatient program does not invest in quality and safety programs, or attempt to understand licensing and regulatory requirements, and loosely oversees the service, then it would appear to be easy, safe, and that anyone could do it.

With this book, we strive to shed some light on the opportunities that abound in outpatient services and to debunk these two myths. Outpatient care is rich with quality offerings, accrediting agencies, and leadership credentialing to promote excellence. However, what is needed is investment in stronger oversight, mandatory licensing, leadership expectations, and standards across states and outpatient service lines.

Maybe someday outpatient quality and safety programs will be prolific and patients will enjoy transparency of information from all care channels and the myths will have taken the path of dragons and fairy tales. Finally, it's our belief that if consumers had a choice, they would not select the care pathway from those that run mythical outpatient programs.

Bad Apples and Apple Pie

An analogy that comes to mind when thinking about healthcare quality has to do with apple pie and bad apples. It's easy to take the bad apple approach, reacting only to errors, egregious acts, and horrific outcomes. This fosters a crisis management quality method. On the flip side, if the good apples are discovered and used, the apple pie created would be desired by all, hopefully decreasing the need to invest so much time with bad apples.

Choose the good apple approach to grow and prosper, but know that bad apples do exist, requiring specific interventions to ameliorate these situations.

Bad Apple Quality can be described as:

1. Punitive and secretive
2. Poor communication
3. Fostering a culture of fear
4. Ostrich quality—burying one's head in the sand to avoid tough issues
5. Doing only what's needed to get by
6. Not having a passion for the work and outcomes
7. Living in a bubble
8. Groupthink behavior
9. Mavericks, heroes, and silos
10. Ceasing to learn or to think that others may do something better

Apple Pie Quality can be described as:

1. Prevention is practiced
2. Patients come first
3. Process oriented
4. Innovative and passionate, but realistic
5. Knows the value of system thinking
6. Deconstructs silos
7. Creates a synergistic culture of quality and safety
8. Huddles daily with staff
9. Believes in measurement and understands variation
10. Benchmarks against the best of the best

Chapter Summaries

This book consists of twelve chapters. Chapter 1 delivers an overview of out-patient healthcare, a high-level view of opportunities, existing national quality programs, and the challenges we face. Chapter 2 outlines the governance, medical staff, and quality structures required to create, implement, and maintain strong outpatient quality programs. Chapter 3 explores the world of human connections, and concentrates on the importance of taking care of our customers.

Chapter 4 provides an outline of needed policies, procedures, and plans, and stresses the importance of the written word to deliver quality healthcare services. Chapter 5 discusses the human resources (HR) factor, and what's essential to properly address the needs of the people who serve our patients in outpatient care settings. Chapter 6 describes measurement examples, and delves into scientific methods and analytic tools.

Chapter 7 introduces medication management strategies, and Chapter 8 delivers infection prevention quality and safety applications for outpatient services. Both are highly complex, but if not implemented appropriately would contribute to potentially deadly outcomes for our patients. Chapter 9 covers clinical documentation and the steps needed to create a comprehensive approach to telling the patient's story.

Chapter 10 continues with safety themes by concentrating on risk prevention and error elimination, thus stirring our thinking about what we can do to enhance our safety programs for all who touch outpatient care. Chapter 11 enters the world of licensing, accreditation, deemed status, and certification for ambulatory programs. Chapter 12 encourages practice, drills, and planning for worst case scenarios.

Appendices augment the chapter information, delivering tools for medical record review, policy and procedure checklists, measurement, and state resources. A glossary covers key terms for outpatient quality and safety.

Purposeful Omissions

Excellent references and teaching tools already exist to help healthcare professionals with their journey. Therefore, the wheel was not created once again. It isn't our aim to retool quality theory or patient safety foundations. Rather, we chose to stimulate the reader with practical applications, stories, and outpatient quality and safety examples.

Caregivers want to drive the way we take care of our patients. We want to wrap our processes around their needs. To drive the care delivery processes requires knowledge of available evidence-based literature and studies. We did not spend a great deal of time on evidence-based medicine. We do think there is value in this knowledge, but didn't feel this book was the proper venue for this information.

Even though we won't cover evidence-based information, we do want to emphasize the importance of reducing variation in care processes. Variation in healthcare contributes to a great deal of cost associated with care. We encourage outpatient leaders to hold weekly meetings to address variation. Map out the process and study the findings. Make it safe to ask questions and to work collegially. We do not cover the theory of transactional leadership as it pertains to physician relationships and variation. We don't believe that physicians are motivated by reward and punishment and a clear chain of command. Physicians do not cede authority for their care delivery decisions to a manager. Instead, we look at partnering with physicians, leaders, and caregivers as the way to reduce unnecessary variation.

We also acknowledge that a *what's in it for me* (WIIFM) mentality can and does exist. WIIFM, fondly known as the radio station of caregivers, is common when anything new is presented in the healthcare arena. We have to attempt to tune in to the needs of the population of caregivers and clearly articulate what's in it for them. There are scores of books dedicated to change management and how to get people to buy in. Once again, that's not the purpose of this book.

We have concentrated on what we believe to be the most pertinent sources for references at the end of chapters, with some imbedded in the chapters or the appendices. It's our hope that this book, along with the references, will ignite a passion for quality and safety application for those who directly and indirectly influence the care of our patients. It's also our hope that our selected omissions do not deter from the path we all need to take to make a difference and to achieve world-class status in all avenues of ambulatory care delivery.

About the Authors

Carole Guinane RN, MBA. Carole's quality journey began in 1989 as a senior leader and Vice President at Parkview Episcopal Medical Center in Pueblo, Colorado. Parkview's success story was published in 1992 by The Joint Commission, with the foreword of the book written by Donald M. Berwick, MD. The book, *Striving for Improvement: Six Hospitals in Search of Quality*, shared the process, methods, and rewards that our leadership team, employees, and physicians experienced. It was magical. Applying quality principles to clinical processes was new to healthcare at the time, but groundbreaking results occurred. Carole took the lessons learned from those early days and continued to grow her knowledge base for operational and clinical improvement application.

Carole has worked as Chief Clinical and Compliance Officer for an ambulatory surgery center company, Vice President of Medical Staff Services and Quality for a healthcare system, Vice President for Applied Business Science and Education for a specialty hospital and healthcare system, Consultant and Clinical Improvement Director for a Center for Continuous Improvement and Innovation, and Vice President for Ambulatory Clinical Improvement and ASC Clinical Operations for an integrated healthcare system. She has had the pleasure of building and growing quality and clinical operations programs for large healthcare systems, small and rural hospitals, ambulatory surgery centers, insurance companies, and ambulatory entities. Carole is a trained Six Sigma Black Belt. She has published books and journal articles on clinical pathways, quality tools, Six Sigma, clinical operations, and consumer-driven healthcare.

Noreen Davis RN, BSN, MPH. Noreen earned her BSN from St. Louis University and her master's in public health from the University of North Carolina in Chapel Hill. Her healthcare journey began in cardiovascular care and heart and lung transplantation. As a trained Six Sigma Black Belt, she is an experienced healthcare quality and operations executive. She has worked as a quality consultant for ambulatory programs, and has experience in assisting with

National Committee for Quality Assurance (NCQA) accreditation. Noreen has several years experience supporting outcomes measurement and analysis for both hospitals and outpatient facilities.

Her management experience includes positions with direct responsibility for transplant, clinical research, patient safety, performance improvement, accreditation for hospital and ambulatory care settings, infection prevention and control, and clinical case management. Her current responsibilities include management and development of evidence-based shared baselines across all service lines for a large healthcare system in conjunction with the development of comprehensive electronic medical records (EMRs) and computerized order entry for ambulatory and acute settings. Noreen has published articles on healthcare quality and Six Sigma.

Acknowledgments

We are greatly indebted to Kristine Mednansky, senior editor at CRC Press, a Taylor & Francis Group. No one helped us more, as this book was brought to life because of her belief in our vision for outpatient quality.

Our gratitude is extended to Marsha Pronin, our project coordinator at Taylor & Francis. As an eagle eye proofreader and editor, she made our job so much easier.

Our sincere thanks are due to Kidist Kassahun, MHA. Chapter 11 and Appendix I required painstaking research, and she exceeded our expectations. Her exhaustive work and prudent skills contributed significantly to the book, and we are grateful.

We can't possibly list all of the people who have touched our lives in the healthcare and quality world. There have been so many teachers along the way. We are eternally grateful to the quality champions and leaders that really do get it. To these heroes and patient safety warriors, thank you.

From Carole

When Kris and I first talked about the possibility of this book, I spent several months living with the idea of outpatient quality and what it means. What motivated me most of all were my grandchildren, as I want their healthcare journey to be awesome and free from life-changing errors and devastating events. They are often touched by outpatient services and healthcare practitioners. They deserve the absolute best and I will champion this cause for as long as I live.

More recently, Coumadin errors nearly killed a loved one. To make matters worse, the physician blamed the patient for the errors, which was not the case. Poor follow-up for this new medication, a lack of lab testing to monitor levels, and blaming the patient while he was in the cardiac care unit (CCU) all spell failure. Why did this have to happen? Mythical outpatient care—promoting errors, insensitive care practices, and lack of an embedded outpatient quality program.

I must thank my husband, Tom. Many weekends were spent on the computer, locked away in my home office, and he kept me sane by providing support, nourishment, and encouragement. My daughter Carissa and I bounced around ideas, and she never seemed to lose her enthusiasm for the spirit of this book. Just talking to her helped to clarify my thinking. Thanks to my son, Jordon, for believing in me. As always, my family offered unending sources of inspiration. Thanks to Noreen, my writing partner and friend. I couldn't have done it without her.

This book is dedicated to my grandchildren, Darcy Elizabeth, Carolyn Rose, William Alexander, and Rowan Grace, with love.

From Noreen

My healthcare journey began as a teen at the hospital where my mom coached and mentored many nursing students. I was not sure I could possibly be as skilled as she was in caring for her intensive care patients. After twenty-five years in healthcare, I have learned that knowledge and skill are not just taught, but are acquired over time from lessons learned along the way. Hopefully this book shares some of those pearls of wisdom.

I want to thank Carole, my true friend, who knows all of my strengths and weaknesses. She inspired me to take this journey and I am truly grateful for the chance to write this book. It is rare to find someone who shares the same passion for life and work.

I also want to thank my husband for his never-ending patience and support in the past year. Many challenges in family and work life have taken time away from us and yet he never questioned my desire to write and spend time on this project.

This book is dedicated to my three children Connor Michael, Brenna Catherine, and Cara Elizabeth Davis.

Chapter 1

Defining Outpatient Healthcare

> I believe strongly and passionately that every American has a right to good health care that is effective, accessible, and affordable, that serves you from infancy through old age, that allows you to go to practitioners and facilities of your choosing, and that offers a broad range of therapeutic options.
>
> —Andrew Weil, MD

Outpatient Quality

Outpatient healthcare is growing rapidly and there continues to be movement of care from inpatient to outpatient locations. It can be said that the majority of care delivered to patients in the United States is provided in the outpatient setting. According to the National Quality Forum, more than one billion outpatient encounters occur ever year.

The outpatient market produces wide variation in quality practices. Inconsistent oversight by regulatory, licensing, accreditation, and benchmarking agencies contributes to variation, as do many other variables. Outpatient quality programs rely on the honor system for the most part.

Economic prosperity for outpatient programs depends on reducing variation, improving efficiencies, and implementing predictive care models within a challenging reimbursement system. Healthcare reform initiatives beg that we think about efficiency and effective care models for outpatient services. Accountable care organizations (ACOs), if successful, will push inpatient and outpatient entities together in a collaborative model to share in Medicare reimbursement. It comes down to savings for Medicare. The jury is out as to whether this will be successful, and what outcomes of care will materialize. Regardless, the quality canvas is changing.

Building and delivering a culture of quality and safety is absolutely necessary if true prosperity is to occur and if we are to make outpatient programs affordable and accessible.

For the purpose of this book, the following definition will be used when speaking about outpatient healthcare:

> Outpatient services consist of treatment performed without requiring an inpatient stay.
> Outpatient care is also called ambulatory care.

The patient may be treated in a variety of settings, including, but not limited to:

- Ambulatory surgery centers (ASCs)
- Minute clinics
- Urgent care facilities
- Physician practices
- Imaging centers
- Oncology centers
- Dialysis centers
- Homecare
- Freestanding emergency centers
- Endoscopy centers
- Chiropractors
- Aesthetician and health spas
- Emergency departments

National Health Statistics Reports

The Centers for Disease Control and Prevention (CDC), National Center for Health Statistics (NCHS), Division of Health Care Statistics conducts surveys of healthcare providers and facilities such as hospitals, ambulatory surgery centers, and physicians. Encounters are tracked, along with the characteristics of those who seek encounters. This "family" of surveys is called the National Health Care Survey (NHCS).

Table 1.1 provides a snapshot of data gleaned from the *Ambulatory Medical Care Utilization Estimates for 2006* survey. Clearly, ambulatory visits overall are increasing, demonstrating a steady climb in numbers since 1996. Medication therapy goes hand in hand with ambulatory visits, presenting a need to manage patient medications across the continuum. Information on medication safety can be found in Chapter 7. Spend some time reviewing your medication practices in your facility, as errors abound in the sector. Volume alone dictates a need for attention to medication practices.

An astounding 300 percent increase in freestanding ASC visits from 1996 to 2006 was explained in the *Ambulatory Surgery in the United States, 2006* report. Table 1.2 displays key findings from this report. The migration from hospital ambulatory surgery programs to freestanding centers demonstrates a healthcare transformation that is underway. This trend will continue to escalate, and

Table 1.1   2006 Ambulatory Medical Care Utilization

Ambulatory Medical Care Utilization	Results
Rate of visits	1.1 billion visits to physician offices, EDs, and hospital outpatient departments— resulting in 381.9 visits per 100 persons annually in 2006.
Visit rates to medical specialty offices	29% increase from 1996 to 2006.
Hospital outpatient department visits	Went from 25.4 per 100 persons in 1996 to 34.7 visits per 100 persons in 2006.
Emergency department visits	Increased from 34.1 per 100 persons in 1996 to 40.4 visits per 100 persons in 2006.
Ambulatory care visits	18.3% of all visits in 2006 were for conditions such as routine checkups and pregnancy exams.
Medications	Seven out of ten ambulatory care visits had at least one medication provided, prescribed, or continued in 2006. Amounted to 2.6 billion drugs overall.
Analgesics	Accounted for 13.6 drugs per 100 drugs prescribed, most often in primary care and ED visits in 2006.

Table 1.2   2006 Ambulatory Surgery Utilization

ASC Utilization	Results
Rate of visits to freestanding ASCs	Increased 300% from 1996 to 2006
Rate of visits to hospital-based surgery centers	Remained unchanged from 1996 to 2006
34.7 million ASC visits with 53.3 million surgical and nonsurgical procedures performed in 2006	Of the 34.7 million visits, 19.9 million occurred in hospitals and 14.9 in freestanding ASCs.
Average times	Higher for hospital-based ASCs than for freestanding ASCs: • 61.7 minutes compared with 43.2 minutes for time in the operating room • 34.2 minutes compared to 25.1 minutes for time spent in surgery • 79 minutes compared to 53.1 minutes for postoperative recovery room time • 146.6 minutes compared with 97.7 minutes for overall time
Gender	Females had significantly more ASC visits at 20 million versus 14.7 million for males.
Discharge disposition	93.1% routine discharge with 0.8 percent admitted as inpatients for 2006.
Anesthesia	30.7% of ASC visits received general anesthesia alone, 20.8% received IV anesthesia only, 20.8% received multiple types of anesthesia
Diagnoses	Leading diagnoses included cataract, benign neoplasms, malignant neoplasms, diseases of the esophagus, and diverticula of the intestine.
Procedures	Procedures performed most often in an ASC: endoscopies of the large intestine and small intestine, and extraction of lens for cataract surgery.
Payors	More than half of outpatient surgery visits were paid by private insurance—54%.

freestanding ASCs will continue to thrive. With the demonstrated efficiencies in time spent for the visit, along with ease of access for freestanding ASCs, attractiveness of these programs will recruit patients, providers, and caregivers alike.

The National Health Statistics Report titled *National Hospital Ambulatory Medical Care Survey: 2006 Outpatient Department Summary* delivers results that demonstrate shifts in utilization patterns. Table 1.3 presents an overview of the outcomes. Nonphysician independent practitioner patient visit numbers are increasing. Sicker patients are using outpatient services. Increases in medication use, along with multiple prescriptions per patient, are highlighted in the report. Visits from patients with diabetes and hypertension are skyrocketing, and overall increases in outpatient visits demonstrate an amplified need for ambulatory care services.

As we see more and more movement to the outpatient sector, a need for stronger quality programs will ensue. Payors are pressuring for reduction of costs associated with care, consumers are demanding more outlets to care to promote health and prevention, and technology and medications will continue to evolve. Per the book published by the Department of Health and Human Services, CDC, *Health Care in America*, the acute care inpatient market shows a decline in community hospitals, from 5,384 in 1990 to 4,915 in 2000. With the decline, an increase in staffing occurred, but not at the bedside. Interestingly enough, many of the additional staff are assigned to management and administration, thus increasing overhead. All of these reasons contribute to the need for more outpatient programs.

Outpatient Quality Initiatives

Advanced technology, speed, improved medication options, shorter medical procedure duration, and the ability to be nimble and cost effective makes outpatient programs attractive to physicians and administrators. Unfortunately, inconsistent support exists from payors for outpatient settings. If we can tack on the ability to demonstrate superb quality and financial outcomes, outpatient care can and would be appealing to a wider provider and payor base.

While there are a few national initiatives underway to measure quality in the outpatient setting, it must be emphasized that the biggest leaps in quality will be at the grassroots level. This means that each practice, surgery center, clinic, and other outpatient entity takes ownership of quality, striving to provide true customer mindedness, enriching their program and producing excellent quality outcomes. Transparency exists, showing that there is nothing

Table 1.3   2006 Outpatient Department Utilization

Outpatient Department (OPD) Utilization	Results
Visits	102.2 million OPD visits in 2006
Gender	Females had higher OPD visits rates at 41.2 per 100 persons versus 28 visits per 100 persons.
Preventive care	Highest for children under one year of age at 43.2 visits per 100 persons at OPD clinics in 2006
Payor information	Private insurance was listed as the most frequent expected source of payment—42.3% of OPD visits. One-third of OPD visits were made by patients using Medicaid or other State Children's Health Insurance Program (SCHIP). Preventive care visits for these programs were almost four or more times higher than for patients using other payment sources. One in eight persons in the USA relies on Medicaid or SCHIP.
Diabetes	Diabetes mellitus is the leading primary diagnosis for adults at OPD visits, ahead of essential hypertension for 2006. Visits increased 43% from 1996 to 2006.
Comorbid chronic conditions	About one-half of OPD visits were made by patients with one or more comorbid chronic conditions.
Hypertension	Visits among adults increased by 51% from 1996 to 2006.
Clinic characteristics	General medicine clinics, internal medicine, family practice, primary care clinics represented 60.8% of OPD visits.
Medications	Ordered or prescribed at 76.7 million OPD visits. Increased from 1996 to 2006 from 60.6% to 75%. Patients requiring six or more medications increased from 5.4% to 14.4%.
Physician assistant or nurse practitioner	Percentage of visits solely attended by a mid-level provider increased by 112% from 5.6% in 1996 to 11.9% in 2006.

to hide, all the while engaging employees, physicians, and stakeholders in the journey.

National initiatives existing today stem from organizations such as the Centers for Medicare and Medicaid Services (CMS), the National Quality Forum, state Medical Societies, the ASC Quality Collaboration, and the Ambulatory Quality Alliance (AQA).

CMS Outpatient Initiatives (HOP QDRP)

The Hospital Outpatient Quality Data Reporting Program (HOP QDRP) includes seven clinical performance measures and four Medicare fee-for-service claims-based measures. In order to receive the full annual update to a hospital's Outpatient Prospective Payment System (OPPS) payment rate, hospitals must report data using the standardized measures as defined by CMS. The measures are publicly reported. The measures can change in future years, as measures can be added or deleted as appropriate to care.

It is the intent of CMS to provide consumers with this data so that better decisions can be made about healthcare choices and care at the hospital level. Regrettably, none of these measures are required outside the hospital setting for outpatient programs that are truly freestanding.

These measures for outpatient are as follows:

- Cardiovascular disease
  - Median time to fibrinolysis
  - Fibrinolytic therapy received within 30 minutes of emergency department (ED) arrival
  - Median time to transfer to another facility for acute coronary intervention
  - Aspirin at arrival
  - Median time to electrocardiogram (ECG)
- Surgery
  - Prophylactic antibiotic initiated within one hour prior to surgical incision
  - Prophylactic antibiotic selection for surgical patients
- Imaging
  - MRI lumbar spine for low back pain
  - Mammography follow-up rates
  - Abdomen computed tomography (CT) use of contrast material
- Thorax CT use of contrast material

Clinical Performance Measures for Ambulatory Care

The Agency for Healthcare Research and Quality posted on the Department of Health and Human Resources website a starter set of measures approved by a team representing the AQA, the American Academy of Family Physicians (AAFP), American College of Physicians (ACP), America's Health Insurance Plans (AHIP), and the Agency for Healthcare Research and Quality (AHRQ). The team consisted of a large group of stakeholders representing clinicians, consumers, purchasers, and health plans. As a work in progress, it's clearly noted by these entities that additional work is needed to expand the data set.

Measures for this initiative cover the following:

- Breast cancer screening
- Colorectal cancer screening
- Cervical cancer screening
- Tobacco use
- Advising smokers to quit
- Influenza vaccination
- Pneumonia vaccination
- Coronary artery disease
  - Drug therapy for lowering low-density lipoprotein (LDL) cholesterol
  - Beta-blocker treatment after heart attack
  - Beta-blocker therapy post myocardial infarction (MI)
- Heart failure
  - Angiotensin-converting enzyme (ACE) inhibitor/angiotensin II receptor blocker (ARB) therapy
  - Left ventricular function (LVF) assessment
- Diabetes
  - HbA1C management and control
  - Blood pressure management
  - Lipid measurement
  - LDL cholesterol level (<130 mg/dL)
  - Eye exam
- Asthma
  - Use of appropriate medications for people with asthma
  - Pharmacologic therapy
- Depression
  - Antidepressant medication management for acute and continuation phases

- Prenatal care
  - Screening for human immunodeficiency virus (HIV)
  - Anti-D immune globulin
- Quality measures addressing overuse and misuse
  - Appropriate treatment for children with upper respiratory infection
- Appropriate testing for children with pharyngitis

ASC Quality Collaboration

Data is collected and submitted with ongoing comparative quarterly outcomes available on their website. Data presented below is for admissions from January 1, 2010 through March 31, 2010. However, graphs on the website demonstrate how improvement has occurred since the inception of these efforts in the second quarter of 2009.

Organizations contributing to this extensive data set include the Ambulatory Surgery Center Association, the Ambulatory Surgical Centers of America, AmSurg, HCA Ambulatory Surgery Division, National Surgical Care, Nueterra, Surgical Care Affiliates, Symbion, and the United Surgical Partners International.

The report displays aggregated data for six ASC quality measures that were developed by the ASC Quality Collaboration with endorsement by the National Quality Forum.

In addition, there are tools available to help improve infection prevention practices for hand hygiene, safe injection practices, and point of care devices. Additional toolkits are underway to help ASCs excel at infection prevention practices, such as for sterile processing.

Measures, along with outcomes, are as follows:

- Rate of patient falls in the ASC. Lower rates are better. 0.149 per 1000 admissions.
- Rate of patient burns in the ASC. Lower rates are better. 0.037 per 1000 admissions.
- Rate of hospital transfers or admissions from the ASC. It's expected that some transfers occur. 1.081 per 1000 admissions.
- Rate of wrong site, side, patient, procedure, implant in the ASC. Lower rates are better. 0.034 per 1000 admissions.
- Prophylactic IV antibiotic timing in the ASC. Higher percentages are better. 95 percent.
- Appropriate surgical site hair removal. Higher percentages are better. 98 percent.

American Medical Association (AMA)

The AMA is working with state and county medical societies to foster collaboration between peers so that improvement in care processes can occur. Physician isolation, appropriate insurance coverage, and physician availability are all concerns resulting in barriers to ambulatory quality initiatives at the local level.

Medical societies do promote quality activities, relying on volunteer time from physicians and staff, along with paid state and medical society staff. Some of the quality and education examples presented in the AMA study, funded by the Robert Wood Johnson Foundation, include:

- The Pennsylvania Coalition to Save Antibiotic Strength
- The Maine Health Management Coalition
- The Michigan Quality Improvement Consortium
- The Ohio Committee on Trauma
- The Diabetes Footprints Campaign in Cleveland, Ohio
- The Health Leadership Task Force in Oregon
- The Michigan health literacy grant project
- Evidence-based treatment information in Pennsylvania
- Practice management seminars to assist physicians with purchasing and successfully implementing electronic medical records as well as understanding state-required quality assurance programs in Washington State.

Safe Injection Practices Coalition

The **Safe Injection Practices Coalition** (SIPC) is a joint venture of organizations that was created to promote safe injection practices in healthcare settings in the United States. The *One and Only Campaign* targets healthcare providers and patients, providing teaching tools and promotional aides so that safe practices are fostered throughout. Regrettably, the leader of the HONOReform Foundation, one of SIPC's founding organizations, Dr. Evelyn McKnight, was infected with hepatitis C virus (HCV) while being treated for breast cancer in 2000. Ninety-nine patients at the oncology clinic became infected with HCV when their provider failed to follow safe injection practices. More information on infection control and prevention can be found in Chapter 8.

The *One and Only Campaign*, driven by the SIPC members, consists of the following organizations:

- Accreditation Association for Ambulatory Health Care (AAAHC)
- Ambulatory Surgery Foundation

- American Association of Nurse Anesthetists (AANA)
- Association for Professionals in Infection Control and Epidemiology, Inc (APIC)
- Becton, Dickinson and Company (BD)
- Centers for Disease Control and Prevention (CDC)
- CDC Foundation
- Covidien
- HONOReform Foundation
- Hospira
- National Association of County & City Health Officials (NACCHO)
- Nebraska Medical Association
- Nevada State Medical Association (NSMA)
- Premier Healthcare Alliance
- The U.S. Food and Drug Administration (FDA) *(ad hoc member)*

Safe Practices for Better Healthcare

The National Quality Forum endorsed thirty-four medical care safe practices. It's noted that errors that create and contribute to harm are based on organizational system failures, leadership issues, and what they call predictable human behavioral factors. We have a long way to go to achieve uniformity in safe care practices, but there is hope. We have to get into the habit of stopping and thinking before doing. We must move the activity to the other side of the brain, to break habits and actions. We have to call "time out" more and more with actions that are taken when planning, delivering, and analyzing care.

These practices can be found on the National Quality Forum website. Many of the practices identified are applicable to the outpatient service setting. Get to know them, as we believe they are worth the effort. The practices are organized into the following seven categories:

- Creating and sustaining a culture of safety
- Informed consent, life-sustaining treatment, disclosure, and care of the caregiver
- Matching healthcare needs with service delivery capability
- Facilitating information transfer and clear communication
- Medication management
- Prevention of healthcare-associated infections
- Condition and site-specific practices

Summary and Key Points

1. Outpatient and ambulatory programs are booming, exploding in numbers and visits.
2. Outpatient settings are varied and widespread, delivering the majority of care in the United States.
3. Healthcare reform and the ACOs will impact outpatient care, reimbursement, and how outcomes are measured.
4. Quality programs exist, but are not as clearly defined or promoted as in the inpatient setting.
5. Grassroots quality efforts, if applied, can significantly contribute to improving quality in the outpatient setting.
6. Resources do exist to assist some outpatient programs with quality measures and initiatives.
7. Take advantage of the free programs that are available, such as the *One and Only Campaign*. Hats off to organizations such as this that have entered the ring, hoping for a knockout when it comes to demonstrated quality and outcome improvements in outpatient care.

Sources

Affordable Healthcare Act. A federal government Web site managed by the U.S. Department of Health & Human Services, 200 Independence Avenue, S.W., Washington, D.C. 20201, http://www.healthcare.gov/law/introduction/index.html

Ambulatory Care Quality Alliance, Recommended starter set: Clinical performance measures for ambulatory care. Agency for Healthcare Research and Quality, http://www.ahrq.gov/qual/aqastart.htm.

American Medical Association. *Advancing ambulatory quality improvement: Results of focus groups with medical societies*, http://www.ama-assn.org/ama1/pub/upload/mm/433/ambulatory-quality.pdf (accessed December 20, 2010).

ASC Quality Collaboration. Quality report, http://www.ascquality.org/qualityreport.cfm.

Cullen, Karen A., Margaret J. Hall, and Aleksandr Golosinksly. *Ambulatory surgery in the United States, 2006.* Department of Health and Human Services. Centers for Disease Control and Prevention (CDC). National Center for Health Statistics, Number 11, January 28, 2009.

Department of Health and Human Services. *Health care in America: Trends in utilization.* Department of Health and Human Services. Centers for Disease Control and Prevention (CDC). DHHS Pub No. 2004-1031. 03-0357 (January 2004), http://www.cdc.gov/nchs/data/misc/healthcare.pdf.

Hing, Esther, Margaret J. Hall, and Jianmin Xu. *National hospital ambulatory medical care survey: 2006 outpatient department summary.* Department of Health and Human Services, Centers for Disease Control and Prevention (CDC). National Center for Health Statistics, Number 4, August 6, 2008.

Irmiter, Cheryl, Susan Mayer, and Susan Nedza. AMA. Advancing Ambulatory Quality Improvement: Results of Focus Groups with Medical Societies. http://www.ama-assn.org/am1/pub/upload/mm/433/ambulatory-quality.pdf.

National Quality Forum. *National voluntary consensus standards for ambulatory care. An initial physician-focused performance measure set. A consensus report,* http://www.qualityforum.org/.

National Quality Forum. *National voluntary consensus standards for ambulatory care part 2. A consensus report,* http://www.qualityforum.org/.

National Quality Forum. *Safe practice for better healthcare—2010 update. A consensus report,* http://www.qualityforum.org/Projects/Safe_Practices_2010.aspx.

Safe Injection Practices Coalition. One needle, one syringe, only one time. http://www.oneandonlycampaign.org/about/coalition/default.aspx.

Schappert, Susan M., and Elizabeth A. Rechtsteiner. *Ambulatory medical care utilization estimates for 2006.* Department of Health and Human Services, Centers for Disease Control and Prevention (CDC). National Center for Health Statistics, Number 8, August 6, 2008.

U.S. Department of Health and Human Services. Center for Medicare and Medicaid Services (CMS). The hospital outpatient quality data reporting program, https://www.cms.gov/HospitalQualityInitiativesGenInfo/.

Chapter 2

Creating a Structure for Quality and Safety

Never doubt that a small group of thoughtful committed citizens can change the world. Indeed, it is the only thing that ever has.

—**Margaret Mead**

Simplicity Is Best

Keep it simple. That is the best approach when creating a superior quality and safety program structure. There isn't a need for numerous committees or layers upon layers of employees to get the work done. Ambulatory means nimble and quick, so using that thinking, let's explore how to make this work.

Most ambulatory programs have the benefit of being small. They don't carry the burden of large hospital overhead or population. At the same time, employees and physicians must wear many hats with responsibilities for multiple roles and responsibilities. Finding the right people to fill these positions is imperative and necessary to achieve and sustain a successful business. For example, if someone does hold an administrator, CEO, or leader role, that person will not have an entourage to support each and every requirement for safety, quality, and financial management.

On the flip side, when outpatient services are imbedded within a hospital, unless the service is receiving hospital-based reimbursement, it would be difficult to financially support the overwhelming structure in place for the hospital and system.

The majority of programs such as this behave more like an inpatient program, with very little in place in the way of true ambulatory/outpatient measures and processes. It's hard to be nimble and quick when policies and procedures are designed for inpatient care and services, multiple departments and programs, extensive clinical documentation, hospital bylaws, and acute care–based quality and safety plans.

Tie Your Quality Strategy to Your Mission, Vision, and Values

One of the most powerful visionary organizations existing today is Susan G. Komen for the Cure, the world's biggest grassroots network of breast cancer survivors and supporters. We all know someone who has battled breast cancer, or another type of cancer. Much of the treatment for cancer occurs in the outpatient setting. All physicians, dentists, and practitioners have touched at least one patient who has or is fighting this horrendous disease. To see and feel the strength behind what the Susan G. Komen stands for is a beacon of life when dealing with such a frightening diagnosis. Women and men know they are not fighting alone.

Here is their vision statement: "Our Vision is a World without Breast Cancer."

What is interesting about this statement is the use of the word *our*. It's not stated that Susan G. Komen's vision is a world without breast cancer. Instead, it enlists everyone to believe that it is *our* vision together. On their website, they offer a promise, alongside the vision and core values, that continue to engage, uplift, and encourage: "Our promise is to save lives and end breast cancer forever by empowering people, ensuring quality care for all, and energizing science to find the cures."

The rationale for presenting an inspiring vision and promise is to encourage you and those involved with your organization to step back and review your existing words and actions that are meant to guide and motivate the people touched by your services. If the mission, vision, and values are nonexistent, engage a committee to create your purpose, direction, and beliefs.

As this work is underway, ask and find the answer to this very important question: How can we translate the vision, mission, and values into safe and high-quality care? Table 2.1 presents a sample prioritization grid that integrates calculated quality and safety initiatives with the strategy of an organization, based on the mission, vision, and values.

Appoint a Governing Body

To meet Medicare, licensing, and other regulatory and state requirements, most freestanding ambulatory programs should have a governing body that

Table 2.1 Quality and Safety Prioritization Grid

Strategic Factor	Importance to Mission, Vision, and Values	Impact on Patients	Clinical Care Impact	State Licensing, Medicare, and/or Regulatory Importance	Patient Safety Impact	Cost and Profitability Impact	Total
Lab Results Turnaround Time and Reporting	◉	◉	◉	◉	◉	○	48
Patient Access	◉	◉	◉	◉	◉	○	48
Referring/Consulting Physician Communication	◉	◉	◉	◉	◉	○	48
Chronic Disease Management	◉	◉	◉	◉	◉	○	48
Copay Collection	◉	◉	△	△	△	◉	30
Scoring Key	◉	Significant	9 points				
	○	Medium	3 points				
	△	Weak	1 point				
	NA	No Effect	0 points				

takes on full legal and fiduciary responsibility for policies that govern the program's operation and to ensure that the policies are implemented and administered so that high-quality and cost-effective care is delivered in a safe environment.

But before this is taken on, please consult legal counsel to ensure that the direction that is chosen for governance matches the contracts, management agreements, and structure of the entities that are in place for your organization and facility.

Due to the size of many outpatient programs, the question arises quite frequently as to why a governing body is needed. Some physician practices have one or two practitioners. Ambulatory surgery centers may have fewer than five surgeons on board or may be office based with only one surgeon and one anesthesia professional.

In the Conditions for Coverage from Medicare for ambulatory surgery centers (ASCs), it states in the interpretive guidelines for §416.41 that, "in the case an ASC has one owner, that individual constitutes the governing body." While that seems small, it can work. Think about inviting two to four other professionals to sit on the board. This allows for an outside perspective and can provide support in ways that would be beneficial for the outpatient program. Examples of those who can be invited are other physicians, the administrator if one exists, community leaders, or healthcare executives from other facilities or programs. Conflict of interest and confidentiality agreements are readily available in the marketplace and can be implemented to protect the intellectual capital of the organization. The chairman of the board and the medical director can be the same person. It just needs to be understood that different hats are worn.

Table 2.2 displays an example of how each governing body member can evaluate their contributions and involvement on an annual basis. Compiling the results and sharing the information at a governing body meeting provides grist for the mill when determining what orientation and training programs to initiate to keep the members up to speed about their responsibilities.

Heartbreaking errors occur in all facets of healthcare. Outpatient programs are not exempt. Without a strong quality and leadership program, it's easy to overlook the structure that needs to be in place to foster and implement safe care.

Leader Selection

A leader always exists, whether appointed or informal in nature. Someone is running the show. The wrong leader can certainly devastate any organization,

Table 2.2   Governing Body Self-Evaluation

I.	*Bylaws, Policies, and Procedures*	*Yes*	*Partially*	*No*	*Comments*
1.	Do you have an understanding of how the facility is governed?				
2.	Has the governing body adopted bylaws that stipulate its fiduciary accountabilities and responsibilities?				
3.	Does the governing body approve all management, clinical, professional, and nonprofessional contracts?				
II.	*Policy*	*Yes*	*Partially*	*No*	*Comments*
1.	Do the policies and procedures address the activities related to delivering quality patient care, patient safety, risk management, medical staff credentialing, and financial management?				
2.	Have you been a part of establishing and reviewing policies and procedures that govern our facility?				
III.	*Quality and Patient Safety*	*Yes*	*Partially*	*No*	*Comments*
1.	Are you involved with establishing and overseeing the quality, safety, infection prevention, and risk management programs for the organization?				
IV.	*Resources, Management, and Planning*	*Yes*	*Partially*	*No*	*Comments*
1.	Have you been involved in the budget and capital budget process?				

(Continued)

Table 2.2 Governing Body Self-Evaluation (Continued)

IV.	Resources, Management, and Planning	Yes	Partially	No	Comments
2.	Is the governing body actively involved in short- and long-term planning processes?				
3.	Is the strategic plan integrated with our mission, vision, and values?				
V.	Roles and Responsibilities	Yes	Partially	No	Comments
1.	Are the relationships and responsibilities of the governing body and of the appointed staff positions clearly defined and followed?				
VI.	Leadership	Yes	Partially	No	Comments
1.	Have you been involved in the appointment and evaluation of the CEO/administrator?				
2.	Is the governing body responsible for medical staff leadership competency and evaluation?				
VII.	Medical Staff	Yes	Partially	No	Comments
1.	Is the governing body responsible for all aspects of appointment and privileging of medical staff members?				
2.	Does the governing body approve and review the bylaws and the rules and regulations of the Medical Staff?				
3.	Does the medical staff participate in the organization's planning, budgeting, safety management, quality, and patient safety programs at the governance level?				

Table 2.2   Governing Body Self-Evaluation (Continued)

VIII.	Auxiliary Organizations	Yes	Partially	No	Comments
1.	Does the governing body provide guidance for the establishment of auxiliary organizations?				
IX.	Investigational Review Board	Yes	Partially	No	Comments
1.	Is the governing body kept abreast about IRB activities, results, and actions?				
X.	Conflict of Interest	Yes	Partially	No	Comments
1.	Does the governing body successfully address the issue of conflict of interest throughout the facility/service and its leadership?				
XI.	Conflict Resolution	Yes	Partially	No	Comments
1.	Does the governing body successfully address conflict resolution at all levels of the organization?				
XII.	Community Needs Assessment	Yes	Partially	No	Comments
1.	Is the governing body actively involved with assessing and determining the direction our organization should take to meet the identified needs of the community?				
XIII.	What is the governing body doing well?				
XIV.	What could the governing body improve?				
XV.	What else would you like to tell us (please specify)?				

department, or service. Leader selection is something that the governing body needs to take very seriously. A physician or group of physicians may own the ambulatory service program, but identification of someone to serve as an administrator, executive director, and/or manager of the business is a critical step for success.

The governing body clearly communicates expectations and updates the goals and expectations to meet the needs of the changing environment. Overall, the expectations should include measurement results from physicians, staff, and patients; financial viability and profitability; clinical and quality measures; and growth and business development. The leader ensures that the staff is competent and that laws, regulations, and standards are met. Figure 2.1 displays a basic organizational chart that can easily be modified to meet your program's requirements. Table 2.3 proposes an effective assessment tool that can be used during the annual evaluation process of the leader(s).

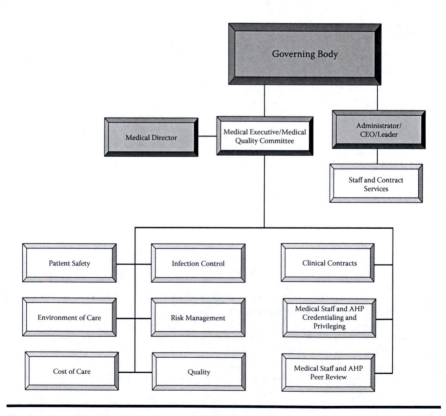

Figure 2.1 Sample Organizational Chart.

Table 2.3 Annual CEO/Leader/Administrator Evaluation

The *leader* is responsible for planning, organizing, and achieving defined outpatient service objectives for regulatory compliance, financial management, human resources management, customer satisfaction, patient and organizational safety, quality improvement, and information management. Utilizing this assessment tool, please circle one number in each of the listed areas that indicates your evaluation of the leader's performance. Provide comments as appropriate.

1.	Plans, prioritizes, continuously assesses, and improves the performance of outpatient service functions and services.	Yes	Partially	No	Comments
2.	Planning includes patient care services in response to identified patient needs and is consistent with the outpatient's service's mission.	Yes	Partially	No	Comments
3.	Fosters communication between and among individuals and components of the outpatient service and coordinates internal activities.	Yes	Partially	No	Comments
4.	Develops and implements policies and procedures that guide and support the operations of the outpatient service.	Yes	Partially	No	Comments
5.	Implements programs to promote the recruitment, retention, development, and continuing education of all staff members.	Yes	Partially	No	Comments
6.	Creates and maintains information systems and appropriate data management processes to support collecting, managing, and analyzing data needed to facilitate ongoing improvement in quality and patient safety.	Yes	Partially	No	Comments

(Continued)

Table 2.3   Annual CEO/Leader/Administrator Evaluation (Continued)

7.	Prepares and submits periodic reports relative to financial (including an annual operating budget and long-term capital expenditure plan), operational, and clinical activities and outcomes of the outpatient service.	Yes	Partially	No	Comments
8.	Attends and is prepared for all meetings of the governing body and committees thereof.	Yes	Partially	No	Comments
9.	Ensures the outpatient service is in compliance with all legal, regulatory, and accreditation requirements.	Yes	Partially	No	Comments
10.	Maintains good working relationships with the governing body, medical staff members, employees, and community leaders.	Yes	Partially	No	Comments
11.	What is the leader doing well?				
12.	What could the leader improve?				

The Medical Staff, Nurses, and Allied Health Professionals

The medical staff is accountable to the governing body or governance entity. To keep the number of committees to a minimum, combine medical staff and quality activities together under one umbrella. This helps protect the data from a peer review perspective. The committee can be called the Medical Executive Committee, or Medical Staff and Quality Committee, or whatever makes sense for your organization. This committee would report to the governing body or governance entity via minutes and verbal reports. The minutes would be approved by the governing body/governance entity with specific action sent back to the committee should additional information or actions be required.

When an outpatient program allows physician and nonphysician practitioners to practice within the services provided, the guidelines for privileges and membership need to be clearly outlined and defined. These practitioners must practice within legal limits and in accordance with state board limitations. Most physician extenders should have medical staff supervision and direction guidelines delineated, with adherence to these protocols steadfast. In addition, the physician that agrees to supervise and direct these professionals must do so within the scope and practice of both of their licenses.

Recently a physician had harsh sanctions imposed on him from the state board due to his lack of adequate supervision of a physician assistant (PA). The PA lost her license and is not allowed to practice in any state because of the freedom she took with her license. She was practicing more like a physician and was performing procedures that she should not have performed. The physician did not review charts or observe care—not once. He blindly believed what she told him. It was because of a patient complaint to the state health department that this came to light. Two practitioners' lives are ruined and a patient is scarred for life due to a PA's lack of common sense and a physician's lack of proper oversight.

The leader/administrator of that clinic had no idea this was going on and is in the midst of a lawsuit from the patient due to the lack of supervision on his part, since the PA was also an employee of the clinic. Processes, protocols, clinical delineations, quality measures, and patient safety plans were nonexistent.

Nurses, in any setting, must work within the state board of nursing requirements and care standards. A physician or other practitioner cannot ask or expect a nurse to do something that he or she is not legally licensed to do. Many times, a licensed professional nurse (LPN) is hired and asked to function as a registered nurse. For example, the LPN is expected to complete nursing assessments, give IV medications, or circulate in an operating room (OR). Maybe some states allow some of these processes to be completed by an LPN, but don't assume. Make sure that all nurses have job descriptions that are legal and accurate, and that the nurse works within their scope of care and practice.

The defined scope and services of the program defines what can and can't be done in each facility where the practitioner will practice. For example, if an ambulatory surgery center has equipment and instruments to care for patients requiring ear, nose, and throat (ENT) surgical and procedural intervention, the physicians would be privileged for the procedures within the scope and service of outpatient ENT. Approving privileges and membership to surgeons that want to perform gynecology procedures would not make sense as the center does not have the necessary equipment, competent staff, or supplies to do this. Nor would it make sense to grant clinical ENT privileges that are high risk and/or acute-care based.

A physician or practitioner who is privileged at a local hospital or other outpatient facility does not automatically qualify for privileges and membership at your outpatient facility. Each program must have its own written protocol, process, and policy for appointment and reappointment of medical staff professionals, physician extenders, and nonphysician practitioners.

In Chapter 5, more details about credentialing, privileging, and employee human resource processes are covered. For this chapter, the big takeaway is to have clearly defined governing body and leadership practices to adequately manage the care processes related to physicians, practitioners, and employees or contract workers.

Table 2.4 presents a checklist that can be used to help remember what should be reviewed, approved, and reported to the governing body or governance entity and/or the medical executive/quality committee.

Meetings, Minutes, and Keeping a Calendar

It's desired that the governing body or entity and medical staff/quality committee meet at least quarterly. Anything less than that makes it difficult to follow the quality outcomes and critical data review necessary to keep a strong program in place.

Both committees keep minutes with signatures and dates demonstrating that they were approved and read. When reading the minutes, it should be clear as to how actions are followed up and closed out. Use a table format with categories as follows:

- Agenda topic
- Conclusions and recommendations
- Actions to take
- Responsibility assigned
- Timeframe for actions to be completed

It helps to keep a running action list at the front of the minutes book. At the end of each meeting, add the actions to the list and cross off closed-out action items. That way, it's difficult to forget about actions that may have been assigned six months back.

A calendar for quality reports and events assists with agendas. Based on the number of times the board and quality committee meet, determine what is reported and when. Think about reporting quality items a minimum of twice a year. It's been found that if a detailed reporting process is in place, all mandatory, legal, and regulatory items are covered. Check your accreditation standards and your state standards and create a calendar to make it your own.

Another reporting tool that is helpful is a credentialing, employee competency, and education calendar. Keep track of all reappointments that are due, as you do not want to exceed the reappointment timeframe for physicians and

Table 2.4   Governance and MEC Review and Approval List

Item Requiring Review and Approval	MEC	Governance	Other
Abbreviations and Symbols	R and A	R and A	
Accreditation and/or Certification Decisions	R and A	R and A	
Allied Health Professional Appointment Forms/Privileges	R and A	R and A	
Appointment of Medical Staff Chairs/Directors	R and A	R and A	
Appointment of the CEO/ Administrator/Leader	R and A	R and A	
Appointment of the Compliance Officer	R and A	R and A	
Appointment of the Infection Prevention Officer	R and A	R and A	
Appointment of the Medical Director	R and A	R and A	
Appointment of the Patient Safety Officer	R and A	R and A	
Appointments of Physicians and AHPs: includes membership, clinical privileges, department assignment	Recommend or Do Not Recommend	R and A	
Blood and Blood Product Criteria and Reviews	R and A	R and A	
Budgeted Income Statement	Review	R and A	
Capital Expenditure Plan—3 Years	Review	R and A	
Certifications and Center of Excellence Programs	Review	R and A	
Clinical Competency for the Staff	Review	R and A	
Clinical Documentation Forms	R and A	R and A	
Compliance Plan and Documents	Review	R and A	

(*Continued*)

Table 2.4 Governance and MEC Review and Approval List (Continued)

Item Requiring Review and Approval	MEC	Governance	Other
Contract Services Discussion, Recommendation, and Approval	R and A	R and A	
Credentialing Verification Organization (CVO) Contract	R and A	R and A	
Credentialing/Privilege Approvals	Review	R and A	
Credentialing/Privilege Forms and Lists	R and A	R and A	
Critical Lab Values	R and A	R and A	
Delinquent Medical Records	R and A	R and A	
Disaster Drills	Review	R and A	
Discharge Plan	R and A	R and A	
Electronic Signatures and Use of Stamps or Faxes	R and A	R and A	
Employee Health Process	Review	R and A	
EMS and Ambulance Services	R and A	R and A	
EMTALA and Transfer Policy and Transfer Agreement	R and A	R and A	
Environment of Care Plans	R and A	R and A	
Governing Body Membership Appointments and Assignments	Review	R and A	
HIPAA Documents	Review	R and A	
History and Physical Format and Timeframes	R and A	R and A	
Infection Prevention Plan and Documents	R and A	R and A	
Medical Staff Committee Chairs	R and A	R and A	
Medical Staff Bylaws and Governing Body Bylaws approval/revision	R and A	R and A	

Table 2.4   Governance and MEC Review and Approval List (Continued)

Item Requiring Review and Approval	MEC	Governance	Other
Medical Staff Meeting and Event Calendar	R and A	R and A	
Medical Staff Orientation	R and A	R and A	
Medical Staff Rules and Regulations	R and A	R and A	
Mission, Vision, and Values	R and A	R and A	
Operating Budget	Review	R and A	
Parking and Wayfinding	Review	R and A	
Patient Care Plans and Clinical Pathways	R and A	R and A	
Patient Education Material	R and A	R and A	
Patient Handbook and Patient Rights	R and A	R and A	
Physician Order Sets	R and A	R and A	
Plan of Care and Staffing	R and A	R and A	
Policy and Procedure Manuals	R and A	R and A	
Professional, Business, and Nonprofessional Contracts/Service Agreements	R and A	R and A	
Quality Education and Orientation	R and A	R and A	
Quality Plan	R and A	R and A	
Quality Reports	R and A	R and A	
Reference Lab Contract	R and A	R and A	
Risk Management Plan	R and A	R and A	
Root Cause Analysis Reports	R and A	R and A	
Sentinel Event Plan and Process	R and A	R and A	

(Continued)

Table 2.4 Governance and MEC Review and Approval List (Continued)

Item Requiring Review and Approval	MEC	Governance	Other
Staff Orientation and OSHA/ Mandatory Training	Review	R and A	
Strategic Plan	Review	R and A	
Surgical and Procedural Case Criteria and Review	R and A	R and A	
Verbal Orders	R and A	R and A	
Waived and Nonwaived Tests	R and A	R and A	

practitioners, which is normally every two years. Once the deadline is exceeded, privileges and membership cannot be extended; the practitioner must reapply all over again. Continuing medical education and mandatory training calendars track what has to be done and when.

Set up your meetings ahead of time and don't stray from the dates and times for these meetings. For example, your governing body or entity would meet the second Tuesday from 6:00 to 7:00 p.m. in January, April, July, and October. The medical staff/quality committee meets prior to that from 5:00 to 6:00 p.m. Emergency meetings or calls can occur anytime to address sentinel events, emergency credentialing, and other important matters. Everyone may not make all meetings, but if you cancel and reschedule, it will often throw off the reporting and accountability needed for adequate and appropriate governance. Don't forget to include staff meetings in this timeline and calendar of events. Keep minutes and report these to your governing body. Remember that all minutes and documents are confidential. Pick them up after each meeting and destroy them.

Keep vendor, physician, employee, and contract service rosters easily accessible to all staff and pertinent stakeholders. Privilege delineation and scope of service should be apparent at all times.

Quality Program Topics

There are numerous ways to set up quality studies, reporting, and outcome measures for an outpatient setting. Take time to define your outpatient program scope of care and practice first and foremost, as this will help with the selection of quality and safety opportunities. Once this is done, use the categories listed below to determine what requires ongoing measurement, what dictates prevention strategies, and what improvement and innovation opportunities exist. Once the calendar is created, implement the strategies. Use the appropriate method-ologies and analytic tools to make the most of your quality and safety initiatives. We will present ideas on many of these topics and strategies throughout the book. These topics include:

- Preventive quality efforts
- Medication safety and practices
- Utilization management of resources
- Infection prevention
- Surgical and procedural case review
- Clinical documentation
- Medical staff processes and peer review
- Competency, skills training, and knowledge based assessments
- Benchmarking analysis
- One level of care studies
- Blood and blood product utilization and outcomes
- Risk management opportunities
- Patient safety opportunities
- Satisfaction results for patients, employees, and physicians
- Human resource initiatives for recruitment, retention, staffing, and contract services
- Facility, equipment, and instrument improvement opportunities
- Efficiency studies

Summary and Key Points

1. Inspiration is needed to build a robust quality and safety program. Take the first step by creating purposeful mission and values statements.
2. Appoint a governing body or governance entity, including a set of bylaws or at least a policy and procedure statement that defines the governance process, delegations, and responsibilities. Invest in training and orienting the members. Implement a yearly self-assessment program.
3. Select leaders who buy into the culture and can champion the vision, mission, values, and quality philosophy of the organization. Demonstrate how governance leads the selection effort and then delegates operational responsibilities to the leader(s).
4. Create policies and procedures that serve to govern the outpatient service. This can include medical staff bylaws, rules and regulations, and physician-specific policies. Appointment and clinical privileging must be spelled out.

5. Incorporate clearly defined job descriptions, competencies, and skills checklists.
6. Appoint a medical director and form a committee that covers the topics mentioned earlier.
7. Determine the scope and services for the ambulatory program. This document defines what can and can't be done within the outpatient service.
8. Write and implement a comprehensive quality and safety plan. Set specific quality goals at the board and administrative levels.
9. Assign responsibilities and hold people accountable.
10. Create a calendar that supports regular, periodic meetings, reports, and assessments. Keep minutes and close-out actions in a timely manner.
11. Always have a tracking system for following up on quality and safety initiatives and metrics. Encourage all practitioners to review, debate, analyze, and identify opportunities for improvement.

Sources

Collins, J. C., and J. I. Porras. 1994. *Built to last.* New York: HarperBusiness.

Collins, Jim. 2001. *Good to great.* New York: HarperCollins Publishers, Inc.

Conditions for Coverage for ASCs. Centers for Medicare and Medicaid Services (CMS), http://www.cms.gov/CFCsAndCoPs/16_ASC.asp#TopOfPage.

Deming, W. Edwards. 1982. *Out of the crisis.* Cambridge, MA: Center for Engineering Study.

Deming, W. Edwards. 1993. *The new economics: For industry, government, education.* Cambridge, MA: Massachusetts Institute of Technology.

Freiburg, Kevin, and Jackie Freiberg. 1996. *NUTS!: Southwest Airlines' crazy recipe for business and personal success.* Austin, TX: Bard Press, Inc.

Fritz, Albert L., Hugh P. Greeley, Eric D. Lister, John C. McGinty, and Richard A. Sheff. 2005. *Orientation to healthcare governance for board members.* Marblehead, MA: HCPro.

Goldratt, Eliyahu M., and Jeff Cox. 1984. *The goal: A process of ongoing improvement.* Great Barrington, MA: North River Press Publishing Company.

Kotter, John. P., and Dan S. Cohen. 2002. *The heart of change: Real-life stories of how people change.* Boston, MA: Harvard Business School Publishing.

Schein, E. H. 1992. *Organizational culture and leadership.* San Francisco: Jossey-Bass.

Schein, Edgar. 1999. *Process consultation revisited: Building the helping relationship.* Reading, MA: Addison-Wesley Publishing Company, Inc.

Starr, Paul. 1982. *The social transformation of American medicine: The rise of a sovereign profession and the making of a vast industry.* New York: Basic Books.

Susan G. Komen for the Cure. http://ww5.komen.org/.

Trout, Jack, and Steve Rivkin. 1999. *The power of simplicity.* New York: McGraw-Hill.

Chapter 3

Engineering the Customer Connection

It is not the employer who pays the wages. Employers only handle
the money. It is the customer who pays the wages.

—Henry Ford

In outpatient services, there are many customers. The patient is our primary
customer, but other customers are the staff, physicians, patient family members,
the community that is served, and healthcare organizations that continue the
care of the patients. Even though the customer groups are different, there are
similarities in what they expect and want from outpatient providers.

The basis of any quality program is to discern the customer wants and needs
while meeting or exceeding their expectations. This belief is not new, but unfortunately it hasn't translated to conviction in much of the ambulatory environment. This chapter was born from the common themes of customer-mindedness
that stem from the healthcare industry and consumer-driven markets.

Each and every day we take away lessons learned, as we are all customers of one
another at some point. Whether it's purchasing a car, visiting a bank, going to the
grocery store, or shopping at the mall, impressions are made as to whether we as
customers were well cared for. Noted are the times when we are cheerfully greeted,
punctually waited on, or overwhelmed with the outcome of the service provided.

There are numerous books, articles, and resources in the marketplace relating to customer service. This includes methodologies that meld science and art

when it comes to customer thinking, such as Lean, Three Types of Waste, Six Sigma, Quality Function Deployment (QFD), Kaizen, and the overall basics of quality principles from gurus such as Shewhart, Deming, and Juran. These methodologies, combined with ten commonsense principles (CSPs) and the takeaways from personal experiences, will deliver a customer-focused culture, if engineered and practiced. Think of the CSPs as the seventh sense, if you will. They are intuitive, but at the same time require practice to achieve perfection. Scientific methodologies and customer tools help us practice the right way.

A Venn diagram (Figure 3.1) is used to show the possible logical relationships among the ten CSPs presented in this chapter. All circles interface, each touching one another in some way. It's simple dependency. When integrating the CSPs with the scientific methodologies mentioned earlier, one can quickly discern how they are staples of these very methodologies that have been known to help build zero-defect products, send shuttles into space, entertain millions of people at theme parks, and create complex communication venues to connect family members from one side of the globe to another.

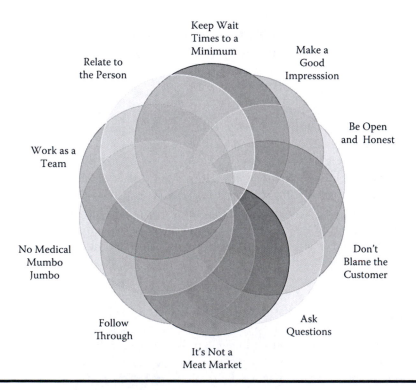

Figure 3.1 Commonsense principles.

Quality Function Deployment

Quality Function Deployment (QFD) is notably called the voice of the customer. It's an effective team approach to designing products and services that involves key stakeholders from the organizations that are responsible for what the customer uses or purchases. It's necessary to distinguish the difference between customer specifications and the specifications representing the voice of the providers, which can frequently conflict with the needs, wants, and expectations of the customer—and in many cases our patients.

QFD and the voice of the customer refers specifically to the development of a meticulous and prioritized set of customer wants and needs in support of new program, service, or care delivery systems. QFD and the voice of the customer belongs at the very beginning of a new initiative; the grey area that kicks off innovation, where the outpatient program endeavors to define precisely what type of program and service it wishes to construct. At the same time, QFD also works to improve existing programs in healthcare.

Providers are encouraged to go to the *Gemba*—the actual and real place where value is created for customers and where service is provided. For us in outpatient services, it is the workplace, where the patients enter, are processed, are cared for, and are discharged. To fully understand the experiences of our customers, walk in their shoes—literally.

Customers, for the most part, aren't very good at identifying solutions or telling you exactly what they want. However, when properly prodded, they're adept at communicating their needs—what they like, what they don't like, what makes their lives hard or easy to stay healthy and disease free, what they wish for from their physician, and what they're trying to achieve for their health. Remember, it's not the customer's job to implement and carve out solutions. That is the responsibility of the healthcare provider who is taking money from the customer for the healthcare services they provide. The customer needs to have the ability to articulate his or her needs and to have someone really listen.

Figure 3.2 displays an actual voice-of-the-customer tool, which takes a great deal of customer input and links it to the processes that are to be implemented within this outpatient program, which happens to be a cardiac catheterization lab. The process is designed to determine how to have a zero-defect outcome for groin injuries postprocedure. The customer for this particular matrix is the physician, who ultimately impacts the patients. Notice the highlighted areas with the top scores in regards to customer expectations and processes believed to be most important. This was based on input from the practicing cardiologists in that cath lab.

Figure 3.3 is another example using the customer voice tool, this time for urgent care admission processes. The customer in this matrix is the patient.

		Output	Customer Requirements: 9 = most important, 3 = important, 1 = least important				
			MD Orders	*Expectations*	*Safety*	*Technique*	*LOS*
Inputs		*Weight*	9	3	9	9	3
Step	*Process*						
Communication	*Assessment*		81	27	81	81	3
			9	9	9	9	1
	Patient Process		81	27	81	81	27
			9	9	9	9	1
	Information in Chart		81	27	27	81	3
			9	9	3	9	1
	Readiness for Procedure		81	27	81	81	3
			9	9	9	9	1
	Competent Staff		81	27	81	81	3
			9	9	9	9	1
Stability/Well-Being							
			81	27	27	81	3
	Positioning		9	9	9	9	0
	Medications		81	27	81	81	3
			9	9	9	9	1
	Patient Education		27	27	27	81	9
			3	9	3	9	3
Injury							
	Device		81	27	81	81	9
			9	9	9	9	3
	Technique		81	27	81	81	9
			9	9	9	9	3
	Orders		81	9	81	81	3
			9	3	9	9	1
	Assessment Results		81	27	81	81	9
			9	9	9	9	3
	Handoff to Caregiver		81	27	81	81	27
			9	9	9	9	9
Total			999	333	891	1053	111

Figure 3.2 Outpatient cardiac cath lab customer requirement matrix.

		Output	**Customer Requirements**					
Inputs		Weight	Timeliness	Accuracy	Knowledge	Competency	Relationship Skill	Total Value
Step	*Process*		5	5	4	5	3	
1	Call RN		25	25	16	25	12	
			5	5	4	5	4	103
2	RN assessment		25	25	20	20	12	
			5	5	5	4	4	102
3	MD assessment		25	25	20	25	15	
			5	5	5	5	5	110
4	Enter orders into computer		20	25	16	20	6	
			4	5	4	4	2	87
5	Process test results		25	25	20	25	9	
			5	5	5	5	3	104
6	Evaluate test results		25	25	20	25	12	
			5	5	5	5	4	107
7	Consulting MD assessment/guidelines		25	25	20	25	15	
			5	5	5	5	5	110
8	Room assignment		25	25	20	25	15	
			5	5	5	5	5	110
9	Discharging patient		25	25	20	25	12	
			5	5	5	5	4	107
Total			225	230	176	220	111	

Figure 3.3 Urgent care example.

All variables are important, but knowledge takes the lead in the columns, while personnel jump ahead when crossing all columns. Outcomes will depend on the knowledge, competency, and relationship skills of our employees and physicians. The interactions of all variables also affect excellence or unfortunately, failure.

Kaizen

Kaizen simply means improvement. It's a way of life in a quality-oriented facility. It embeds scientific method, experiments, lean, and overall improvement in day-to-day work life. It humanizes the workforce, providing workers with empowerment, tools, and resources to really excel and elevate productivity, ultimately increasing profitability. Nurturing, praising, encouragement, and participation are all words one thinks of when Kaizen is properly implemented. Input is garnered from frontline workers on up. To be totally successful, the focus is on understanding the customer and fostering teamwork to meet and exceed their expectations in the workforce.

Plan, Do, Check, and Act (PDCA) and Six Sigma

Known as the Deming cycle, the Shewhart cycle, or Deming wheel, PDCA is commonly used for healthcare quality improvement efforts. It's recognizable and elegant. DMAIC is the Six Sigma methodology. It stands for Define, Measure, Analyze, Improve, and Control. The latter is not used as much in healthcare because it's much more resource intense and requires what are called highly skilled Six Sigma Black Belts to manage and lead projects. When Six Sigma is applied, it's potent, producing incredible outcomes.

Based on the scientific method, iteration is perpetuated. It's a continuous improvement methodology, seeking high-quality outputs and operations. Perfection is the goal. Identifying and measuring customer specifications are required with scientific methods. Reasoning, the testing of hypotheses, experiments, and predictions make scientific methods strong and sustainable. It is the antithesis of pseudoscience.

Three Types of Waste

What's referenced as "waste" in quality thinking consists of three Japanese terms that were made popular by the Toyota Production System. Lean improvement methodologies capitalize on the elimination of waste within work and personal space. It makes sense and it's really pretty easy to accomplish. For the most part, you don't need statistical process control tools to make this happen.

1. *Muda* is an activity that is wasteful and doesn't add value to the customer or to the organization. Muda exercises are profound and concentrate on reducing and eliminating seven wastes: overproduction, unnecessary transportation, inventory, motion, defects, overprocessing, and waiting. Determining what adds value and what does not leads to clean and streamlined processes that are focused on our key customers. For example, patients don't like it when a bad outcome occurs and we as healthcare

providers don't wish for that either. Eliminating medication errors and unnecessary steps, getting the caregivers to spend more time with the patient, and reducing wait times are all examples of how muda reduction works.

2. *Mura* refers to inconsistency in process, people, or human spirit. Just-in-time inventory and systems play a big part in eliminating mura. Kanban is a favorite in healthcare because it's an effective way of communicating inventory control. Kanban is simply a sign or board in a visible area that posts important information for all users associated with the work processes. It tells you what to produce, when to produce, and how much to produce. Using kanbans for patient servers inside the patient rooms is a great use of mura reduction. See Table 3.1 for a patient server example. Keeping supplies that are used frequently close at hand reduces the need for staff to leave a room to find a needed patient care item. Also, posting a kanban outside or inside of surgery and procedure rooms helps to log patient safety issues, equipment needs, or other important items as noted in Table 3.2. Important for any success with kanban boards or cards is to engage the employees, physicians, and caregivers in keeping up with counts, information, and to actually use the boards.

3. *Muri* is based on unreasonableness or absurdity in work and system processes. Concentrating on making systems and processes logical is critical

Table 3.1   Nurse Server Kanban Example

Item	Product Number	Minimum	Maximum	Quantity
10-cc syringe	S123	5	10	6
Washcloths	W123	5	10	7
Emesis basins	E123	3	5	4
Alcohol pads	A123	25	100	50
Ace bandages	AB123	4	6	6
Steri-strips	SS123	10	20	15
Band-Aids	B123	25	100	65
Tongue depressors	T123	25	100	75
Thermometer covers	TH123	25	40	27

Table 3.2   Kanban Surgery Suite Patient Safety Example

Patient: Cece Better OR Room: 3	Product, Equipment Number or Name	Comments
Phaco	#57468392	Used in room 2 for an earlier case
Lens implant for right eye	L12345	Obtained and logged in
Surgeon	Dr. Vision	
Anesthesiologist	Dr. Nitrous	
Anesthesia	MAC	
Allergies	Latex	
Antibiotics	No	
Medical clearances	Cardiology	In chart, no issues noted
Special needs	Hearing aids are not in	She reads lips when her hearing aid is not in and this will be a problem in the OR suite with everyone wearing masks.

for success. For example, muri standardizes workflow. Reducing process steps to the simplest elements and knowing how handoffs and next steps work produces systems that patients, staff, and physicians can easily navigate. Figure 3.4 displays a throughput map that shows the relationships of inputs and outputs and cleverly narrows down what is most important to the users and customers of the process. It's a picture of an electronic medical record (EMR) process, harvesting what's most important to making the EMR successful in the way of inputs and outputs. The map is based on the formula, $Y = f(x)$, or y is a function of x. A function can be likened to a machine that converts the inputs into outputs; the outputs are the things on which the customer passes judgment.

Now that a quick review of some of the key methodologies has been presented, let's look at the CSPs, learning from patients who shared their experiences when seeking and obtaining ambulatory healthcare.

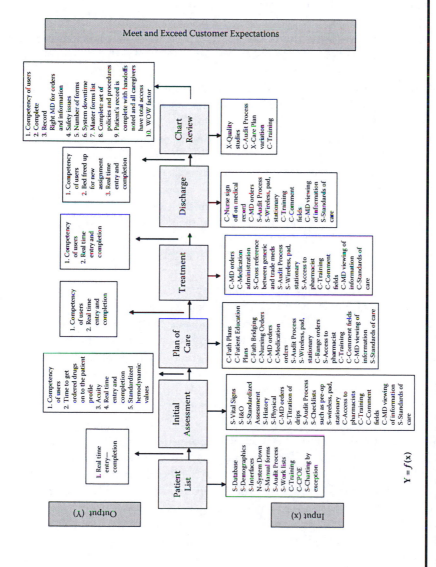

Figure 3.4 Electronic documentation throughput.

CSP Number 1: Keep Wait Times to a Minimum

Mrs. S was referred to an orthopedic surgeon by her family practice physician. The surgeon group was well known and serviced the professional football team in the city. Mrs. S arrived for her appointment thirty minutes early. She was neither greeted by the front desk personnel nor was there any communication about wait times or paperwork necessary for the visit. Two and a half hours later she was taken back to the exam room. Sixty minutes later, the orthopedic surgeon arrived to perform the exam.

During the wait time, it was noted by the patient that the office staff were not communicating well, the handoffs were clumsy, and the nurse that assisted the surgeon messed up on the radiology procedure that he ordered and then blamed the patient for the error. All the while the patient heard this dialogue occurring, along with hearing the surgeon dictate his findings about other patients he previously saw. And at no time was a patient history taken by the nurse or surgeon, not even a baseline set of vital signs.

When the patient let the surgeon know what she experienced, he commented that the office was a mess and that he had difficulty getting information he needed. Mrs. S chose another surgeon based on the office staff's lack of teamwork, the unnecessary wait time, and the potential for errors, not because of the surgeon's qualifications, which were impeccable.

Mrs. T, new to the city, made an appointment with an internist. The appointment time was 9:00 am. She was ten minutes late as she was still learning to navigate her new surroundings. She was cheerfully greeted and welcomed. It was then explained to her that the doctor sees all of her patients on time and that in the future she should arrive on time. They have a palm print identification system, so a baseline print was obtained for future use.

Mrs. T had filled out the necessary new patient paperwork, as it was available online via the physician's website. After paying the copay, she was taken right back to the exam room. She was weighed in a private hallway, not out in the open. The nurse processed her, completing a history and taking vital signs. In addition, a list of all medications requiring prescriptions was taken so that it could be entered into the system for future refills. The paperwork that the patient had filled out asked whether there were any issues, problems, or questions that the patient had so they could be properly addressed during the visit.

At 9:20 a.m. the physician was in the exam room with the patient. The first ten minutes were spent getting to know one another, and with the physician confirming and adding to the history. The physical was then completed. It was noted that vaccines were needed, so they were given during the visit. Also, the patient was over fifty, so the physician confirmed that a colonoscopy had been done. In addition, a mammogram and a bone scan were ordered.

The exam was over at 10:00 a.m., and the patient was walked to the checkout desk by the nurse. The appointments for the mammogram and bone scan were made and the annual visit appointment was set up. The patient was in her car at 10:10 a.m., with all of the information needed for continuity of care.

When reviewing the two patient encounters, it's clear as to which one provided the greatest value and patient satisfaction. Mrs. S experienced waste and the office would benefit from applying Lean methodology to their practice. On the other hand, wait time was nonexistent for Mrs. T, and in a follow-up chat with her it was confirmed that after three years, subsequent visits were still as efficient, friendly, and wonderful as the first visit. We later found out that the practice had invested in a customer service consultant to help them be the best they could be, and it seems to be working.

Providing consistency in practice lets the users know what to expect, which makes it easy to schedule time out of their busy day. Wait times for patients can be one of the biggest barriers to satisfaction. In addition, most office staff members tend to be poor communicators, not letting the patients who are waiting know when they will be seen or what is going on. In true emergencies, all patients are forgiving, but not when it's due to inefficiencies and downright bad business practices.

Lesson learned: Keep wait times to a minimum for your customers. Overcommunicate if necessary. Keep the customer in the loop so they can work with you. If a patient's appointment is for 8:00 a.m., then the patient should be in the exam or procedure room at that time. But that doesn't mean they wait there for a long period of time for the doctor, tech, or nurse. Keep the processes moving, and if there is a delay, let the patient know why.

CSP Number 2: Make a Good Impression

Mr. E had an appointment for a colonoscopy. The staff behind the glass never looked up to greet the patient, and the glass partition was not opened to talk directly to the patient. He was told to take a seat and someone would call for him. In addition, the endoscopy group had several locations in which they saw and treated patients, so preadmission visits were scheduled for the convenience of the doctors, and not due to the travel time of the patient. When the patient arrived for the procedure, he had to fill out the forms regarding his history and medications once again. He inquired about this and said he already had done that. He was told by the glass partition worker that their computers do not speak to each other and that it would take someone's time to deliver the medical records from site to site. Therefore, the patient had to redo the forms.

There are so many things wrong with this encounter that it's hard to know where to begin. Clearly, friendly, helpful people do not exist at this practice. First and continuing impressions were dismal. However, the patient didn't directly question this as it was a referral from his doctor and he was brought up to respect the physician's choices. That doesn't mean that Mr. E has kept quiet. He shared his story with anyone that would listen, relating how poorly he was treated and to beware should the listeners require the same kind of service.

Personnel in the front office, and those who answer the phone and greet customers, are usually the least trained and lowest-paid individuals in any ambulatory setting. This takes a toll on that business as they are the face of the practice, surgery center, or other ambulatory program. It's said that over 50 percent of a patient's opinion of the doctor or business is based on the first impression. Unfortunately, these first impressions last a very long time. They essentially leave a scar, and the patients and other users are wary from that point on and expect the worst, should they decide to return.

A friend shared that he kept a mirror at his desk, looking at himself when he spoke on the phone. That reminded him to smile. Even though the person on the other end of the phone couldn't see him, he projected more enthusiasm, and was happier. This rubbed off because his phone calls were so much more positive. It then became a habit and he found himself smiling more and more at work. Smiling is highly contagious, and a smile goes a long way when greeting someone. He also said that he practiced making eye contact when greeting or talking with people. That way they knew they had his attention and that they were important.

Lesson learned: Work on creating fantastic first and continuing impressions, starting with those who answer the phones, to those who greet and admit patients, all the way to the discharge and final disposition and follow-up phone calls. If answering machines are used, make sure that patients have access without hassle to a caregiver or staff member. Hire secret shoppers if necessary to determine what impressions are out there about your business. Practice Kaizen!

CSP Number 3: Be Open and Honest

Mr. and Mrs. J had traveled to another state to attend a relative's wedding. Their one-year-old daughter came down with a fever, which was persistent. The child's pediatrician said to take the baby to an emergency department as the baby had been treated for previous urinary tract infections (UTI). After waiting two hours in the emergency waiting room, without any information regarding timeframes to be seen, they were taken to an exam room. A pediatric nurse processed the baby. A history was taken and the parents clearly articulated the UTI background.

When the emergency room physician examined the baby, he felt that nothing was wrong and sent the parents on their way. The fever persisted, so that when the parents and child returned home, the pediatrician ordered a urine culture and started the little girl on antibiotics. Due to the extended period of time with the UTI, additional invasive tests were required to ensure that kidney or other damage had not occurred. Needless to say, the pediatrician was furious.

The physician and the nurse in the emergency department did not pay attention to the history that was given for the child. Standards of care were not followed, as the parents found out later. The child had to have additional painful tests done because of the breakdown in communication.

Patients, and their family members, want honesty, even if the news is bad. Information is critical for the well-being of our patients. They want self-control if at all possible. The level of detail shared depends on the patient, so that's something that should be assessed and honored. Communication is a two-way street, and while so much information is going out to the patient and family, the caregivers must also learn to listen and be open and honest in return regarding the patient's feedback and questions.

Lesson learned: There are few choices for children and adults who become ill when traveling. Pediatricians and local physicians will not see them and the emergency departments are so overwhelmed that mistakes happen. Honesty and communication is so important in all patient care situations. Physicians need to read the history and story of the patients regularly. The outcome for this child could have been much worse because of the communication breakdown, and thankfully it wasn't. Lean application would be helpful for the emergency department, and the pediatrician could have also called ahead to alert the emergency department about the patient so that handoffs would have been much smoother.

CSP Number 4: Don't Blame the Customer

In CSP Number 1, Mrs. S was blamed because the wrong radiology test was done. When confronting the doctor about this accusation, the surgeon then went to find the nurse to seek clarification and to admonish the nurse for her mistake. This conflict occurred in front of Mrs. S.

Blaming the customers and users of your program is never a good idea. It's better to just acknowledge the mistake and to ask how things could be fixed, or to just fix it right then and there. It comes down to respect and dignity for the patient.

Lesson learned: Gestures of kindness and support are fundamental when attempting to establish excellent customer relationships. Patients generally have a high level of fear when visiting any type of healthcare facility, and blaming them for something that went wrong does nothing to help support them or to allay this fear. Revealing confidence and trust from the caregivers is a necessary skill set for anyone who works in an ambulatory setting.

CSP Number 5: Ask Questions

Mrs. T in CSP Number 1 experienced the perfect visit. She had a chance to collect her thoughts prior to her appointment because the paperwork she filled out asked her questions to prepare for the exam with her physician. For future visits, the paperwork is updated and the patients are asked to consider what they want to talk about and what questions they have about their health. That way, the physician has this document and a true conversation can occur.

The receptionist doesn't necessarily know what to do when a question is asked. When clear directions aren't given, it goes back to the patient or family member to try and figure it out. Training front desk staff can ward off rework and waste, and if they know what to ask and how to respond to patients, then a clearer understanding of their needs is brought forward. All in all, it prevents the exportation of chaos down the line.

Lesson learned: By giving everyone the opportunity to ask questions, an individual care plan that is dynamic and pertinent for the patient can be created and implemented.

CSP Number 6: It's Not a Meat Market

Mr. M went to an outpatient imaging center for a radiology test. The center was crowded and very busy, and it was understaffed. Ten patients were there for the same appointment time. The receptionist brought out the paperwork and handed it out to the patients and told all of them to fill it out as they wouldn't be seen if the paperwork was not complete.

The next step was to take the patients back to a hallway, where they sat in chairs. They were told that a tech would come out to call their name and take them back. There was no greeting or any other acknowledgment that the patients were actually people. Do this, do that, don't do this, stand here, not there, now we have to redo because you moved, and on and on.

The results from the exam took several weeks to come back to the patient. The time spent worrying about the outcome was long and arduous for Mr. M, and, clearly, taking care of the patient's needs was not a priority for this center.

Lesson learned: It's okay to be efficient, effective, and lean, and to process high volumes in any setting. What requires work and attention to detail is the fact that we aren't fixing computers or working on televisions. We are treating people, and it's not a meat market. People have thoughts, feelings, and voices. Taking time to be human is needed in any outpatient setting.

CSP Number 7: Follow Through

Mrs. T in CSP Number 1 was referred for a mammogram. When she arrived, her paperwork was there from the referring physician. Again, they were expecting her, greeted her warmly, and showed her to the dressing room to prepare for the test. She waited only five minutes and was taken back to the room. The technician was friendly and cheerful, providing education about the exam and what to expect.

The technician was careful about her comfort level during the exam. Once finished, Mrs. T was shown to a meditation room that had a beautiful fountain, soft lights, and hot herbal tea to enjoy while waiting to make sure the results were clear for the physician to read.

The entire visit took thirty minutes. The referring physician sent a letter to Mrs. T with the results within the week, and a personal note was on the bottom, hoping that Mrs. T was doing okay and to call if she had any questions.

Mrs. T is a lucky woman as she is receiving stellar care.

Lesson learned: Help people navigate the system. If you say you are going to do something, do it. Don't put it all on the patient or family members' shoulders to continually track down information or referrals. Communicate with referring doctors in a timely manner so they can care for their patients appropriately.

CSP Number 8: No Medical Mumbo Jumbo

Mrs. B is a seventy-two-year-old woman with Type II diabetes. She's respectful of her physicians and will not ask questions. She's highly educated, having earned a doctorate in education. This doesn't mean she understands medical mumbo jumbo. To her, the clinical terms and big words are just that—big words. They have little meaning because she can't relate these words to the full impact on her health.

Mrs. B wanted to lead an active and normal life, but she didn't know how. Due to the lack of communication between her and the physician, the treatment plan left her feeling tired and sluggish. She also had a difficult time controlling her glucose levels.

Without ongoing support for chronic disease management, and because of broken communication systems, Mrs. B chose to find another doctor. This change gave her a support system via the nurse and office staff. Skilled in asking questions, they were able to find nutrition, medication, and exercise programs that worked for Mrs. B.

Lesson learned: Taking time to find out how the patient is doing, how things are going at home, and to alleviate anxiety builds the confidence and trust that patients need. Say what you mean in language that nonclinical people can understand. Patients and family members aren't stupid—most are highly educated or experienced, and they shouldn't be treated as if they didn't have a brain in their head.

CSP Number 9: Work as a Team

Finding out how handoffs work, how the team works, and how deliverables occur is fundamental to system and process improvement. A one-page process map forces us to put on paper what is really important. The X variables contribute to the outcomes, which are the Y variables. The Y variables are important to the customer, so therefore we need to know how the X variables are behaving so that the Y variables meet or exceed our customers' expectations.

No one is an island when it comes to providing healthcare in any setting. Customers, in general, can sense when teamwork is not in place. As Mrs. S found out in CSP Number 1, the teamwork was nonexistent in the orthopedic surgeon's office.

Lesson learned: Create a process map as noted earlier in this chapter. Identify handoffs that impact your customers and outcomes. Learn how to work as a team and how complexity, rework, unnecessary steps, and delays can be averted.

CSP Number 10: Relate to the Person

As shown in the examples shared throughout the CSPs, the successful encounters capitalized on exhibiting humanistic behaviors. We are different, our patients are different, and caregivers are different. Expressing concern, giving support, and knowing when things are tough at home for the patient and family delivers the WOW factor in outpatient settings.

Lesson learned: Show that you care and revisit the other lessons learned in this chapter.

Summary and Key Points

We have endless possibilities to take fantastic care of our customers in the outpatient environment. No more excuses for any of us; instead let's work to make the experiences for new mothers, sick grandparents, ailing parents, and scared children caring, humane, and positive. It's time to figure out how to engineer the customer connection throughout outpatient settings.

1. Make it a point to know who the customers are for your outpatient program.
2. Keep customer-mindedness on the agenda when meeting with staff.
3. Learn how to apply the methodologies presented in this chapter.
4. Implement a CSP of the week and make it a fun and engaging activity. Tell your stories and share them widely. Celebrate your successes.
5. Walk in your customer's shoes. Know what it's like to sit in your waiting room. Are your front desk staff warm and open, making strong, positive first impressions? Do you project a healing environment? Is your service setting age appropriate? Be critical and truly assess your organization from your customer's eyes and experiences.

Sources

Conca, Maria Gisella, and Antonella Pamploni Scarpa. 2004. *Quality and customer satisfaction*. Salem, NH: Goal/QPC.

Deming, W. Edwards. 1986. Out of the Crisis. MIT-CAES.

Gerteis, Margaret, Susan Edman-Levitan, Jennifer Daley, and Thomas L. Delbanco. 1993. *Through the patient's eyes*. San Francisco, CA: Jossey-Bass.

Graban, Mark. 2009. *Lean hospitals: Improving quality, patient safety, and employee satisfaction*. New York: Productivity Press, Taylor & Francis Group.

Guinane, Carole S. 2008. Interview with a quality leader: Regina E. Herzlinger on Consumer-driven healthcare. *The Journal for HealthCare Quality* 30: 17–19.

Herzlinger, Regina. 1997. *Market-driven health care: Who wins, who loses in the transformation of America's largest service industry*. Reading, MA: Perseus Books.

JCAHO (Joint Commission on Accreditation of Healthcare Organizations). 1995. *Understanding the patient's perspective: A tool for improving performance*. Oakbrook Terrace, IL: JCAHO.

JCAHO (Joint Commission on Accreditation of Healthcare Organizations). 2006. *Doing more with less: Lean thinking and patient safety in health care*. Oakbrook Terrace, IL: JCAHO.

Juran Institute. http://www.juran.com/about_juran_institute_index.html

MacInnes, Richard L. 2002. *The lean enterprise memory jogger*. Salem, NH: Goal/QPC.

Quality Council of Indiana. 2007. *LSS (Lean Six Sigma) primer*. West Terre Haute, IN: Quality Council of Indiana.

Shewhart, Walter. 1980. Economic Control of Quality of Manufactured Product/50th Anniversary Commemorative Issue. American Society for Quality Control. Milwaukee, Wisconsin.

Studer, Quint. 2003. *Hardwiring excellence: Purpose, worthwhile work, making a difference.* Gulf Breeze, FL: Fire Starter Publishing.

Venturelli, Joseph. *The informed patient.* 2005. http://itunes.apple.com/us/book/the-informed-patient/id388632819?mt=11.

Weil, Andrew. 2009. *Why our health matters: A vision of medicine that can transform our future.* New York: Hudson Street Press.

Chapter 4

Policies, Procedures, and Plans

Find out who you are and do it on purpose.

—**Dolly Parton**

Staying True to Your Mission, Vision, and Values

Dolly Parton knows who she is and has stayed true to herself. It doesn't mean she was stagnant by any means; in fact, quite the opposite. She has earned the love and admiration of loyal fans throughout her career, as well as proved her mettle as a savvy and respected businesswoman. She is a successful songwriter, musician, singer, and actress. Her philanthropic nature is well known, especially for the promotion of literacy through gifting of books to children. One doesn't hear bad things about Dolly; in fact, she is consistently amazing and certainly delights her ever-growing number of customers over and over. Spanning generations, she has earned her legendary status.

Dolly's words are important for this chapter: "Find out who you are and do it on purpose." That certainly sums it up. If we don't know who we are, then it's tough to be purposeful. Documents play a heavy role in healthcare as they help expand on who we are, and once that is defined, we undoubtedly should do it on purpose.

Creating Lean and Useful Documents

The importance of providing guidance to employees, physicians, and patients contributes to the essential value of communication. Users of any document within your outpatient setting should be able to easily read the document and to comprehend its intent. Ensure that documents are readily available, up to date, and consistent.

Most importantly, documents should matter. Work to convey what you do and why you do it. Written documents provide formal expectations for anyone who's directly or indirectly in contact with your healthcare services. If done correctly, policies, procedures, and plans will help improve, sustain, or revamp processes within any organization. Written documents clearly reflect and support the organization's mission, vision, and values.

Policies replicate the standards governing the execution of the facility's processes.

Procedures represent a realization of policy and will vary over time as new information, resources, and technologies emerge, new processes are created, and the risks associated with an area change in response to the internal or external environment. Procedures should be dynamic. Institute regular reviews and update outdated procedures. Quality improvement efforts, in part, help to identify potential process opportunities.

Plans, on the other hand, offer a series of steps. They are attached to goals that define what the organization is to accomplish. Plans are action oriented and much more detailed than policies. The following plans are critical for all healthcare organizations, whether outpatient or inpatient: quality, patient safety, risk management, infection prevention, environment of care, and compliance.

It's recommended that all documents are reviewed at least yearly, unless the scope of care and service has changed. Governance formally approves these documents every two years unless state or other regulatory agencies dictate otherwise.

Regulatory Requirements for Documents

The Medicare Conditions for Coverage for ASCs, §416.41, informs users about what is expected from the governing body and management.

> The ASC must have a governing body that assumes full legal responsibility for determining, implementing, and monitoring policies governing the ASC's total operation and for ensuring that these policies are administered so as to provide quality health care in a safe environment. When services are provided through a contract

with an outside resource, the ASC must assure that these services are provided in a safe and effective manner.

While this is just one snippet of information, similar wording and meaning can be found throughout other Medicare requirements, for services such as home care or rehab, or in accreditation or state licensing standards. This information links to Chapter 2. Integrate documentation with your structure to operate and govern the outpatient program.

The Users of Policies, Procedures, and Plans

Users of your documents include clinical and nonclinical staff, and customers of your services. Users include, but are not limited to, the following:

- Nursing staff
- Clinical and professional staff
- Credentialed physicians
- Referring physicians
- Allied health professionals
- Business office staff
- Transcription staff
- Contract services
- Vendors
- Students
- Volunteers
- Patients
- Patient families and significant others
- Management and administrative staff

Make your policy and procedure information widely accessible as appropriate to all audiences listed. This will provide a basis for accountability on all levels.

Remember, it's impractical to define all processes in a document. That would make the manuals cumbersome. Instead, keep the documents concise, factual, and current. Spell out all acronyms the first time you use them in a document.

Use Reference Manuals and Association Books

Don't make it too technical, unless it's necessary for patient care or operational processes. If technical and specific is appropriate, don't reinvent the wheel.

Use what's out there in the marketplace. It's much more productive to find an excellent resource that can be referenced as the detailed step-by-step tome. Purchase the books or manuals and then reference the appropriate section of the resource in your policy or procedure. Search the association and specialty sites that pertain to the outpatient services specialty. Look on Amazon.com, as just about everything is available for purchase.

Here are some organizations that offer resources in the form of books or manuals:

1. The Association for Operating Room Nurses (AORN) has excellent resources. A physician office performing procedures or an ambulatory surgery center benefits from having standards of care and practice available for all nursing staff. Following AORN's practice standards promotes patient, staff, and physician safety in any surgery or procedure suite. AORN resources are available at http://www.aorn.org.

2. ASPAN is the American Society of Perianesthesia Nurses, and like AORN offers succinct and helpful standards of care and practice. ASPAN represents the interests of more than 55,000 nurses practicing in all phases of preanesthesia and postanesthesia care, ambulatory surgery, and pain management. ASPAN resources are available at http://www.aspan.org.

3. The Medical Group Management Association (MGMA) provides information and resources for professional administrators and leaders of medical group practices. MGMA resources are available at http://www.mgma.com/.

4. The American Nurse Association (ANA) is the only full-service professional organization representing the interests of the United States' 3.1 million registered nurses through its constituent member nurses associations, its organizational affiliates, and its workforce advocacy affiliate, the Center for American Nurses. An extensive catalog of books can be viewed for purchase, covering nursing practice and standards of care at http://www.nursingworld.org/.

5. HCPro offers books, manuals, webinars, and other resources linked to accreditation, care processes, infection prevention, medical staff affairs, and quality. HCPro resources are available at http://www.hcpro.com.

6. The Association for Professionals in Infection Control and Epidemiology (APIC) boasts more than 13,000 members. Their primary responsibility is for infection prevention, control, and hospital epidemiology in healthcare settings around the globe. APIC offers an ambulatory e-newsletter that focuses specifically on the outpatient setting. APIC resources are available at http://www.apic.org.

7. The Ambulatory Surgery Center Association (ASC) provides benchmarking data, information on financial management for ASCs, HIPAA workbooks, a

Conditions for Coverage manual, and other resources specific to ambulatory surgery centers. ASC resources are available at http://www.ascassociation.org.
8. The American Society for Healthcare Risk Management (ASHRM) offers handbooks and other resources at http://www.ashrm.org.
9. The American College of Radiology (ACR) provides practical guidelines and standards along with other resources at http://www.acr.org.

Document Format

Determine how your policy and procedure manual will be set up. Once the organization is complete, the actual document would be created and assigned to a category. Standardize the format for policies and procedures. Figure 4.1 displays the information in a document format example.

TITLE	LOCATION	
NUMBER	APPLIES TO	
I. SCOPE/PURPOSE		
II. POLICY STATEMENT		
III. APPLICABILITY AND DEFINITIONS		
IV. EQUIPMENT		
V. PROCEDURE		
VI. DOCUMENTATION		
VII. RELATED DOCUMENTS		
VIII. REFERENCES AND RESOURCES		
IX. SUBMITTED BY		
X. EFFECTIVE DATE		
XI. DATES REVISED		
XII. DATES REVIEWED		
XIII. APPROVED BY:		DATE:
SIGNATURE (NOT ALWAYS REQUIRED)		
XIV. COMMITTEE APPROVAL		DATE:

Figure 4.1   Policy and procedure template.

Documents to Create and Have on Hand

When an outpatient service is licensed, accredited, or given deemed status by Medicare, document review is required. Having an effective plan in place as to what documents to create, implement, and review is key, plus it provides a starting point. Appendix A offers a table of contents listing policies, procedures, plans, and forms that will help an outpatient program meet the regulations and standards for most regulatory and licensing entities.

There are specialty certifications, centers of excellence, and organization-specific requirements that will require additional documents. Edit the table of contents as needed to conform to your needs.

If you choose to keep your documents electronically, allowing easy access for staff and physicians, make sure you have at least one hard copy available. Equipment failure, lost electronic files, and theft do happen.

It's helpful, in some cases, to create scenarios that supplement the documents. These are particularly valuable when running drills for malignant hyperthermia, patient codes, allergic reaction to a medication, patient falls, impaired physician/practitioner, intruder and potential violence event, fire drills, and disruptive individuals. Scenarios are essentially a script that is written and then acted out, with employees, physicians, and other invited guests taking on the characters in the script. When completing scenarios, make it as real as possible, using the rooms where the event would happen, and making sure everything works down to the equipment, emergency generator, 911, staff, and physicians.

A glossary of terms can be found in Appendix B to assist with the definitions needed for your documents. Chapter 12 provides more information about scenarios.

Reviewing and Revising Your Documents

A good rule of thumb is to review documents yearly. Table 4.1 is a procedure assessment tool example that can be used to elicit input from staff members at your organization. The information received can help determine if the documents in place are working and are being used. Add a couple of additional lines to obtain information about specific problem documents, and to ask what documents need to be added.

Think about assessing any written document against a set criteria base such as the following:

- Application to your mission, vision, and values
- Necessary to meet state, federal, or regulatory requirements

Table 4.1   Procedure Assessment Tool

	Statement	Strongly Disagree	Disagree	Neither Disagree nor Agree	Agree	Strongly Agree
1	Most procedures don't apply to me.	1	2	3	4	5
2	I know where the policy and procedures manual is kept.	1	2	3	4	5
3	Some procedures are difficult to understand.	1	2	3	4	5
4	Some procedures conflict with one another.	1	2	3	4	5
5	I have better ways of doing things than those written in the procedures.	1	2	3	4	5
6	Some procedures contribute to unsafe practices.	1	2	3	4	5
7	I have read the procedure manual in the last year.	1	2	3	4	5
8	I have not been trained on the procedures that pertain to my job.	1	2	3	4	5
9	It's necessary to work around procedures to get the job done.	1	2	3	4	5
10	Compliance with procedures is not enforced.	1	2	3	4	5
11	Procedures are not kept up to date.	1	2	3	4	5

(Continued)

Table 4.1 Procedure Assessment Tool (Continued)

	Statement	Strongly Disagree	Disagree	Neither Disagree nor Agree	Agree	Strongly Agree
12	I often encounter situations where a procedure is not available to help me.	1	2	3	4	5
13	Some procedures are impossible to comply with.	1	2	3	4	5
14	Peer pressure exists to work around the procedures.	1	2	3	4	5
15	My supervisor does not comply with procedures.	1	2	3	4	5

- Needed to enhance competency
- Required to define quality and safety for the organization
- Guides employees and physicians on how to care for patients

Summary and Key Points

1. Create documents that matter. Be succinct and make the documents user friendly.
2. Governance and management are owners of these policies, procedures, and plans.
3. Use materials in the marketplace for your technical procedures and reference them in your documents.
4. Keep a consistent document format throughout.
5. Use the checklist provided to create your table of contents and documents.
6. Incorporate facility-specific documents in the table of contents.
7. Review and update your documents at least once a year.
8. Use the documents as a teaching tool for the staff and physicians.
9. Keep at least one hard copy of the documents available to the staff.
10. Evaluate policies, procedures, and plans yearly if possible.

Chapter 5

The Human Resource Factor

The greatest tragedy in America is not the destruction of our natural resources, though that tragedy is great. The truly great tragedy is the destruction of our human resources by our failure to fully utilize our abilities, which means that most men and women go to their graves with their music still in them.

—Oliver Wendell Holmes

Overview

The human resource (HR) factor in outpatient settings promotes a preventive and systematic people program that results in successful outcomes for the patients that we serve. The HR factor covers employees, physicians, allied health professionals, contract workers, vendors, and volunteers. Each group requires different levels of oversight and management when it comes to meeting state, federal, and regulatory requirements. In addition, the HR factor can make or break any business. The HR factor relies on alignment with specialized workers to deliver care and service as it relates to the mission, vision, and values of the organization.

The elements of human resource management include coaching, interviewing, hiring, competency and skills assessment, orientation, ongoing education and training, job descriptions, job qualification, performance reviews, privileging, credentialing, proctoring, contracting, worker's compensation, separation management, and benefits. Organizational development, which contributes to the culture, is not included in the HR factor as it's a separate science with its own unique set of quality measures. It's important to note that the HR factor and organizational development significantly influence one another. In addition, keep in mind that physician and allied health practitioner privileging, staff competency, and scope of care/service are synergistic, relying on one another to create an HR factor that influences the care process.

To adequately cover human resource management in one chapter is not possible, nor would that be the intent of this book. However, human resource management is the nuts and bolts of the HR factor. To create a dynamic, value-added HR factor, the nuts and bolts are critical for success. The items that will be covered in this chapter relate to the quality side of the HR factor equation—it's what puts rocket boosters on the nuts and bolts structure, allowing it to fly.

One can look at a successful HR factor mathematically. HR Factor (Y) = quality × HR management. If quality (x) is lacking or stumbling, we produce a weak or negligible HR factor (Y). If the management program for HR (x) is lacking or stumbling, we again produce a low performing HR factor (Y). Alignment and leverage are needed between human resource management and quality to produce a highly functional HR factor.

Quality and the HR Factor

During the late 1980s at a Deming Institute course, Dr. W. Edwards Deming, the father of quality advancement, asked a group of healthcare leaders how they convey their mission, vision, and values to employees. He expressed his dismay regarding leadership dropping the ball with constancy of purpose. Essentially, his message was short and gruff. If an employee can't relate what the mission is, the purpose as to why the organization exists, then why on Earth did that person accept the job? There isn't a link between the organization and employee, but rather, it's just a job, a filling of a slot. The employee is there in body; punches in and out on the time clock, cashes his or her paycheck, and performs the minimum to get by each and every day. The connection, the soul, the fire in the belly is sadly missing. Does that sound familiar? If so, then a wake-up call is needed in your facility.

Finding and retaining the right people in any organization is vital. Take time to create well-thought-out policies, procedures, job descriptions, and other documents to adequately articulate what is expected from any individual who decides to join your organization. People want to know what they are required to do, as well as what makes up their workday. Make sure the HR factor links to your mission, vision, and values, as few workplace offerings are worse than inconsistency in what is written and also what is transmitted through actions. A dynamic quality program is thoughtful, as words and actions are powerful contributors to HR outcomes.

The following information can provide important information to leaders and stakeholders when determining the quality component of the HR factor. These items are not all-inclusive. Create your own plan, adding and deleting as necessary to make the program effective for your facility.

1. Define what constitutes a complete file for the following:
   a. Employee HR
   b. Employee health
   c. Employee education and training
   d. Physician appointment and privileging
   e. Physician quality and peer review
   f. Volunteers
   g. Vendor contracts
   h. Professional and non-professional contracts
2. Monitor, collect, and analyze data for the following:
   a. Employee, physician, and contract service satisfaction
   b. Complete files, including authentication
   c. Up-to-date tracking of licenses, certifications, mandatory training, and orientation
3. Determine internal and external benchmarks for the following:
   a. Productivity
   b. Clinical man-hours
   c. Overall man-hours
   d. HR vacancies and turnover
   e. Worker's compensation claims
   f. Needle sticks and injuries and Occupational Safety and Health Act (OSHA)-required outcomes

Appropriate language in job and position descriptions, application attestation, and/or contracts that specifically require adherence to state and federal law, regulatory requirements, and licensing standards apply to all employees, physicians, practitioners, contract workers, and vendors.

Creating Complete HR Files

Recordkeeping is by far one of the most important functions of any human resource and medical staff services department. The file contains a record of every action that was taken for employment or privileging and credentialing. Keep a file for each person who is associated with the outpatient facility. This includes contract services, vendors, and volunteers. Volunteers are found in many outpatient programs. As they can influence the safety and quality program, they must be vetted; therefore, their files are the same. Students may serve in some capacity at the location, so initiate appropriate school/program paperwork. Precise and ongoing measures ensure that the files are exact, complete, and current.

Files that concern medical examinations and information, disability, worker's compensation, and other related items are to be kept separate. In addition, employee health files may include:

- Results of tests required under OSHA
- Participation in wellness programs offered by the organization
- Hazardous work environment medical inspections
- Substance abuse monitoring and testing records
- Fitness for duty examination information
- Medical leave information
- Physician and nursing notes regarding absences and other health matters
- Results of psychological tests
- Requests for family leaves to care for a sick family member

An employee's HR file contains personnel documents that have a direct relation to the employee's job and responsibilities, including licenses, certifications, performance evaluations, employment application, salary adjustments, and other associated documents. Access to the employee files is limited to those who are supervisors of that employee, or those who need to know from a regulatory or legal need. The HR file is kept separate from the employee health file and the education/training file. Please remember that if physicians or other practitioners are employed, they require employee files, along with a credentialing file, which is detailed later on in this chapter.

Included in the HR files are the following:

1. Job application, resume, and job description, verification of references, background check results, criminal background checks, and credit checks
2. Conflict of Interest signed form
3. Evidence of appropriate licensure and certification

4. Performance appraisals and results per policy and procedure
5. Compensation reviews, updates, and adjustments
6. Signed form acknowledging receipt of the employee handbook, and that it was read
7. I-9 (immigration and naturalization form), visas, and other documents. Many times this information is kept separately due to the confidentiality of the information.
8. Documentation of how the licensure, certification, and information are updated to ensure that expirations do not occur.
9. National Practitioner Data Bank (NPDB) report for all clinical professionals
10. Office of Inspector General (OIG) and state report on sanctions
11. Education and training file contains the following:
    - Completion of compliance and Health Insurance Portability and Accountability Act (HIPAA) training
    - OSHA mandatory training
    - Orientation and training to the organization and department
    - Evidence that employee was orientated to the policies, procedures, and processes of the organization
    - Advanced cardiac life support (ACLS), pediatric advanced life support (PALS), basic life support (BLS), ATLS training
    - Skills checklist per job description
    - Competency assessment and results
    - On-the-job orientation and training for the position, including timeline, assessment as to readiness, and ongoing monitoring and evaluation
    - Education and training plan based on assessment needs, competency, and skills checklist. For example, the plan can include the results of the National League of Nursing medication exam.
    - Continuing education and college course information pertinent to the job
    - Proctoring requirements
12. Separate employee health file includes the following:
    - Employee physical exam results
    - Signed hepatitis B immunization record, vaccination, or declination of vaccination
    - Immunization record per state and organization requirements; for example, H1N1, flu, rubella, rubeola, or varicella zoster.
    - Tuberculosis screening questionnaire
    - TB screening, which includes the two-step skin test and/or chest x-ray
    - Any other medical information that is specific to the employee or family member

Medical staff and allied health professional files are different from employees' as they are governed by medical staff policies, procedures, bylaws, and rules and regulations. Verification of credentials must be in line with the policies, procedures, bylaws, and rules and regulations of the organization. Primary and secondary source verification is appropriately used. Also in place is a clear definition regarding the timeframes for reappointment, which should not be longer than two years. If the timeframe passes, the practitioner's membership and privileges cannot be extended, as they have lapsed and appointment is to occur once again. All files are reviewed by an appropriate peer prior to signing off on membership, privileging, and competency.

Included in the medical staff and AHP files are the following:

1. Complete, signed application for appointment and reappointment
2. Signed liability release form
3. Signed attestation form
4. Primary source verification of education, training, board certification, and current competency
5. Board certification is monitored as applicable with current information documented
6. State medical license or AHP license is verified and monitored with current information documented
7. DEA registration validated/verified and is monitored, with current information documented
8. Proof of current medical liability coverage per governing body requirements as appropriate and applicable
9. National Practitioner Data Bank report on the practitioner
10. OIG reports regarding sanctions
11. Signed clinical privilege request form
12. Review and approval form from medical staff leadership and the governing body, with specific approval for clinical privilege recommendations from the medical staff leadership
13. Quality and Health file contains:
    a. Professional liability claims history information
    b. Peer review results
    c. Quality profiles used for appointment and reappointment. See Table 5.1 for an example of a physician profile
    d. Disciplinary action taken based on behavior, quality outcomes, or health issues
    e. Sanctions by any organization, including Medicare and Medicaid
    f. Complaints filed against the practitioner by local, state, or national organization or licensure board

Table 5.1   Physician Reappointment Example

Physician: Timeframe:	Number	Facility Benchmark	External Benchmark	Comments
American Medical Association Reappointment Profile	N/A	N/A	N/A	
NPDB Report	N/A	N/A	N/A	
Consults Performed—volume				
Surgical Procedures—volume				
Other Procedures—volume				
Meeting Attendance				
Medical Record Delinquencies				
Suspensions				
Malpractice Claims				
Criminal Actions				
OIG Sanctions				
Other Sanctions				
Patient Grievances and Complaints				
Staff Complaints				
Complications				
Number of Deaths				
Disciplinary Actions				
Infections				

(Continued)

Table 5.1 Physician Reappointment Example (Continued)

Physician: Timeframe:	Number	Facility Benchmark	External Benchmark	Comments
Readmissions within 30 days				
Surgical and Procedure Appropriateness				
Facility Measures: Compliance				
Medication Management Issues				
Continuing Medical Education Current and Meets Facility/State/Specialty Requirements				
Other:				

    g. Refusal or cancellation of professional liability coverage

    h. Denial, suspension, limitation, termination, or nonrenewal of privileges at any hospital, ambulatory program, health plan, medical group, or other health care entity

    i. U.S. Drug Enforcement Agency (DEA) and state license action against the practitioner

    j. Conviction of a criminal offense

    k. Health information:

        i. Chemical dependency, including monitoring and evaluation by an approved organization

       ii. Verification of current physical and mental health

     iii. Required vaccinations or tests per the organization's policies and state/federal requirements

These files are highly confidential and many laws, regulations, and standards are in place to protect individuals in the workplace. Therefore, knowing and understanding the law as it relates to employees, credentialed practitioners, and contract workers associated with the outpatient program is necessary.

Health Care Quality Improvement Act (HCQIA) of 1986

Most physicians and healthcare leaders, if asked, could not explain the intent or purpose of this act, and many would be unaware of its existence. Unfortunately, the act that was created to protect the public and physicians has been abused. Monopolies made up of powerful physician committees practice with economic and political interests and intent instead of leading with quality improvement and safety initiatives. Hundreds of physicians and independent practitioners are locked out of certain practice venues due to this inappropriate use of this act. The National Practitioner Data Bank is also abused with data reporting from silos of errant and misguided decision makers.

It can't be stressed enough that fair practices in credentialing and peer review are mandatory when fostering high-quality standards in outpatient settings. If this is not the plan, then physicians will not get involved, as the incentives are nonexistent. Peer review and medical staff quality programs should focus on the good apple approach, with the patient at the beginning of the decision-making passageway.

Vendor and Contract Files

Vendors and contract services can contribute to a quality program in an outpatient setting. Some are better than others, and some are downright horrible. Whether it's linen services, generator preventive maintenance, an engineer, or any number of services required, doing your due diligence will pay off and you will get a reputation that you only do business with high-quality organizations.

When setting up a relationship with a vendor or contract service, there are several steps to think through and to complete. A contract with a vendor or contract service is a legal document and, depending upon what is signed, it could be difficult to get out of the contract should a bad outcome or relationship ensue. Read each and every contract in detail and make sure the proposal matches what the contract ends up saying.

Corroborate the language of timeframes to ensure that they are in sync with what your organization requires. Look for proper names from all parties, as sometimes a vendor or contract service will place another name in the contract, and when it comes down to filing a complaint or discontinuing the contract, it may be difficult due to the names used in the contract.

Check for an out period, as both sides should have the ability to discontinue the contract, but take care of your organization first. Less than 90 days is a good timeline. Often, one will find that the contract is binding for years. Don't let that happen to you.

Ask whether the contract can be serviced by other entities. If so, get counter bids, at least two others. Also, obtain references from those that have used or are using the service. Search the company on Google to see what's out there. It's surprising what you can find on the Internet nowadays about any company or individual.

Determine who in your organization can and should sign off on contracts. All clinical contract services need to go before your medical staff and governing body for approval, as they do potentially impact care.

If a contract is in place for longer than one year, ensure the pricing is consistent for all years and does not increase after each year. Every vendor or contract service is to provide proof of insurance with the proposed contract. Keep a copy of the signed contract and set up a file to monitor the deliverables, as well as any expiration dates.

Clinical Contract Employee Requirement and Files

The following documents must be provided by the contracting individual(s) for inclusion in the contractor files:

1. Copies of documentation proving that the following has been performed or verified:
   a. Preemployment drug screening with a negative result
   b. Applicant health assessment results are obtained and kept in a separate file. Follow your policy for health assessment, tests, and vaccines.
   c. Highest level of education as required by job description
   d. Licensure/certification/registration/accreditation as required by job description. Verify that licensure and all other documents are in good standing.
   e. Professional references (preferably three) have been contacted.
   f. Criminal background check has been completed and is negative.
   g. Credit check has been completed if required for the position.
   h. Database checks have been done as required by the OIG and NPDB.
2. Copies of prior and ongoing performance reviews. Performance reviews performed while in the employ of your facility must utilize your organization's job description featuring the contractor's logo/name.
3. Copy of current license/certificate/registration/accreditation as required by the job description. The contractor must provide a current copy prior to expiration of the license.

4. Copy of documentation of all training/education—prior and future.
5. Completion of Certification of Religious, Ethical, and/or Treatment Conflicts form, Conflict of Interest form, and Confidentiality form.
6. Copies of initial and ongoing competency assessments as follows:
   a. Includes competency checklist, which must be completed during orientation
   b. The job description assessment, which should be completed according to your policy
7. Training and Education Files are the same as noted for the employee file in this chapter.
8. Contractor must provide a copy of the following policies for review. If any policy is found to be inadequate, you must reserve the right to require the contractor to institute a comparable policy for the contractor's employees who are assigned to your facility. The following is a list, but it is not all-inclusive.
   a. Care plans, coordination of care, and all policies relating to how they will perform their service at your facility
   b. Substance abuse policy
   c. Antiharassment policy
   d. Workplace violence policy
   e. Application for employment (to include requirement for background checks)
   f. Hiring policy
   g. Grooming and dress code policy
   h. Personal behavior policy
   i. Bulletin boards policy
   j. Company property policy
   k. Confidentiality policy
   l. Conflict of interest/commitment policy
   m. Electronic data system policy
   n. Identification badges policy
   o. Inclement weather policy
   p. Solicitation, distribution, and posting policy
9. Evaluation process of the contract service includes the following:
   a. Supervisor evaluation at 30 days or a timeframe that suits your organization
   b. Supervisor evaluation every year as per HR employee evaluation policy
   c. Medical Staff evaluation with contract selection and renewal

Monitoring, Collecting, and Analyzing Data

There are many ways to monitor and analyze data to fulfill the quality side of the HR factor equation. Software programs exist to help with the credentialing of physicians and practitioners. Human resource programs are also in existence. If you cannot invest in a program, simple Excel files can be used.

Some simple items to track are the following:

1. Job descriptions that are signed and dated by the employee and supervisor
2. Privilege forms that are signed and dated by the practitioner and medical director or designee
3. Appointment/reappointments that are signed and dated by medical director or designee
4. Completion of checklists that accompany each file
5. Audits of files are performed on a regular basis
6. Keep an Excel file that shows what is needed regarding updates for licenses, certifications, board renewals, training, competencies, and reappointments

Figures 5.1 and 5.2 display control charts that track man-hours per case. While the control chart is the same data, the histograms are different. Figure 5.1 shows the data prior to improvement regarding reduction of overall man-hours to bring it more in line with national and internal benchmarks. The analysis of the data is noted in Table 5.2. The average decreased significantly, as did the process sigma and control limits. The histogram has narrowed, showing the reduction in variation as well as a shift in the overall process average and distribution.

Figure 5.3 shows how to collect data on contracts for services rendered by companies, individuals, or vendors that are not employees. The form allows for monitoring and evaluation of key clinical and nonclinical services.

Figure 5.4 presents a Pareto diagram that shows the variables that contribute to needle sticks at an organization. Since all needle sticks are considered defects, control charts are not needed. Each defect is to be investigated with appropriate actions taken to protect the person who was stuck from potential bloodborne pathogen transmission. While the goal would be zero defects (Y), the variable data (x) requires analysis. A Pareto chart helps determine what variables are producing 80 percent of the problems, which in this case is recapping syringes and blades/needles in place when cleaning instruments. The improvement plan would concentrate on the 80 percent initially, with improvements continuing until a zero defect environment is obtained.

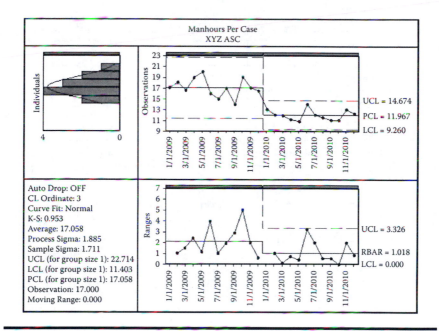

Figure 5.1 **Manhours per case before improvement.**

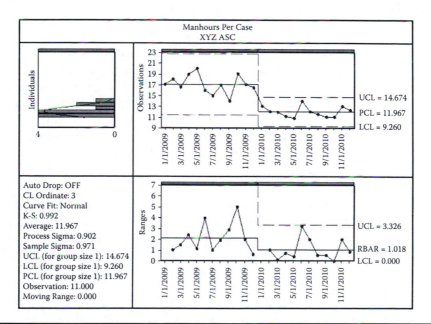

Figure 5.2 **Manhours per case after improvement.**

Table 5.2   Results of the Man-hours Improvement Effort

	Before	*After*
Average	17.058	11.967
Sigma	1.885	0.902
Upper Control Limit	22.7	14.674
Lower Control Limit	11.4	9.26

Table 5.3 offers another data collection tool, this time for analyzing over-time, breaks, and lunch. Have employees turn in the completed form with the timecard. The results provide pertinent information about overtime and whether employees are taking breaks and lunches. Some states have strict requirements in place for payment when lunch and breaks are not taken.

Create a data collection plan that works for your facility. Make it dynamic and make it pertinent.

HR Training to Promote Safety and Quality

OSHA requires that employees and other individuals affiliated with your facility complete training before starting work and yearly thereafter, unless situations arise requiring more frequent training. Fortunately, products and programs exist that are ready to go for most organizations in this area. The training and surveillance does not have to be overwhelming. Once again, tracking adherence is important. In addition, if done correctly, training and education can facilitate a safer envi-ronment, leading to improved and sustained quality outcomes. It's important to check your state OSHA requirements, as they do differ in many cases.

Training that is essential consists of the following:

1. *Infection prevention* training can help prevent unnecessary transmission of deadly organisms through proper hand washing and hygiene, instill-ing precautions and prevention, and learning respiratory hygiene when sick. This can extend to your patient population, as many patients treated are sick, so there is a need to prevent transmission through preventive practices.
2. *Personal protective equipment (PPE)* training includes the use of goggles, shoe covers, masks, hats, gloves, and other protective devices and gear.

Complete this summary, and submit with all the appropriate paperwork/information to your supervisor for approval, including additions or addendums. When completed, file with contract.

Vendor/Provider/Co.:		Service :	
Initial Effective Date:	How many days are required to cancel the contract?	Who's Resp.	
Exp Date or Auto Renewal (circle one)	Date:	Leader Name:	
Description of Contract:			

Forward Copies to: (1) Leader　　　　　(2) Copy To　　　　　(3) Copy To

- ACTION REQUIRED -

1. ☐ New/ ☐ Renewal　　　2.☐ Annual Review　　　3. ☐ Addendum　　　4.☐ Amendment　　　5. ☐ Cancellation

1. NEW/RENEWAL: *Note any pertinent information relating to this contract in the Comment section below.*

Comments:

2. ANNUAL REVIEW: *Evaluate the following categories and provide detail in the comment section if a category is unacceptable.*

a. Provides timely, complete and accurate services.	☐ Acceptable	☐ Unacceptable
b. Provides appropriate and competent staff.	☐ Acceptable	☐ Unacceptable
c. Responds to requests and problems effectively.	☐ Acceptable	☐ Unacceptable
d. Complies with organization, legal, licensing, and regulatory requirements.	☐ Acceptable	☐ Unacceptable

Comments:

3. ADDENDUM: if additional information is required to complete the contract evaluation, please detail what is attached and why

Addendum : ☐ Yes ☐ No:

What and why?

4. AMENDMENT: *Must include reason and effective date of amendment.*

Reason for Amendment:	**Amendment Date**
	/ /

5.CANCELLATION: *Must include reason and effective date of Cancellation/Intent To Cancel.*

Cancellation Letter Required:　　　☐ No ☐ Yes: Explain below.	**Cancellation Date**
Reason for Cancellation:	/ /

Notice of Intent to Cancel Letter Required:　　　☐ No ☐ Yes: Explain below.	**Intent To Cancel Date**
Reason for Intent to Cancel:	/ /

- APPROVAL SECTION -	**Date Approved**
a. **Leader:**	/ /
b. **Other Signature:**	/ /

- ADMINISTRATIVE USE ONLY -

Contract No.:	No.	**Annual Review Date:**	Date	Addendum Sent:	Y/N	/ /
				Addendum Received:	Y/N	/ /
Contract Type:	Type	**Leader Rev Date:**	Date	Amendment Sent:	Y/N	/ /
				Amendment Received:	Y/N	/ /
Clin/ NonClin:	C/NC	**Last Review Date:**	/ /	Cancellation Letter Sent:	Y/N	/ /
				Proof of Delivery Received:	Y/N	/ /
Business Assoc:	Y/N	**Next Review Date:**	/ /	Intent to Cancel Letter Sent:	Y/N	/ /
				Proof of Delivery Received:	Y/N	/ /

NOTES:

Figure 5.3　Contract summary sheet.

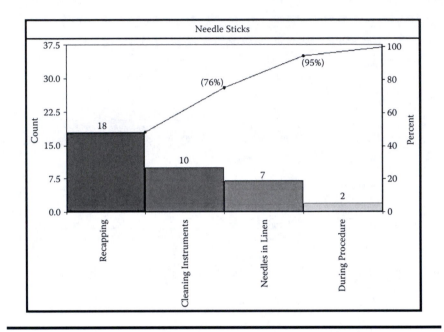

Figure 5.4   Needle stick Pareto chart.

Assessing your facility to determine what is needed helps to understand what training to provide and what equipment to have available for your staff.

3. *Ergonomics* training and implementing a program to reduce work-related musculoskeletal disorders caused by repetition, forceful exertions, awkward positions, contact stress, and vibration.

4. *Workplace violence* trains those who are associated with your facility with information about how to stay safe and how to promote a safe environment. This includes terrorism and what to do should this occur. Also included is family and domestic violence, as many incidences of workplace violence can trend back to people that employees know. Included in the training is how to report any signs of abuse to local, state, or federal law enforcement agencies or to a designated abuse line. The law requires that this information is available to your employees and physicians so they know how to report abuse.

5. *Harassment* training shows how to create an environment free of sexual and other harassment in the workplace.

6. *Fire safety*, which includes fire hazards, prevention, and rescue, activate alarm, contain the fire, and extinguish or evacuate (RACE).

Table 5.3   Data Tracking Tool for Overtime and Breaks

Check One or More Boxes as They Apply for Each Day of the Payroll Period and If Another Reason for Overtime, No lunch, or Break Occurs, Please Explain:	M	T	W	T	F
Overtime due to late case					
Overtime due to MD request					
Overtime due to staffing issues					
Overtime due to workload					
Overtime due to leadership request					
Overtime due to caseload					
Other for overtime:					
No lunch break due to MD request					
No lunch break due to staffing issues					
No lunch break due to caseload					
Other for no lunch breaks:					
No break(s) due to MD request					
No break(s) due to staffing issues					
No break(s) due to caseload					
Other for no breaks:					
Employee Signature					
Date					
Supervisor Signature					
Date					

7. *Portable fire extinguisher use,* unless it's required that employees evacuate due to the small size of the business.
8. *Bloodborne pathogens,* which covers safety needles and sharps. Employees in most healthcare organizations are or could be exposed to bloodborne pathogens. Include in your training basic safety requirements, such as the use of self-sheathing needles, gloves, masks, and gowns. That is why vaccinations are important, to protect employees, physicians, and patients.

9. *Hazard communication and emergency preparedness* upon hire. Since healthcare facilities usually have hazardous chemicals and drugs on premises, having a safety plan addressing hazardous material is vital. Employees have a right to know details about any dangerous chemicals with which they may come in contact. Employees also have the right to information regarding what safety measures are required to prevent adverse effects from occurring as a result of these hazardous materials. Material safety data sheets must be available to help employees with information about any hazardous material on site.

10. *Radiation safety.* OSHA requirements for healthcare facilities regulate the use of x-ray machines or other devices that may cause a radiation threat to workers. Any facility using radiation-emitting technology must disclose the type and create a floor plan, so that restricted areas can be clearly marked to allow only authorized personnel in the area. Those working in the areas must wear radiation monitors. Proper warning signs are posted to inform workers of the threat of potential radiation. Also include magnet safety programs to ensure that facilities using magnetic resonance imaging (MRI) have promoted safe practices in their organization.

OSHA requires that businesses keep records that show compliance with all safety and health standards. By carefully maintaining an OSHA file in a place accessible to any OSHA inspector, you should be able to avoid the heavy fines that may accompany noncompliance.

You can log onto the OSHA website to download all forms needed for recordkeeping compliance. Always keep a pulse on OSHA and what is required. For now, under the recordkeeping requirements an employer must:

■ Maintain exposure records for the duration of the exposed employee's employment plus 30 years
■ Record needle sticks (if medical treatment is necessary) on their Form OSHA 200
■ Maintain training records for three years
■ Maintain records (healthcare) sharps injury log.

Not all training that is provided is OSHA required. There will be programs offered in your facility to meet or exceed safety and quality standards. Such training programs could cover quality and safety, patient rights, advance directives, customer service, and scenarios.

Audits and Auditors

Audits and auditors are invited into healthcare organizations on a regular basis. At the same time, some are not invited, but they show up. Either way, it's appropriate to validate and vet them just as we would anyone else who has access to sensitive and confidential information. When working with auditors who are invited, check out their credentials. Are they certified? Should they be? Call references and complete reference checks. Look online for any information about the company and individuals who will be working in your facility. Check them out on the OIG site. And most importantly, have an out clause; if they are not doing what they should be doing, you want the option to terminate the contract.

Define expectations for any audit that you choose to put into place. Have an action plan with timeframes assigned. Both sides should know what the expectations are and what you determine to be value added for your facility.

Summary and Key Points

1. Laws, regulations, and oversight abound in the world of human resource management. Be aware of your local, state, and federal laws and the regulations that govern your particular organization.
2. Carefully select and train the individual(s) who is responsible for administration of the files, paperwork, and oversight of your human resource program.
3. Keep meticulous and current records for all of your employees, physicians, practitioners, contract workers, volunteers, vendors, and students.
4. Invest in your HR factor through training, policies and procedures, and process. Competent workers elevate the quality of care for patients.
5. Use appropriate quality tools to analyze your HR data.
6. Collect and analyze data to know if your program is producing the quality and safety outcomes that are desired in a world-class outpatient environment.
7. Vet auditors who come into your facility.
8. Take time to appreciate the people who work in your organization. Create an environment that fosters teamwork through great communication networks and customer orientation.
9. Even if your organization is small, it doesn't mean you can bypass the HR factor.

Sources

Deutsch, Sheryl, and Christine S. Mobley. 1999. *The credentialing handbook.* Gaithersburg, MD: Aspen Publishers, Inc.

Finkler, Steven A., and Mary L. McHugh. 2008. *Budgeting concepts for nurse managers.* St. Louis, MO: Saunders Elsevier.

Guinane, Carole S. 1999. Esprit de corp: Is work something you really believe in? *The Journal for HealthCare Quality* 21:28–34.

National Association Medical Staff Services, http://www.namss.org/.

Rollo, James. 2009. *Performance management 2nd edition: A pocket guide for employee development.* Salem, MA: Goal/QPC and Competitive Advantage Consultants, Inc.

Rozakis, Laurie E., and Ellen Lichtenstein. 1995. *21st century Robert's Rules of Order.* New York: The Philip Lief Group, Inc.

Chapter 6

Measuring Quality and Safety

Nothing in life is to be feared. It is only to be understood.

—**Marie Curie, physicist and
first woman to win the Nobel Prize**

Measurement

Measuring data need not be feared, nor should looking at what the data's story represents. Measuring what matters is fundamental because success, failure, and mediocrity are identified only when creating and using a robust and elegant measurement program. This is a strategic necessity for the formation and continuation of an effective and high-performance quality and safety program. Knowing leads to moments of inspiration and ah-ha's, and this then leads to improvement and innovation, and ultimately integration throughout the organization.

Keep in mind that scorecard measures are to be aligned with the mission, vision, and values of the organization. What is learned from the data will help leaders with their strategy for the business and to maintain a competitive advantage.

To assist with understanding measurement in the outpatient setting, a scorecard example, along with ways statistical and analytical tools can be used, will be covered in this chapter. As important as strategic measures are to the organization, even more powerful are grassroots measures. This means that those closest to the process, the owners of the work, know what is done, when it's done, and how it's done, and what it all means as it relates to customer expectations.

At times the data is soft, meaning it isn't numerical. That doesn't mean it's not usable or powerful. A great example of the latter is customer murmurs. Some of the greatest leaps in improvement and innovation have to do with documenting what the customer says by observing their interaction with the processes and systems they encounter in the *Gemba*.

As mentioned in Chapter 3, customers don't always know what they want, so it's up to the business owners to figure out what to do to exceed their expectations. With the patient cancellation case study in this chapter, the front desk personnel listened to the customers and documented what they said as to why they were canceling. In addition, when patients came in for their appointment, they documented the murmurs, the things the patients or family members and caregivers were saying, such as:

"Why aren't you open on Saturdays? It would make my life so much easier."
"Is there any way to set up appointments online or with a real person?"
"Why does it take so long to get an appointment? I shouldn't have to wait three weeks to receive care when I don't feel well."

Reviewing the customer murmur data at staff meetings on a regular basis is a wonderful way to identify new opportunities for improvement and innovation. Take this thought process even further by applying it to employees and physicians. What are they really saying? What murmurs are going on in the break rooms or when chatting in the hallway? How many times does someone ask you for help to fix the same broken process? You will be amazed as to what you hear when you really listen. Create an open communication channel with those around you.

Induction, Deduction, and the Scientific Method

Induction and deduction are both needed for critical thinking and logic. In healthcare, fostering critical thinking is important to patient care and quality outcomes. When we use logic, we put on our scientist hat and we use science to guide our decision making. A scientific method consists of the collection of data through observation and experimentation, and the formulation and testing of hypotheses.

A common method used in healthcare is the PDCA cycle, otherwise known as plan, do, check, and act. Some may refer to it as PDSA, or plan, do, study, and act. This methodology was created in the late 1920s by Dr. Walter Shewhart, a Bell Laboratories scientist, with further use and clarification from Dr. Deming. Dr. Deming considered Dr. Shewhart to be his friend and mentor.

Figure 6.1 provides a nice example of a PDCA worksheet. Figure 6.2 displays the definitions of the terms referenced in Figure 6.1. Notice that **Accreditation Association for Ambulatory Health Care** (AAAHC) categories are used in this example. You can change this section to meet the needs of whatever accrediting agency is selected for your organization. If you choose to use this worksheet, make it two-sided to help users remember the definitions, and make it available so everyone feels they can improve the processes they own. It's a great tool and has been effective in day-to-day use by employees and physicians in many outpatient settings.

Case Study

If you haven't had specific training on quality tools and methods, sign up for training, or find a reasonable consultant to assist you with your transformation journey to the quality and safety side of business. Learning the ins and outs of data measurement, analysis, and how to understand variation leads to achieving stability and high-performing systems.

Figures 6.3 through 6.8 show the results of a study initiated by staff members to reduce patient cancellations. Figure 6.3 tells the story of the improvement effort, summarizing the actions identified and the use of statistical and decision-making tools to determine what the process was producing for the center. Figures 6.4 and 6.6 are before and after control charts, demonstrating that common cause variation exists in both charts. It can be said that on any given day, cancellations would be between 3.718 and 12.784 based on the control limits, reducing to zero to 5.717 based on the control limits after the improvement. Of note is that the lower control limit for the after control chart is actually a negative 1.984. For this data set, we can't have a negative number of cancellations, so it reverts to zero as the lower control limit (LCL).

The analysis of variance (ANOVA), Figure 6.8, of the before and after data shows a statistical shift in the processes as the p value is less than .05. Figures 6.5 and 6.7 are before and after Pareto charts, lending important information regarding the days of the week where cancellations were occurring frequently, helping to point the improvement efforts in the right direction.

What is most powerful about this data and study is that blame didn't occur. The process was broken and it needed to be fixed, as is usually the case in most situations. Employees were empowered to collect the data and to really figure out what was going on to improve the process for patients. What is beautiful about

Process Owner and Team Members: Date:

PLAN

Aim and Improvement Opportunity:

Customer(s):

Performance Measure: *(see definitions on back of form)*

• Volume + Flow	• Cost + Efficiency	• Process + Output	• Outcome
• Risk Management/Safety/Infection Control		• Customer Satisfaction	

Dimensions of Performance Monitored: *(see definitions on back of form)*

• Efficiency • Safety • Timeliness • Other_____	• Continuity • Availability • Respect and Caring	• Appropriateness • Efficacy • Effectiveness

AAAHC Application: *(see definitions on back of form)*

• RP • GOV • ADM • QC • QMI • HIM • PI • F&E • ANES • SURG

• PHARM • LAB • RAD • EDUC

DO   Data Collected/Method Used?   Time Frame:

Sample Size: Data Source:

UCL, LCL, mean, p value, sigma value, correlation coefficient, or other:

Benchmark (external and internal):

Data Display/Analysis Tool(s):

• Regression Analysis	• ANOVA	• Crystal Ball	• Cause and Effect
• Flow Chart(s):	• Control Chart	• Pareto	
• Seven Management Tool(s):		• Variability Chart	• Other:

CHECK   What was found/Results (note all the changes in variability) and

Opportunities for Improvement

ACT   Follow Up?

Peer Review Referral? Project team launched? Hold the Gain? Management Action?

Referred or reported to MEC—date to be done?

Please describe all that was done to complete or continue the PDCA process:

   • Data collection plan?
   • Actions to take
   • Report to:
   • Continue PDCA or other methodology?

Figure 6.1   PDCA worksheet.

Performance Measures:

- **Volume and Flow Measures:** Volume activity, utilization, and flow patterns in the department or service area.
- **Cost and Efficiency Measures:** Show operating costs and how resources are being used.
- **Process and Output Quality Measures:** Measures that delineate the capability and performance of a **service** or team's key systems and processes.
- **Risk Management/Safety/Infection Control Measures:** Aspects of care and/or services important to **meeting** risk management, infection control, and safety standards.
- **Customer Satisfaction Measures:** Clarify the customer's needs, expectations, and satisfaction with the care or service received.
- **Outcome Measures:** Help to explain the results (outcomes) based on customer's experience with the **service** or product.

Dimensions of Performance Monitored:

- **Efficacy:** The degree to which the care/intervention used for the patient has been shown to accomplish the desired/projected outcome(s).
- **Continuity:** The degree to which the care/intervention for the patient is coordinated among practitioners, between organizations, and across time.
- **Appropriateness:** The degree to which the care/intervention provided is relevant to the patient's clinical needs, given the current state of knowledge.
- **Safety:** The degree to which the risk of an intervention and the risk in the care environment are reduced for the patient and others, including the healthcare provider.
- **Availability:** The degree to which the appropriate care/intervention is available to meet the needs of the patient served.
- **Efficiency:** The ratio of the outcomes (results of care/intervention) for a patient to the resources used to deliver the care.
- **Timeliness:** The degree to which the care/intervention is provided to the patient at the time it is most beneficial or necessary.
- **Respect and Caring:** The degree to which a patient or designee is involved in his or her own care decisions, and that those providing the services do so with sensitivity and respect for his or her needs and expectations and individual differences.
- **Effectiveness:** The degree to which the care/intervention is provided in the correct manner, given the current state of knowledge, in order to achieve the desired/projected outcome(s) for the patient.

AAAHC Application:

RP—Rights of Patient
F&E—Facilities and Environment
ADM—Administration
QC—Quality of Care Provided
QMI—Quality Management and Improvement
HIM—Clinical Records and Health Information
PI—Professional Improvement

GOV—Governance
LAB—Pathology and Lab Services
ANES—Anesthesia Services
SURG—Surgical and Related Services
PHARM—Pharmaceutical Services
RAD—Diagnostic Imaging
EDUC—Health Education and Wellness

UCL/LCL, p value, correlation coefficient, sigma—This is not an arbitrary number. It is what the process produces. It could be the UCL/LCL of a control chart or histogram, the mean/median of a run chart, the Pareto analysis 80/20 results, the correlation coefficient for regression analysis, the p value and/or the response measure/variable outcome from a DOE.

Benchmark—A benchmark is what the industry, whether local or national, produces. It is the best for this particular process/measure. It could also be the best within the facility; for example, one MD's cost/outcome is considered the best for a procedure. He/she then becomes the benchmark for the facility. The team can also use an upper and lower specification level as noted in a capability analysis.

Figure 6.2   Definitions for Figure 6.1.

OPPORTUNITY: To reduce the number of patient cancellations; this will increase patient satisfaction and center profitability.

DATE: January 2010 through March 2010 for before study   **CUSTOMERS:** Patients

PLAN:

Measure(s): # of patient cancellations per day, day of week influence, reason for cancellations
Performance Measure: Volume + Flow and Cost + Efficiency
Dimensions of Performance Monitored: Efficiency, Availability and Timeliness
AAAHC Application: ADM, QC, and QMI

DO: **Time Frame: January–February 2010**

Sample Size: All cancellations for 30 consecutive business days starting on January 4, 2010
Data Source: Front desk personnel captured data on data collection tool
Data Display and Analysis Tool(s): ANOVA, Control Chart, and Pareto Chart

CHECK

1. UCL 12.784, LCL 3.718, mean 4.533
2. Pareto Analysis shows that Wednesday and Thursday have the highest numbers of cancellations.
3. Reasons for cancellations are:

   ■ Patients not consulted about time and day of appointment
   ■ Could not get out of work for the time given for the appointment
   ■ Could not find a driver or a babysitter

ACT

Management action taken based on data presented.
Referred or reported to MEC on February 17, 2010—management actions supported
Please describe all that was done to complete or continue the PDCA process:

1. Extend operating hours on Wednesday and Thursday to accommodate late appointments/procedures.
2. Instead of leaving voice messages with an appointment date and time, the patient was consulted about what day and time would work.
3. Collect 30 more days of data to determine if an improvement occurred: 3/1 through 4/9.
   a. Results from the follow-up data collection:
      i. UCL 5.717, LCL zero, mean 1.867. ANOVA of before and after shows a statistical shift with a p value of 0.048 and variance decreased from 213.7 to 23.7. The actions taken resulted in a significant improvement.
      ii. Pareto analysis shows that Wednesdays and Thursdays have the highest number of cancellations.
4. Actions to take:
   a. Continue the study for another 30 days to determine if cancellations can reduce even more.
   b. Impact on patient satisfaction and center profitability improved, but continue to measure to ensure that this holds true for a longer period of time:
      i. Patient satisfaction for access to care increased from 88% to 97%.
      ii. Profitability improved due to improved use of resources and increased volume by 3%.

Figure 6.3   Reducing patient cancellations PDCA.

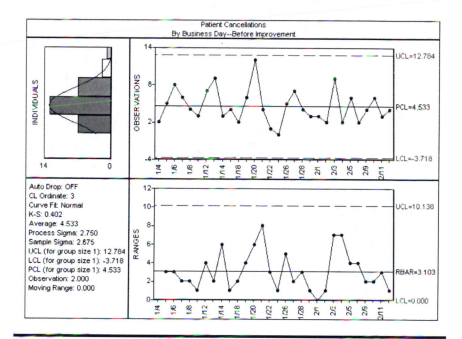

Figure 6.4 Control chart of patient cancellations before improvement.

this study is that patient cancellations were decreased, patient access improved, and there was a positive impact on business and financial outcomes.

Scorecards for Outpatient Services

When creating a scorecard for your organization or facility, think about what is important from financial, operations, salaries and benefits, clinical, customer feedback, benchmarking, regulatory, licensing, and safety perspectives. You don't need to make it complex. Keep it streamlined, but make it count and make it consistent. Tie it in tightly with your mission, vision, and values. If it can't be linked back, then reevaluate whether it's really important and if some other measure can contribute.

Figure 6.9 provides an example of a scorecard for ambulatory surgery centers. One scorecard is used for all of the ASC data, while each facility has its own individual scorecard with the same measures. Once the data is collected, it's easy to find best practice results within any organization or system. Input timeframe elements such as month to date, quarter to date, year to date, or comparative

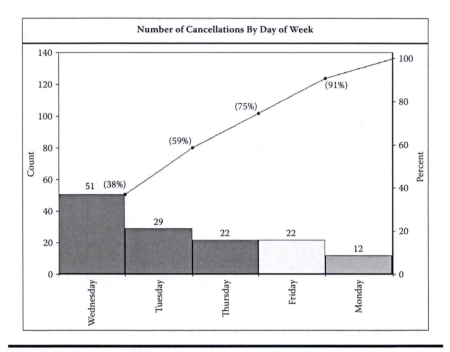

Figure 6.5 **Pareto chart for patient cancellations prior to improvement.**

years into the scorecard. Also, incorporate internal and external benchmarks as well as targets. Replicate what works and eliminate what doesn't.

When determining targets and benchmarks for your measures, take into account what is achievable, what is a stretch target, and also what the industry is producing. Sometimes a dry run for a period of time is needed to really understand how your organization is behaving. Using good analytical and statistical tools will help guide you in the right direction.

Having a strong financial or business analyst or CFO is critical, as the data has to have integrity. Too often, financial leaders do not connect with the clinical leaders, or decisions are made without clinical operations input. Team effort is absolutely necessary to prevent suboptimization for our customers. Garbage in is always garbage out for any data set. Here are some of the measures to consider for your scorecard.

Financial measures:

1. Profitability
2. Revenue per patient
3. Rate per case by specialty and procedure type
4. Cost per case broken out by physician or provider

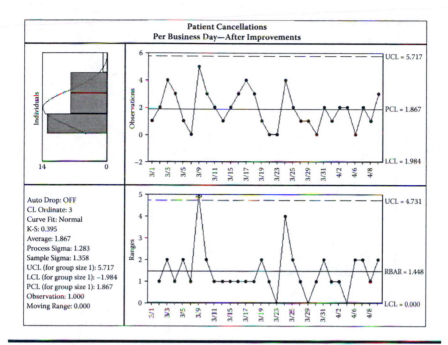

Figure 6.6 **Control chart for patient cancellations after improvements.**

5. Payor mix
6. Supply cost
7. Cash flow
8. Collections as a percent of billings
9. Aging greater than 60 or 120 days
10. Cash receipts daily

Operations measures:

1. Case volume per day
2. Actual cases per day
3. Cases per physician
4. Cases sorted by Current Procedural Terminology (CPT), International Classification of Diseases (ICD)-9, or diagnosis-related group (DRG)
5. Block utilization by physician and room
6. Clinical and nonclinical man-hours per patient
7. Length of stay (LOS)
8. Voice of the customer
9. Block time utilization

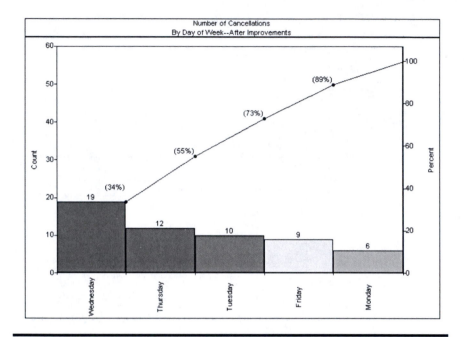

Figure 6.7 Number of cancellations after improvements.

Anova: Single Factor						
SUMMARY						
Groups	Count	Sum	Average	Variance		
Before	5	136	27.2	213.7		
After	5	56	11.2	23.7		
ANOVA						
Source of Variation	*SS*	*df*	*MS*	*F*	*P-value*	*F crit*
Between Groups	640	1	640	5.391744	0.048766	5.317655
Within Groups	949.6	8	118.7			
Total	1589.6	9				

Figure 6.8 Analysis of variance for cancellations.

10. Regulatory, licensing, and other certification measures
    a. DEA license
    b. AAAHC accreditation
    c. The Joint Commission accreditation
    d. Medicare and Medicaid deemed status
    e. Clinical Laboratory Improvement Amendments (CLIA) license
    f. State license

Scorecard for ASC			
Factors	**Objectives**	**Measure(s)**	**Indicators**
Quality and Safety			
	QS1 Best practice for patient safety	Mortality, Patient Experience, Safety Events	1) Overall mortality rate
			2) Patient experience with care
			3) Safety events
	QS2 Best practice for incidence of complications	*Complications*	1) Number of clean surgical site infections/number of clean surgical procedures per month
			2) Number of complications/number of procedures per month
			3) Medication error rate
	QS3 Outcomes are better than external benchmark data	National Quality Forum Endorsed National Voluntary Consensus Standards and Facility Choice Measures	1) Patient burns
			2) Prophylactic intravenous antibiotic timing
			3) Patient fall
			4) Wrong site, wrong side, wrong patient, wrong procedure, wrong implant
			5) Selection of prophylactic antibiotic, first-or second-generation cephalosporin
			6) Timing of prophylactic antibiotics, ordering physician
			7) Timing of prophylactic antibiotics, administering physician
			8) Discontinuation of prophylactic antibiotics, non-cardiac procedures
			9) Hospital transfer/admission
			10) Facility choice for additional measures
Growth			
	G1 Increase revenue	LOS is less than or equal to defined benchmarks	Eye procedures
			ENT procedures
			GI procedures
			Spine procedures
			Pain Management procedures
			Podiatry procedures
			Gynecology procedures
			General Surgery procedures
		Procedure Volume	Volume overall
			Procedure cancellations
			# of ER admits as a % of total ER cases
	G2 Increase market share		ENT volume
			Orthopedic volume
			GI volume
			Ophthalmology volume
			Spine, Pain Neuro volume
			All Other volume
		New Physicians and New Specialties Acquired	Percent of increase in volume per new physicians
			Percent of increase in specialty volume
Business Process			
	B1 Decrease and manage expenses	Salaries, Wages and Benefits	SWB as a percent of net patient revenue
			SWB per case
			Clinical Manhours per case
			Nonclinical Manhours per case
			Manhours per case
			Overtime as a percent of SWB
			Temporary Contract labor as a percent of SWB
	B2 Manage resource allocation proactively	Supply Cost	Supply cost as a percent of net pt revenue
			Supply cost per case
			Days in Inventory
			Implant cost per case for ophthalmology
			Implant cost per case for orthopedic
Customers			
	C1 Number one choice for physicians to practice	MD Satisfaction Scores	Percent of excellence as the place to practice
	C2 Provide excellent timeframes for surgeries and procedures	Block Time Utilization and OR Room Usage	Greater than 80% use of block time and OR room use
	C3 Excellent Patient Satisfaction Scores	Patient Satisfaction	Would you return?
			Would you recommend?
	C4 Employees seek us out as the	Employee Satisfaction	Overall satisfaction rate

Figure 6.9   Scorecard example for an ASC.

Clinical measures:

1. Errors of any kind
2. Serious events/sentinel events
3. Complications
4. Transfers to another facility or hospital
5. Sterilization of instruments—compliance
6. National data from organizations like the National Quality Forum
7. National Patient Safety Goals
8. Healthcare Effectiveness Data and Information Set (HEDIS®) measures from National Committee for Quality Assurance (NCQA)
9. Clinical documentation
10. Infection prevention compliance

Appendix C illustrates a detailed list of quality checks and balances. As a checklist, it guides the users to confirm that safety, regulatory, and quality processes are reviewed at least monthly. If this is of interest to you, edit it to make it your own. The list can look overwhelming, but essentially it helps cover tasks that need to be done anyway. It serves as a memory tool. The source column is one that you would fill out for each check. Determine where the information is found. Is it from a log book? Or can it be located in the medical record? Assign a person to be responsible for each checklist item, and hold that person accountable. Determine how you want the months to be filled out. A checkmark can be used for completion. A number can be used, such as a percentage. Make sure it's clearly noted. Use this as a guide for staff meetings, and to report to the quality committee for your organization.

Rewarding Based on Performance

In many industries and business practices, leaders, employees, physicians, and shareholders are rewarded based on the results and outcomes of the measures put into place. Healthcare is not any different. If scorecard results are to be used to financially reward any individual or team, it's important to develop a nonbiased approach to making this happen. In addition, the data in place requires some kind of audit process so that those on the giving and receiving end can honestly and in good faith give or withhold distributions, bonuses, salary increases, or other financial incentives.

Legal and regulatory compliance is absolutely required when linking financial incentives and scorecards. Unfortunately, it only takes one bad apple to manipulate the system with bad data to rake in financial gain to ruin it for everyone. Weave in checks and balances, and don't leave it in the hands of just one person to do it all. Find authenticity and promote truth.

Summary and Key Points

1. Build a scorecard that meshes with your mission, vision, and values.
2. Grassroots measures and efforts are powerful and should be promoted throughout your organization.
3. Measurement is important to create, achieve, and maintain a profitable, compliant, and great business.
4. Provide training on measurement and scientific methodologies for everyone in your organization.
5. Measure what is important to your customers.
6. Use scientific methods for improvement and innovation opportunities.
7. You don't know if something is better or worse unless it's measured.
8. If scorecard outcomes are tied to financial incentives, create a program that can speak to integrity and is compliant with all laws and regulations that govern this kind of reward.

Sources

AAAHC. 2006. *Quality improvement and benchmarking: A workbook of strategies and tools for success.* Skokie, IL: AAAHC Institute for Quality Improvement.

Box, George E. P., William G. Hunter, and J. Stuart Hunter. 1978. *Statistics for experimenters: An introduction to design, data analysis, and model building.* New York: John Wiley & Sons.

Brassard, Michael, Lynda Finn, Dana Ginn, and Diane Ritter. *The Six Sigma memory jogger II: A pocket guide of tools for Six Sigma improvement teams.* Salem, NH: Goal/QPC.

Brassard, Michael, and Diane Ritter. 2010. *The memory jogger 2: Tools for continuous improvement and effective planning.* Salem, NH: Goal/QPC.

Duncan, Peggy. 2008. *The time management memory jogger: Create time for the life you want.* Salem, NH: Goal/QPC.

Ginn, Dana, and Evelyn Varner. 2004. *The design for Six Sigma memory jogger: Tools and methods for robust processes and products.* Salem, NH: Goal/QPC.

Goal/QPC. 2002. *The black belt memory jogger: A pocket guide for Six Sigma success.* Salem, NH: Goal/QPC and Six Sigma Academy.

Goal/QPC. 2008. *Memory jogger II healthcare edition: A pocket guide of tools for continuous improvement and effective planning.* Salem, NH: Goal/QPC.

Guinane, Carole S. 1997. *Clinical care pathways: Tools and methods for designing, implementing and analyzing efficient care practices.* New York: McGraw-Hill.

Guinane, Carole. S. 2006. Interview with a quality leader: Mikel Harry on Six Sigma in healthcare. *The Journal for Healthcare Quality* 28: 29–36.

Harry, Mikel, and Richard Schroeder. 2000. *Six Sigma: The breakthrough management strategy revolutionizing the world's top corporations*. New York: Doubleday.

Ishikawa, Kaoru. 1971. *Guide to quality control*. Tokyo: Asian Productivity Organization.

Kaplan, Robert S., and David P. Norton. 1996. *The balanced scorecard: Translating strategy into action*. Boston, MA: Harvard Business School Press.

Keller, Paul A. 2001. *Six Sigma deployment: A guide for implementing Six Sigma in your organization*. Tucson, AZ: QA Publishing, LLC.

Martin, Paula, and Karen Tate. 1997. *Project management memory jogger: A pocket guide for project teams*. Salem, NH: Goal/QPC.

Martin, Paula K. 2009. *The innovation tools memory jogger: Generating customer buy-in and solutions that flourish*. Salem, NH: Goal/QPC.

Mizuno, Shigeru. 1984. *Company-wide total quality control*. Tokyo: Asian Productivity Organization.

Pelletier, Luc R., and Christy L. Beaudin. *Q solutions: Essential resources for the healthcare quality professional*. Glenview, IL: NAHQ.

Shewhart, W.A. 1931. *Economic control of quality of manufactured product*. New York: D. Van Nostrand Company, Inc.

Sloan, M. Daniel, and Carole S. Guinane. 1999. *Analyzing clinical pathways: 3-dimensional tools for quality outcomes measurement & improvement*. New York: McGraw-Hill.

Wheeler, Donald J., and David S. Chambers. 1992. *Understanding statistical process control*. Knoxville, TN: SPC Press, Inc.

Chapter 7

Medication Safety

Efforts and courage are not enough without purposeful direction.

—John F. Kennedy

Safety Overview

Preventing harm from medications requires much consideration and attention. Ultimately, a human delivers the medication, and we must ensure proper safety checks are in place to prevent common yet consequential mistakes. It takes considerable effort to plan and implement a safety program, so know what direction you are headed, and have the courage to faithfully apply safe medication practices.

The number of medical errors related to adverse drug-related events is frightening and sorely underreported in the ambulatory world. For ambulatory healthcare (AHC) there are areas of particular focus. This chapter will identify those high-risk areas and also enlist strategies and tools to reduce the chance of error. The areas of utmost risk are high-alert medications such as insulin and anticoagulants, in particular Warfarin and Coumadin; labeling of medications and containers; look-alike sound-alike (LASA) medications; medication reconciliation; safe prescription writing; and safe use of sample medications. In addition, keeping prescription pads under lock and key also contributes to safe medication practices.

Integrate all medication safety processes into your quality and safety program. Report on the results of your quality efforts at least quarterly. Use the process that you have in place for sentinel events, should a medication occurrence be responsible for that outcome.

Formulary, Consulting Pharmacist, and Tools

One of the first steps to take is to know what medications you have in your facility. Inventory these medications room by room. Table 7.1 shows a format that can be used to create this inventory. Once you have an idea about what is on board, determine if each and every medication is required for your particular scope of care and service. Also, look at the numbers of medications that are kept and ask the following: Is it too much or not enough? Once this due diligence is accomplished, you now have the basis for creating a fully functional formulary for your care practice setting.

In most ambulatory settings, especially surgery centers, a contract with a pharmacist is required. If this is the case, use the pharmacist to help define the formulary; help determine where to stock the medications and how to keep the medications locked; and to help write the policies, procedures, and plans needed to make your practice safe. Figure 7.1 provides an overview of what a consulting pharmacist can do. If a pharmacist is not required, the physician or medical director takes on that role. Keep to a plan, and ensure that however the

Table 7.1 Medication Inventory Form

Location	Medication Name	Generic? If so, List Other Names for Medication	Dosage	Type	Number
Nursing Station 1—cabinet above sink	Omeprazole	Yes Prilosec	20 mg	Capsule	4 sample packets with 7 capsules in each packet
Nursing Station 1—cabinet above sink	Celebrex	No	200 mg	Capsule	10 sample packets with 7 capsules in each packet

1. Provides the facility with appropriate information regarding applicable pharmacy and medication information for federal, state statutes and licensure, accreditation and rules, or regulations.
2. Ensures safe storage of all controlled substances, medications, syringes, and other associated supplies in the facility.
3. Works with the center's leaders to acquire and maintain registration with the state board of pharmacy and the U.S. Drug Enforcement Agency (DEA).
4. Establishes requirements for purchase and storage of all medications and pharmacy materials, including drugs, chemicals, biologicals, and syringes.
5. Helps nursing leaders in the development of a formulary, subject to approval of the medical executive committee and the governing body.
6. Helps write and implement pharmacy policies, procedures, and plans.
7. Continually evaluates, using medical record reviews, the distribution of drugs to be administered to patients according to an original or direct copy of the practitioner's medication order. Writes up the results of the reviews, using the approved scientific methodology for quality and safety, and prepares the report for submission to the quality/medical executive committee.
8. Ensures that the center has a sufficient inventory of antidotes and other emergency drugs, and has current antidote information, telephone numbers of the regional poison control center, and other emergency assistance organizations available throughout the organization. Trains the staff on these processes.
9. Performs audits of all transaction records, as required by state and federal law, and as necessary to maintain accurate control over and accountability for all pharmaceuticals.
10. Participates as requested in patient-care audits that relate to medication utilization and effectiveness.
11. Educates the staff on medication safe practices at least twice a year.
12. Provides and updates information for policies, procedures, and plans for obtaining, storing, administering, and disposing of all medications within the facility.
13. Reviews and updates medication policies, procedures, and plans to meet state and federal laws on at least a yearly basis.
14. Continually evaluates the labeling, storage, and distribution of all drugs, including maintenance of information in the pharmacy and nursing station where such drugs are administered, regarding dosage form, route of administration, strength, actions, uses, side effects, adverse effects, interactions, and symptoms of toxicity. This includes sample medications and investigational drugs.
15. Ensures that a process is in place for the admixture of parenteral products.
16. Conducts the required DEA controlled substances inventory.
17. Checks the controlled substances logs, whether manual or in Pyxis, at least monthly for accuracy and for policy adherence.
18. Works with nursing leaders in conducting medication surveillance, which includes refrigerator temperatures, out-of-date drugs, crash cart inventory accuracy, security of the controlled substances storage area, and other items at least monthly.
19. Reports to the nursing leaders any problems related to pharmaceutical deficiencies, errors, or inaccuracies. These problems will be reviewed and evaluated by the nursing leaders and consultant pharmacist, and reports of findings and actions will be reported to the medical executive committee and the governing body committee.

Figure 7.1   Consulting pharmacist requirements.

20. Ensures that the facility meets all inspections, surveys, and other pharmacy requirements.
21. Audits medication and pharmacy records at least monthly.
22. Reviews, evaluates, and audits controlled substance processes (e.g., ordering, storage, and documentation of use) at least monthly.
23. Hazardous substances are identified and the staff is trained.
24. Inventories all medications at least twice a year.
25. Leaves a detailed report after each visit, with action plans, timeframes, and follow-up. Has an exit conference with the appointed nursing leader prior to leaving the center.

Figure 7.1 (Continued) Consulting pharmacist requirements.

Table 7.2 Expired Medication Log

Completed the First Monday of Every Month:	Nurse:	Location:
Medication that Expired	Disposition of Medication	Actions Taken to Replace Medication

medication safety program is designed for your outpatient program, it's the best it can be, and that everyone is doing what they are supposed to do.

Tables 7.2 and 7.3 offer some suggestions on how to monitor expired medications and medications that are kept in a refrigerator. Both reviews are to be done in any setting that keeps medications. Remember that medication refrigerators must not have anything else kept in them, such as food or personal items. Keep the refrigerator locked and secure.

High-Alert Medications

A *high-alert medication* is any medication that, if used in error, has a high risk of causing significant harm. The errors with these medications are often related to the processes involved in preparing them, either in the wrong concentration, mislabeling them, or administering a wrong dose.

Table 7.3   Medication Refrigerator Log

Date (Month, Day, Year)	Time	Temperature	Signature	Action Taken If Variation Exists

For example, heparin, administered in the wrong concentration, was delivered in a flush to the twin babies of well-known Hollywood actor Dennis Quaid. They were accidentally given 1,000 times the common dosage of this blood thinner. While the errors did not result in known permanent harm, it could have easily contributed to their death. The errors received a great deal of national attention, and the actor and his wife filed a lawsuit against the makers of heparin, Baxter International Incorporated, saying that the packaging of the drug confused nurses and physicians. They also filed a lawsuit against Cedars Sinai Hospital, resulting in a $750,000 settlement.

Sadly, other newborns weren't as lucky in their outcomes with heparin miscalculations, as this error had fatal consequences in the previous year.

To begin with, use the following commonsense risk reduction strategies for all ambulatory settings when using high-alert medications:

- Standardize preparations of all diluted solutions—have them ready to use prior to procedures.
- Use only prepared solutions.
- Do not dilute medications on the sterile field.
- Limit the number of medication concentrations.
- In the operating room (OR), have clinicians call out and verbally verify all doses of medication to be given with the surgeon or anesthesiologist.
- Educate your staff, including nurses, clinical, and unlicensed personnel, about how to safely handle and administer medications.
- Include safe medication practices in the annual competencies check off and training for clinicians.
- Walk around units and observe staff, and coach on safe behaviors.

Look-Alike Sound-Alike Medications (LASAs)

LASAs are medications with generic or trade names that can sound or look similar. The Joint Commission requires organizations to annually review their list of these medications and revise practices to continually reduce risk.

Some tips to remember are the following:

- Do not store LASA medications alphabetically by name; store them out of order.
- Use uppercase letters or a bold font when labeling bins.
- Create alerts in electronic dispensing systems like Pyxis that alert staff when overriding medications or doses.
- Limit the supply of some medications.
- Place caution labels on bins.
- Use different color bins for storage.
- Create check points, like verifying both generic and brand names.
- Make two independent checks, with two person checks.

Contrast Media

Traditionally, imaging medications called *dye* required a physician or licensed independent practitioner (LIP) order but were not handled as a true medication. In today's world, contrast agents and radiopharmaceuticals are treated as medications. The reasons were to require the same medication safety controls as applied to prescribing, dispensing, storage, security, administration, and monitoring.

The specifics of this change require an order before dispensing, with only two exceptions: when there is an urgent need for the medication, or when a LIP controls ordering, preparation, and administration of medication.

Services are to be defined through protocol or policy for the role of the LIP in direct supervision of a patient during and after imaging medication is administered. The protocol or policy must be approved by medical staff, and the role of LIP must include timely intervention in the event of an emergency.

There are many licensing and regulatory entities that look for adherence to safe practices in outpatient settings when it comes to contrast solutions, not to mention companies that insure the organization. Monitor the dosages used, the history of the patient, and the medication safe practice processes at your facility. It's wise to treat contrast solutions just like any other drug, knowing that it can harm a patient if given inappropriately, and that it has a street value, meaning that theft of this substance, like all drugs and drug paraphernalia, can be sold or used for gain outside of the organization.

Documentation of allergy histories is also imperative in the communication between patients in contrast administration and medication safety. Use guidelines or questionnaires when reviewing patient histories, including identification of previous allergic-like reactions to iodinated contrast material, multiple allergies to other substances, and/or history of asthma.

Electronic medical records can also be designed to trigger alerts. It's also imperative to educate patients and families on the risks related to iodinated contrast-related procedures.

Anticoagulants

The Institute for Safe Medication Practices has issued guidelines and patient education tools for use of anticoagulants because of their significant risk for life-threatening bleeding or clotting if used improperly. The Joint Commission dedicated National Patient Safety Goal (NPSG) Number 3 to safe practices and requires standardized protocols, guidelines, and standing orders for Warfarin and other anticoagulant medications. The National Quality Forum (NQF) states in its twenty-ninth safety objective: "Every patient on long-term oral anticoagulants should be monitored by a qualified health professional using a careful strategy to ensure an appropriate intensity of supervision." This intense supervision is difficult if you are a stand-alone physician office. Many healthcare systems have opted to standardize their anticoagulation services by centralizing a clinic to serve a multitude of patients. This allows for use of consistent monitoring, consistent use of protocols, as well as patient and family education services.

Insulin

Diabetes care has improved with the advent of point-of-care testing devices. Insulin products are often similar in names, strengths, and concentration ratios, which inherently can contribute to medication errors. Limit the variety of insulin products stored in medication refrigerators and segregate them in separate labeled bins. Place double checks and balances policies where two persons read back and verify doses before administering. Include in patient teaching clear instructions on the differences in insulin names and actions.

Chemotherapy

Chemotherapy administration is one of the top high-alert medications. Medication preparation and administration is often individualized, and weight- or age-based, making the risk for error greater. States also regulate the licensing requirement on who can administer chemotherapy. Advanced certification may be required, and any task of administering cannot be delegated to less-qualified staff. The ordering of chemotherapy is complex, and preprinted orders and protocols are recommended. These types of orders should not be taken verbally. Review relevant patient history, allergies and related laboratory test results before administration. Another confounding factor is that treatment orders and protocols may change based on the patient's reaction to previous treatment. Have a double check in place to verify orders and dosages. Patients should be in view and under close monitoring during the administration of chemotherapy.

Injection Safety and Multiuse Medication Vials

The Safe Injection Practices Coalition defines a *multiuse vial* as a bottle of medication or injectable that contains more than one dose of medication and is approved by the Food and Drug Administration (FDA) for use on multiple patients. You must always use a new sterile needle and syringe to access the medication in the multidose vial. When this practice is not followed, cross-contamination from person to person can occur with life-threatening consequences.

When using a multidose vial, you must also follow the labeling requirements as required by licensing and regulatory agencies. This requires all stored medications to be labeled, including an expiration date. How do you define the expiration date? It is defined by the last date the vial was used. The manufacturer expiration date must be relabeled once the vial has been used, unless this date is shorter than the relabeled date. The discard date for multiuse vials is 28 days after the first use. The only exception to the 28-day rule is vaccines, which are to be discarded according to the manufacturer's expiration date.

Unsafe injection practices have led to transmission of hepatitis C and human immunodeficiency virus (HIV) in recent cases. Reuse of syringes and needles is prohibited, and yet it is still a root cause of these tragedies.

For more information on safe practices related to multiuse vials, see the Safe Injection Practices Coalition One and Only One Campaign, which is a public awareness campaign led in conjunction with the Centers for Disease Control (CDC) (http://www.oneandonlycampaign.org).

Labeling Medications and Containers

An emergency department is an outpatient setting, and an experience with an unlabeled bin involved a life-threatening medication error. A paralytic had been placed in the drawer parallel to another that contained a key for a cardiac medication that was kept in the refrigerator. The medication was clearly labeled correctly; however, the key that had to be obtained from the Pyxis drawer was to unlock the cardiac medication located in a refrigerator. Since the drawer was not labeled, a new nurse did not realize that the vial she grabbed was from the wrong drawer and was not the medication she intended. Failing to perform the five rights in this emergency situation allowed this error to reach the patient.

Labeling can be confusing when it is in small print or in similar colors, as noted in the case of the heparin vials that led to errors involving newborns. Some of the most common contributing factors in labeling errors are illegible handwriting, using unsafe abbreviations, handwritten protocols instead of preprinted orders for complex ordering, using nicknames for medications instead of their generic or trade names, and inappropriate use of verbal orders.

In an OR setting, medications and medication containers must be labeled whether they are on and off the sterile field. Potential medication errors around labeling have been attributed to illegible handwriting. To alleviate this risk, one endoscopy center ordered preprinted labels for all of the most common containers and medications used in their procedure rooms. The cost was minimal, but the error prevention was priceless.

Medication Reconciliation

Medication reconciliation is defined by the Institute for Healthcare Improvement as "the process of creating the most accurate list possible of all medications a patient is taking, including drug name, dosage, frequency, and route, and comparing that list against physician admission, transfer, and/or discharge orders, with the goal of providing correct medications to the patient at all transition points."

This is a difficult standard to meet, however, and is also a process with much variation, even across like settings such as ambulatory surgery centers. For this reason, focus on the commonsense tips that can be applied to prevent the errors of transcription, omission, duplication of therapy, and drug–drug interactions.

Begin your assessment at the patient encounter with open-ended questions in clear, lay terms.

Encourage patients to keep an ongoing list. One community hospital, county EMS, and home care introduced the vial of life for capture of home medications. The vial was a prescription bottle, and inside it held a sticker with key patient demographics and conditions to place on the outside of the freezer or refrigerator. Inside the vial was a list of current home medications and any key medical information readily available for the first EMS responders to the home.

Another healthcare system had a clever campaign called It Could Be the Most Important Thing in Your Wallet that mimicked a credit card commercial for "What's in Your Wallet," where cards were provided to be kept in one's wallet. There are numerous ways to be creative. A medication prototype developed by the Massachusetts Coalition for Prevention of Medical Errors is available from the coalition website: http://www.Macoalition.org/Initiatives/docs/PatientMedCard.doc.

What do you need to reconcile for your setting if you are an imaging center? When a medication that a patient is taking is not relevant to the services your center is providing, you do not have to document that medication. For example, on discharge after an outpatient CT with contrast, the contrast that the patient received does not have to be documented on a discharge medication list. However, if the patient had an adverse reaction to the contrast, that fact should be documented.

Safe prescription writing has improved with the use of electronic prescribing systems. Illegible handwriting can be misinterpreted. The following safety tips can be helpful. When taking a telephone order, spell out the name of the drug when reading it back, describe the indication to the patient, and ask whether it makes sense for the patient's condition. Remind patients to read the label of the prescription when they pick it up; prescriptions are often filled with a generic name. Educate your staff to monitor for abbreviations that should not be used and abbreviations that could be unsafe, as listed in Figure 7.2.

Sample Medications

Sample medications need to be handled and secured using specific policy. This can be a difficult process to manage if you are in a busy office and do not have storage space or an automated way to control the use of sample medications. An office is required to follow safe storage requirements, including proper temperature and lighting, segregation of look-alike sound-alike medications, and tracking receipt and dispensing of all medications. A secured area or cabinet should be set aside and locked. Establish a clear process to document how and who can receive the medications. If you are a part of a larger organization, check the facility-wide policy before you accept the responsibility of handling sample medications.

Unsafe Abbreviations

Do Not Use!

These abbreviations should not be used in any of their forms—upper- or lowercase, with or without periods. These *Do Not Use* abbreviations apply to **ALL** clinical documentation including all types of orders, progress notes, consultation reports, and operative reports.

Abbreviation/ Intended Meaning	Misinterpretation	Acceptable Format
U or u (units)	"U" may be mistaken as a zero, a "4", or "c" leading to overdoses	Write out "units."
I.U. (international units)	I.U. has been interpreted & mistaken as I.V. or 10 (ten)	Write out "international units."
Trailing zero (X.0mg); lack of leading zero (.Xmg)	Decimal point can be missed	Never write a zero by itself after a decimal point (Xmg) and always use a zero before a decimal point (0.Xmg).
Q.D. (daily)	May be mistaken as QID if the period or another mark is inserted between the "Q" and "D."	Write out "daily."
Q.O.D. (every other day)	May be interpreted as QID	Write out "every other day."
MS (morphine sulfate)	Has been interpreted as magnesium sulfate	Write out "morphine."
MSO_4 (morphine sulfate)	Has been interpreted as magnesium sulfate	Write out "morphine."
$MGSO_4$ (magnesium sulfate)	Has been interpreted as morphine sulfate	Write out "magnesium sulfate."

Figure 7.2   Unsafe abbreviations example.

Storing and Securing Medications

Follow state regulations, Accreditation Association for Ambulatory Health Care (AAAHC), and/or Joint Commission medication management requirements related to medication storage and security. Use your contract pharmacist to help set up a program for you. If you don't use a contract pharmacist, think about a yearly assessment program to help ascertain whether medications are stored and secured appropriately. Ambulatory settings need to be cognizant of securing medications during both open office hours and during closed times. If house-keepers or other contract workers have access to your facility after hours, then medications, syringes, tourniquets, and other patient items are to be under lock and key, with narcotics in a double-lock system as approved by most state licensing entities for pharmacy and medication oversight.

Medication Safety Reporting

We only know about errors if they are reported, but how do you know what should be reported? Create policies for reporting medication errors for all settings. Have a clearly delineated process for staff to report either on a paper or electronic log to track medication errors and adverse drug events. Review these events on a routine basis through a performance improvement or pharmacy and therapeutics committee, and routinely evaluate risk reduction strategies. Figure 7.3 provides a form that can be used for tracking medication errors and adverse drug event tracking.

In summary, include the following in your daily work:

- Routinely record all medication errors.
- Complete medication incident reports per the policy for your setting.
- At a minimum, track the following:
  - Incorrect patient received medication
  - Incorrect medication given to a patient
  - Incorrect time of medication
  - Incorrect route of medication
  - Incorrect dose of medication
  - Missed dose of medication

Adverse Drug Reaction Reporting

What is the difference between a medication error and an adverse drug reaction? An adverse drug reaction is considered to have occurred if it results in any of the following:

- Reaction requires treatment with a prescription medication
- Temporary or permanent disability
- Rash, shortness of breath, or any anaphylactic symptoms

2010 Dashboard

Measure		Office or ASC	Benchmark	Goal	Jan	Feb	Mar	1st Q	Apr	May	Jun	2nd Q	Jul	Aug	Sep	3rd Q	Oct	Nov
Medication Event Occurrence Report	Medication errors per 1000 administered closes		<2	<1				0.00				0.00				0.00		
	Class D Errors (as % of total errors)		<3.8%	<3.8%				0.00%				0.00%				0.00%		
Medication Event Occurrence Report	Adverse Drug Events		Internal	N/A				0				0				0		

Figure 7.3 Medication errors and adverse drug event tracking.

- Hospitalization or death
- Discontinuation of a prescribed medication because of unanticipated symptoms

Track adverse drug reactions by doing the following:

- Create an adverse drug reaction log
- Record events in detail on any side effect, injury, toxicity, or sensitivity reactions associated with the use of a drug. See Table 7.4 for an example of a governing body report on medication safety and events.

Table 7.4 Governing Body Report

Governing Body Report Item	When to Report	Actions Taken
Identify medication incidents by category according to the risk management plan.		
Describe risk reduction strategies and actions taken, when the actions were taken, and the outcomes that occurred from the actions.		
Display all educational in-services and CMEs that were delivered relating to medication safety.		
Summarize staff competency initiatives and outcomes on medication safety.		
List all policies, procedures, sentinel event alerts, and other knowledge-based materials related to medication safety and outcomes that were shared with the staff, physicians, and other stakeholders and caregivers.		
Summarize quality and safety efforts that occurred from a preventive approach for medication safety.		
Attach a copy of the Medication Surveillance Rounds summary and results.		

Summary and Key Points

- Create a formulary.
- Know what is in your medication inventory at all times. Perform the necessary daily counts for your medications.
- Hire a pharmacist as a consultant to help oversee your medication safety program.
- Medication errors in ambulatory care can cause harm.
- Pay close attention to high-risk high-alert medications.
- Label all medications.
- Follow safe practices regarding multiuse vials. Use single-use medications if at all possible.
- Reconcile medications at point of entry and care transitions.
- Track, trend, and report medication errors and adverse drug events.
- Secure all medications as required by law, licensing regulations, and accrediting organizations.

Sources

Institute for Healthcare Improvement, http://www.ihi.org.

Joint Commission. 2006. *Safety in the operation room.* Oakbrook Terrace, IL: Joint Commission Resources.

Joint Commission. 2009. *Patient safety handbook for ambulatory care providers 2nd edition.* Oakbrook Terrace, IL: Joint Commission Resources.

Joint Commission. 2009. *The handbook on storing and securing medications.* Oakbrook Terrace, IL: Joint Commission Resources.

Reconciling medications: A learning collaborative on safe practice recommendations. Massachusetts Coalition for Prevention of Medical Errors, http://www.macoalition. org/Education/Reconciling_09-03_Overview.shtml.

Reuters. 2010. Dennis Quaid sues heparin maker for twins overdose, May 25, http://www.reuters.com/article/idUSTRE64O6R220100525.

Schulmeister, L. 2006. Look-alike, sound-alike oncology medications, *Clin J Oncol Nurs* 10: 35–41.

Chapter 8

Infection Prevention in the Ambulatory Setting

Dream as if you'll live forever and live as if you'll die today.

—**James Dean**

Infection Prevention and Control

Virulent strains of antibiotic-resistant bacteria and potent viruses can change a person's life at the drop of a hat, thus emphasizing the need to invest in strong infection prevention practices. A dream perhaps, that prevention can positively influence the transmission of infections? We think not, as infection control and prevention practices when applied appropriately and continuously do work.

The intent of infection prevention is to develop strategies to design, control, and provide a culture where infections are identified early and transmission is minimized. The challenges of infection prevention in ambulatory care have been highlighted recently in the media. An endoscopy center in Florida and a surgery center in Nevada were found to have multiple infection practice violations, spotlighting the need for more oversight and reporting for these centers. These violations included reuse of syringes, sharing of medications from single-use vials, and poor sterilization technique. Thousands of patients were exposed to bloodborne pathogens, with many testing positive.

The first goal of this chapter is to detail the must haves for your program and give you template plans and tools that can be adopted for your particular setting. The second goal is to enlighten you on the regulatory requirements behind these plans and the upcoming future of public reporting.

Care in the ambulatory setting can be as brief as a consultative visit or as invasive as surgery. The care is delivered in a variety of settings, ranging from primary care medical offices, surgery and medical clinics, endoscopy suites, diagnostic magnetic resonance imaging (MRI) and computerized tomography (CT) centers, and physical therapy centers. All have a varied degree of infection prevention requirements. The information outlined in this chapter can be adapted to all of these settings.

Don't wait to implement a strong infection control and prevention program. Too often it takes a tragic outcome, a death of an innocent or a poor survey rating, to pay attention to what matters. Do it now to make a difference. The lives that are touched by the care delivered in your facility deserve the best care possible.

Infection Control and Prevention Structure

A successful program decreases risk to your patients and employees, monitors for the occurrence of infection, implements appropriate control measures, identifies and corrects problems related to infection control practices, and maintains compliance with federal and state regulation as they relate to infection control. This program includes activities in the following areas:

- Surveillance of infection and control and prevention measures
- Outbreak investigation
- Policy and procedure review and revision
- Staff education
- Quality assurance
- Consultation

These are the essentials or "must haves" to begin your program:

- A disaster plan that is specific to your care setting.
- An infection prevention committee that comprises multidisciplinary team members.
- An infection prevention and control plan, policies, and procedures that spell out requirements for the program.
- Most states and accrediting bodies require a licensed healthcare professional trained in infection control and prevention and designated to direct the

infection program. While this service may be contracted out to a certified infection practitioner, someone on site must be designated as the day-to-day practitioner for surveillance and other activities. The consultant would train this person(s) and sign off on all competencies. These activities must be included in the job descriptions for those who are assigned and trained.

An excellent resource for how to design an ambulatory infection prevention program is the *Infection Prevention Manual for Ambulatory Care, 2009, ICP Associates, Inc.* (Bennet 2009).

Disaster Planning and Outbreak Investigation

Medicare's Conditions for Coverage requires compliance with Standard § 416.41 (c)—disaster preparedness planning at all Medicare-certified or deemed status ambulatory surgery center (ASC) facilities. The requirements include a comprehensive written plan. The plan must include coordination with external agencies, safe evacuation plans, practice drills, evaluation of the effectiveness of the plan, and any plans for correction.

A disaster plan includes outbreak investigation. An outbreak is defined as two or more cases over the usual number of cases of healthcare-associated infections. The infection is usually caused by the same organism such as the H1N1 influenza strain. The H1N1 pandemic flu outbreak in 2009 tested the plans of every ambulatory practice including those caring for the unexpected population of pregnant women. Cough kits may traditionally be found in a physician's office, but N92 masks or fit-tested personnel were not. Plan ahead and keep the following items in mind:

- Develop a disaster planning committee or assign key staff with the responsibility for preparedness.
- Establish contacts with your local and regional emergency preparedness organizations (i.e., county agencies, close hospital facilities, or affiliations).
- Identify triggers for activating your plan. If you are part of a larger organization, ask to be included in communication from their command center.
- Define roles and responsibilities prior to implementing a disaster plan.
- Develop a triage plan and an evacuation plan. Include where you would send patients if you reach capacity.
- Develop a plan for vaccine or antiviral distribution; contact your county health department.

- Inventory supplies and identify resources for needed supplies.
- Have a strategy for handling death of patients, which may require assistance from the medical examiner's office.

For disaster plan examples, our recommended resource is the Centers for Disease Control (CDC) website and contacting your state agency. An example pandemic flu plan is available at the website of the Department of Health and Human Services (http://www.hhs.gov/pandemicflu/plan).

Infection Control and Prevention Committee

An Infection Control and Prevention Committee is tasked with investigation, control, and prevention of healthcare-associated infections. Membership, even in a small ambulatory setting, should include administrative, nursing, and medical staff representatives. The committee's responsibility includes the approval of an annual plan and review of relevant policies, procedures, and data for your particular setting. They have delegated authority to take necessary action to prevent infections and harm to patients and personnel.

Keep minutes of your meetings and use a format that clearly states the topic discussed, the recommended actions, and the responsible parties and expected completion dates. This committee can be combined with your Medical Executive or Medical Advisory Committee.

Infection Control and Prevention Plan

All programs for prevention begin with an infection control and prevention plan that seeks to minimize infections and communicable diseases. The infection control and prevention plan guides the activities of the service. The plan must include an assessment of risk, the services provided in your setting, the population served, and strategies to reduce the risk of infection. It requires an annual review at the minimum. The required components of the plan are as follows:

- Assessment of risk
- Assessment of services provided
- Assessment of the population served: adults, pediatrics, and/or seniors
- Prioritization of strategies
- Evaluation of the effectiveness of your strategies
- Surveillance based on past years, or if a new service line, historical data for your specialty. Data, data aggregation, and analysis live here.

- Sample infection prevention plan (Appendix D)
- Sample risk assessment (Appendix E)

A risk assessment is an essential part of your plan. This first step is to assess the current risks in your setting. If you are a new center or a physician's office, consider your geographic location, community environment, and the care and treatment services you plan to provide for the population you serve. Gather data appropriate for your setting; determine your highest risk item and your high-volume area to establish the priorities to be addressed by your risk assessment. Once you prioritize your risks, spell out your goals and strategies to reduce risk, the responsible party or personnel, the time frame for completion, and how you will measure if the strategy was effective.

An example goal for an ambulatory surgery center could be to reduce the rate of surgical site infection (SSI) post knee arthroscopy. You would want to take into consideration your community acquired *methicillin-resistant staphylococcus aureus (*MRSA) rate as a risk factor. Your patient population is young high school athletes because your center is located next to a sports medicine practice. A strategy to reduce the transmission of infections may also reduce MRSA-induced SSI. In this case, use of chlorahexadine scrub to the affected knee prior to surgery could be your strategy.

To measure your effectiveness, you would monitor your rate of SSI in this patient population for one year through a surveillance program. ASCs must follow their patients for infections, and this example shows why this is true. Working hand in hand with physician practices to track outcome data is necessary. Sending follow-up letters to the surgeon's office is one way to track infection rates post ASC surgery.

Surveillance

Infection surveillance requires tracking and trending of infections. It includes ongoing monitoring for infection within your patient population as well as the personnel who come in contact with the patients. Public reporting has placed a high priority on the identification of healthcare-acquired conditions (HACs). In the ambulatory care setting, these are infections temporarily associated with the ambulatory visit or with the care provided during the visit. You will need to track and report any HACs to your Infection Prevention Committee. Also, depending on your home state, you may have mandatory reporting. See Table 8.1 for an example of a HAC tracking tool.

Targeted surveillance or focused surveillance on high-risk areas is recommended. An example of these is catheter-related bloodstream infections, surgical

Table 8.1 Example HAC Sentinel Event Tracking Log

Patient Identifier	Date of Symptom of HAC	Diagnosis and Condition	Related Surgical Procedure	Admitted to Acute Care Facility? Yes or No	Permanent Injury or Loss? Yes or No	Death? Yes or No	Comments

site infections, or dialysis-associated infections. Surgical site infections need postdischarge surveillance, as infections that occur within a year of the original procedure can be attributed to poor surgical technique or ineffective antibiotic prophylaxis. Surveillance data can include lab and culture results, symptom tracking, and logs of visits to healthcare facilities.

The American Recovery and Reinvestment Act (Recovery Act) provided funding to the Department of Health and Human Services (HHS) with the purpose of reducing HACs.

Include environmental rounds in your surveillance; clinical areas should be surveyed at least twice a year and nonclinical areas once a year. However, keep it top of mind for all employees as they work. Don't wait until the surveillance rounds occur to fix problem areas.

Bloodborne Pathogens

The Occupational Safety and Health Administration (OSHA) requires all settings to have an exposure control plan (ECP) with the goal of preventing transmission of bloodborne pathogens. These pathogens are hepatitis B, hepatitis C (HCV), and human immunodeficiency virus (HIV). Be sure to review both the federal and your local state OSHA requirements. State requirements are often more strict.

Your ECP's purpose is to eliminate or minimize occupational exposure to bloodborne pathogens and provide a safe and healthy work environment for each employee in accordance with OSHA Standard 29 CFR 1910.1030, Occupational Exposure to Bloodborne Pathogens.

Your exposure control plan must include the following elements:

- Determination of employee exposure (including log of injuries—for example, sharps)
- Exposure control measures:
  - Standard precautions, which include hand hygiene, personal protective equipment, needle stick and sharps prevention, cleaning and disinfecting, respiratory hygiene, waste disposal, and safe injection practices
  - Work practice controls and engineering controls (this would include specific safety devices on needles)
  - Personal protective equipment includes gloves, gowns, masks, shoe covers, and goggles
  - Required vaccinations such as hepatitis B
  - Housekeeping and cleaning requirements
  - Postexposure assessment and followup (patients and staff)
  - Orientation and communication of workplace hazards
- Procedure for evaluating an exposure event (i.e., root cause analysis)

Standard precaution tools abound in healthcare and continue to proliferate rapidly. Hats off to the CDC, World Health Organization (WHO), and Society for Healthcare Epidemiology of America (SHEA) organizations for making infection control and prevention practices a global concern and initiative.

Take some time to read the WHO guidelines on hand hygiene in healthcare. The *Clean Hands are Safer Hands* document is incredibly powerful. In addition, the WHO started the fire with the First Do No Harm thinking, stemming from the world alliance for patient safety. Their work on safe injection practices is worth reading. The checklists that this organization provides are priceless for all safety initiatives.

The Centers for Disease Control, in conjunction with the Association for Professionals in Infection Control and Epidemiology (APIC) and SHEA delivered a terrific guide on improving hand hygiene. The CDC began this initiative in 2002, and it's still going strong. The Institute for Healthcare Improvement (IHI) took the ball and ran with it, using the Model for Improvement, developed by the Associates in Process Improvement, to roll this out. Practical tools are available and are free. They include training, information about alcohol-based hand hygiene products, supply needs, demonstrations, routine visits to the units, marketing and educational materials, and patient and family member engagement. In addition, measurement tools are included to track progress, variation patterns, and improvements.

Sharps: Engineering Safety Mechanisms

All percutaneous injuries in a facility occurring from a contaminated sharp must be recorded. The log must be kept in addition to the illness and injury log required by OSHA Standard 29 CFR 1904. This log must include all injuries by year and must be kept for up to five years. All sharps in use must be engineered, including syringes, lancets, intravenous systems, and others. If a sharp is in use that is not safety engineered, you must have documentation to prove there is not a device that is currently manufactured for use.

Multiuse Vials and Single-Use Vials

Reuse and sharing of vials of medication can have devastating consequences for outpatients, as seen by an investigation in 2008 in Nevada surgery centers resulting in the spread of hepatitis C. These violations have prompted site visits by the Centers for Medicare and Medicaid Services (CMS) to these facilities. All injections, including medications, saline, and other infusates, must be administered using the following practices for use with only one patient:

- Needle and syringes are single use.
- Medication vials are always reentered with a new needle.
- Medications are predrawn and labeled at the time of draw, including the initials of the person drawing the medication, the medication name and strength, the expiration date and time.
- Single-dose or (single-use) medication vials
- Prefilled (manufactured) syringes
- IV solutions are single use and bags are not spiked until ready to use
- Medication tubing and connectors
- Disinfect multidose vials with an alcohol swab
- Dispose of all sharps in a puncture-resistant sharps box after use

A recommended resource is the CMS Infection Control Surveyor Worksheet, which can be found on the CMS web site (http://www.cms.gov/). Ambulatory surgery centers are required to use this form, and they will be surveyed against it.

Environmental Cleaning and Disinfection

Proper cleaning and disinfection of equipment and environmental surfaces in the ambulatory setting is critical. The number of outpatient encounters per day increases the number and types of microorganisms that encounter the environment. The Medicare Conditions for Coverage §416.44, (a) Standards for Physical Environment, require in particular that ASCs establish a program for identifying and preventing infections, maintaining a sanitary environment, and reporting results to required agencies. To maintain a clean and safe environment and equipment, a good starting point is the CDC recommendations for disinfection:

- Select EPA-registered disinfectants.
- Do not use high-level disinfectants or liquid chemical sterilants for disinfection of noncritical instruments and devices.
- Follow manufacturers' instructions for cleaning and maintaining noncritical medical equipment.
- Use a written schedule for cleaning and disinfecting.
- Wear gloves while cleaning.
- Maintain material safety and data sheets (MSDS) on the cleaning materials used.

Disinfection of devices such as scopes needs to have a clear process for precleaning, sterilization, and high-level disinfection.

Sterilization, Disinfection, and Cleaning

The Association for the Advancement of Medical Instrumentation (AAMI) provides definitions for sterilization and flash sterilization. Changes are occurring, however, and Medicare, the CDC, and other organizations are saying that the term *flash sterilization* is archaic. These groups believe that the critical steps for disinfection and sterilization must be used and that technology dictates the way that this is to occur. It's important to ensure full competency of staff for all steps taken with cleaning, disinfecting, and sterilizing instruments and equipment.

Rapid cycle/short cycle steam sterilization is considered acceptable for processing cleaned patient care items that cannot be packaged, sterilized, and stored before their use. It's important to note that no biological residue is to be present on the instruments prior to disinfection and sterilization steps. Recommended parameters to consider when deploying this process are as follows:

- Proper cleaning, decontaminating, inspecting, and arranging of instruments in the sterilization tray. Please note the CDC guidelines for disinfection and sterilization, as this document provides detail about expectations.
- Keep in mind the storage of clean equipment (i.e., utilize 5 S Lean concepts to keep items from being displaced).
- Train staff on rapid cycle sterilization techniques. Technicians trained in central processing and nursing staff may not have equal training on the technique. Do not assume that anyone has the knowledge required to adequately and competently clean, disinfect, and sterilize instruments and equipment.
- Be aware of equipment contraindications for using the technique.
- Obtain manufacturing guidelines for everything associated with rapid cycle sterilization. Obtain validation from each manufacturer that rapid cycle sterilization is approved per U.S. Food and Drug Administration (FDA) guidelines. Include information for:
  - The sterilizer
  - The trays
  - The containers
  - Instruments
  - Equipment
  - Anything else used for this process
- Deploy safe practices to avoid complications associated with rapid cycle sterilization.
- Have defined and written protocols to include specifying when your facility can and cannot deploy this type of sterilization.
- Use visual cuing by taking pictures of sterile trays to build in efficiencies.
- Dedicate a trained and competent staff member to the task.

- Seek outside support if rapid cycle steam sterilization is used frequently throughout the day.
- Use a closed system or patented system.
- Follow your processes using tools such as supply, input, process, output, and customer (SIPOC); infection tracers; and failure modes and effects analysis (FMEA) to help prevent errors and gaps in process.
- Keep a steam sterilization log that includes the following elements:
  - Sterilization identification and cycle number
  - Items that were sterilized
  - Temperature of the cycle
  - Type of cycle used
  - Name of the staff member who performed the cycle
  - Date and time of the cycle
  - The results of the chemical integrator
  - Any process indicator uses
- Patient identification

Remember that medical devices and instruments must be visibly inspected for residual biologicals and recleaned as necessary until all biological residue is gone.

Recommended Sterilization Resources

1. Guideline for Disinfection and Sterilization in Healthcare Facilities, 2008 from the Healthcare Infection Control Practices Advisory Committee of the CDC (http://www.cdc.gov).
2. Association for Operating Room Nurses (AORN).
3. CMS Flash Sterilization Clarification Memo. Fiscal Year 2010. Ambulatory Surgical Center (ASC) Surveys Memo. https://www.cms.gov/SurveyCertificationGenInfo/downloads/SCLetter09_55.pdf

Measurement

How do you measure the effectiveness of your plan? This can be done by tracking outcome measures as well as process measures. An example of an outcome measure would be a surgical procedure that results in no known infections at one year post procedure. Process measure examples include monitoring of hand washing by observation; secret shoppers to observe without notice; tracking immunization rates for certain infections (for example, hepatitis B or hepatitis A); and timing of surgical antibiotic prophylaxis. Figure 8.1 is a sample outpatient scorecard. Figure 8.2 provides an example of an infection prevention scorecard.

Ambulatory Care/Surgical Services Scorecard							
Indicator	Benchmark	Target	1st Quarter FY 20XX	2nd Quarter FY 20XX	3rd Quarter FY 20XX	4th Quarter FY 20XX	Overall 20XX
Patient Satisfaction							
Ambulatory surgery							
Patient perception of pain control							
Clinical Processes							
Turnaround time (room clean time)							
On-time starts (first start)							
Occurrences							
Unexpected returns to OR cases							
Appropriate Care Score (SCIP)							
Antibiotics within one hour of cut							
Rate of appropriate antibiotic selection							
Appropriate hair removal							
Normothermia documented in PACU							
VTE prophylaxis ordered							
Infection Prevention and Surveillance							
Surgical site infection rate (# of infections Per 100 procedures)							
Hand hygiene (30 observations/month)							
Patient Safety Initiatives (Observational Audit)							
Appropriate use of patient identification							
Telephone/verbal orders read back and verified (documented in record)							
Unapproved abbreviations compliance							
Critical test in PACU reported to provider (within 10 minutes)							
Handoff communication between PACU and anesthesia							
Hand and hygiene							
Universal protocol (time out completed)							

Key
    Green = at or above the target
    Yellow = plus or minus 5% of target
    Red = below 5% of target or may not meet target this year
    Pass = Green
    Fail = Red (correction plan required)

Figure 8.1   Ambulatory surgery infection scorecard.

Infection Prevention and Control Department: Surveillance and Outcome Measures Scorecard (Current through _____)							
Current rates (by quarter) are compared to the previous year and target/goal rate		> target		>= previous CY year < target			> = target
Category/Measure with Calculation	Previous CY Rate	Industry Benchmark	Target / Goal	Q1	Q2	Q3	Q4
TJC National Patient Safety Goals	Industry Benchmark—MRSA						
MRSA Rate per 1,000 patient days	0.00	0.00	0.00				
VRE Rate per 1,000 patient days	0.00	None	0.00				
C Difficile Rate per 10,000 patient days	0.0	None	0.00				
ESBL (Extended Spectrum Beta Lactamases) per 1,000 patient days	0.00	None	0.000				
Surgical Site Infections	Industry Benchmark—NHSN pooled mean						
Knees arthroscopies # interactions per risk index category per all total knee cases in risk index category							
Risk Index 0	0.00	0.00	0.00				
Risk Index 1	0	0.00	0				
Risk Index 2, 3	0	0.00	0				
Current rates (by quarter) are compared to the previous quarter and target/goal rate		<previous CY rate		>= previous CY rate < target			> = target
SSI Best Practice Compliance	Industry Benchmark—TJC						
SCIP Appropriate Care Score	90.3	100.0	00.0				
Current rates (by quarter) are compared to the previous quarter and target/goal rate using the following color codes		<previous CY rate		>= previous CY rate <target			> = target
Employee Exposures							
Bloodborne pathogens (BBP)		None					
Category / Measure with calculation	Previous CY Rate	Industry Benchmark	Target / Goal	Q1	Q2	Q3	Q4
Current rates (by quarter) are compared to the previous quarter and target/goal rate		<previous CY rate		>= previous CY rate <target			> = target
Hand Hygiene Compliance	Industry Benchmark—TJC						
Hand Hygiene Rate, % compliance per observed	95.0	90.0	97.0				
Interventions/Comments:							

Figure 8.2 Infection prevention scorecard example.

Chapter 10 manages sentinel events in the ambulatory care setting, but certain healthcare-associated infections are classified as sentinel events. The purpose of investigating HACs as sentinel events is to identify cases of death and major permanent loss of function attributed to a healthcare-associated infection. During your surveillance you may identify a case that you want to review to identify potential causes. Tools to use include a cause-and-effect diagram (fishbone diagram) and root cause analysis (RCA). Root cause methodology is sensitive and specific and allows staff to identify process and subprocess detail that can lead to failures.

Mandatory Staff Training in Infection Prevention

Reducing the risk of spreading infection in the ambulatory setting is certainly a safety and infection prevention priority. Each ambulatory setting is required to pay specific attention to their patient population and setting. Begin with the basics as outlined in the following text.

Hand Hygiene

Provide initial and annual staff training on infection prevention and control. Start with the basic etiquette of hand hygiene. Observe staff directly involved in patient care and throughout the facility. Educate staff on appropriate use of soap and water versus alcohol-based hand rubs. Tips on the CDC guidelines from the Clean Hands Saves Lives campaign are:

- Hands that are not visibly soiled can use an alcohol-based hand rub; or wash hands a minimum of 15 seconds with warm water and antimicrobial soap when not visibly soiled.
- Visibly soiled or contaminated hands should be washed 15 seconds or longer with warm water and antimicrobial soap.
- Before putting gloves on and after removal, wash with an alcohol-based hand rub.
- Artificial nails are unacceptable.
- Only facility-approved hand lotions should be used.

Isolation Considerations

Standard precautions need to be implemented for all patients with regard to exposure to patient blood, body fluids, excretions, and secretions, except for sweat. These precautions include the following:

- Gloves should be worn whether exposure is planned or unplanned.
- Masks and eyewear should be worn.

- Gowns and aprons should be worn.
- Treatment or exam rooms should be private.
- Resuscitation equipment, such as a mouth piece, is available.
- Sharps containers are accessible.
- Lab specimens are in leak-proof containers.
- Blood spill plan or kit for clean up must be available.
- Notice to patients to cover their face when coughing.
- Personal protective equipment (PPE) should be available along with instructions in patient care areas

To address specific isolation needs for your setting, keep the following in mind:

- Waiting room setup—separate well patients and sick patients.
- Scheduling of patients with suspected infections.
- Train staff to ask patients to identify suspected illnesses. Place patients in a room with a closed door (i.e., tuberculosis, RSV, measles, mumps, rubella, meningitis, and chickenpox/shingles).
- Have a plan for transferring patients if hospitalization is necessary.
- Droplet precautions may be needed in addition to standard precautions to avoid transmission through coughing, sneezing, talking, or by procedures.

Multidrug-Resistant Organisms (MDRO)

Multidrug-resistant organisms are also a consideration. Be prepared for prevention of transmission if a particular organism is identified in your practice. Track and trend for identification of the most common MDROs, including MRSA and *vancomycin-resistant enterococcus* (VRE), which are extremely difficult bugs to eradicate and can be transmitted quickly among the elderly. Use the CDC recommendations for hypochlorite-based germicidal cleaning agents.

Infection Prevention Resources

There are many infection prevention resources available through regional and national organizations, including the following:

- Centers for Disease Control and Prevention (http://www.cdc.gov)
- Society for Healthcare Epidemiology of America (http://www.shea-online.org)
- Association for Professionals in Infection Control and Epidemiology, Inc. (APIC) (http://www.apic.org)

- The Joint Commission on Accreditation of Healthcare Facilities (http://www.jointcommission.com)
- U.S. Department of Health and Human Services (http://www.hhs.gov/pandemicflu)
- OSHA (http://www.osha.gov)
- World Health Organization (http://www.who.int/en/)
- Local and state health departments
- Medicare Conditions for Coverage (www.cms.gov/CFCs And CoPs/)

Summary and Key Points

- Assign one or more people in the organization to be responsible for day-to-day infection control and prevention activities.
- Train all of the staff, physicians, and patients on safe practices.
- Have a plan that includes a risk assessment and emergency preparedness.
- Meet all regulations relating to infection control and prevention.
- For ambulatory surgery centers, comply fully with Medicare's Conditions for Coverage and the infection control and prevention survey guidelines.
- Track potential and real infections through planned surveillance.
- Document known exposures to infections and bloodborne pathogens.
- Track and trend your data.
- Know your state and federal rules for reporting.

Sources

Association for Professionals in Infection Control and Epidemiology, Inc. 2009. Ambulatory care. In *APIC text of infection and control and epidemiology: 3rd edition*. Washington DC: APIC.

Bennet, Gail. 2009. *Infection prevention manual for ambulatory care*. Rome, GA: ICP Associates, Inc.

Centers for Disease Control and Prevention (CDC). 2010. Hand hygiene in healthcare settings, http://www.cdc.gov/handhygiene/.

Centers for Disease Control and Prevention (CDC), Association for Professionals in Infection Control and Epidemiology, Inc. (APIC), and Society for Healthcare Epidemiology of America (SHEA). *How-to guide: Improving hand hygiene: A guide for improving practices among health care workers*, http://www.shea-online.org/Assets/files/IHI_Hand_Hygiene.pdf.

Rutala, William A., David J. Weber, and the Healthcare Infection Control Practices Advisory Committee. *Guideline for disinfection and sterilization in healthcare facilities, 2008*. Centers for Disease Control and Prevention, http://www.cdc.gov/hicpac/Disinfection_Sterilization/acknowledg.html.

World Health Organization (WHO). Infection prevention and control in healthcare, http://www.who.int/csr/bioriskreduction/infection_control/en/.

World Health Organization (WHO). November 2002. *"First do no harm": Introducing auto-disposable syringes and ensuring injection safety in immunization systems of developing countries*, http://www.who.int/vaccines-documents/DocsPDF02/www704.pdf.

World Health Organization. 2005. *WHO guidelines on hand hygiene in health care: A summary. Clean hands are safer hands*, http://www.who.int/gpsc/tools/en/.

Chapter 9

Clinical Documentation

It's not enough that we do our best, sometimes we have to do what's required.

—**Sir Winston Churchill**

History

Accurate and complete health record documentation in ambulatory care is critical to the quality of the care provided. A medical record should tell an all-inclusive story of a patient's history and care. The basic elements must include patient demographics, reason for the visit, list of past and current problems, results of physical exam, results of diagnostic testing, treatments, plans of care, and follow-up care. For a list of core documentation requirements, refer to Table 9.1.

The U.S. Department of Health and Human Services (HHS) published the first uniform ambulatory data set in 1976. It established standards that providers, third party payors, and professional organizations use for policy, research, and data comparison. In 1996 the subcommittee on Hospital Statistics of the National Committee on Vital and Health Statistics added to the data set and required a socioeconomic indicator to include years of education, injury codes, and place of patient encounter. Today, the Meaningful Use regulation outlines key elements of health information that must be captured in an electronic health record.

Table 9.1   Ambulatory Health Record Requirements

Core Requirements for Ambulatory Health Records
■ Health history
■ Problem list (Routine and updated)
■ Medication allergies and adverse reactions
■ Appropriate treatment
Guidelines for Medical Record Documentation
■ Patient name and ID on every page
■ Personal demographic data
■ Address, employment, contact information
■ All entries data and times
■ Legible
■ Significant past and current illnesses
■ Allergies and adverse reactions
■ Past medical history
■ Working diagnosis
■ Treatment plans
■ Encounter forms
■ Follow-up
■ Consult notes and letters
■ Lab and other diagnostic test results
■ Immunization records for pediatrics

Meaningful Use

The American Recovery and Reinvestment Act was signed into law on February of 2009 by President Barack Obama, allocating over $19 billion under the law's HITECH Act to expedite the implementation of electronic health records (EHRs). The HIT Policy Committee and the HIT Standards Committee were given the responsibility of defining *meaningful use* and setting a course of action for this portion of the law.

Meaningful use is important for ambulatory quality programs as it directly impacts most physicians along with other practitioners in office and practice settings. While other ambulatory programs are not part of the rollout program, it doesn't mean that future applications will not occur. Hospitals and critical access hospitals are the other entities that are targeted for adoption of Meaningful Use regulations.

Five goals guide the vision of Meaningful Use. While these are specific to this program, the goals are universal in their significance and application for any healthcare quality program. These goals are:

1. To improve quality, safety, and efficiency
2. To engage patients and families
3. To improve care coordination
4. To improve population and public health
5. To ensure and protect privacy and security of personal health information

There are three stages that currently define the Meaningful Use program. More information can be found on these stages at the Centers for Medicare and Medicaid website (http://www.cms.gov/EHRIncentivePrograms) and the website of the Office of the National Coordinator for Health Information Technology (http://healthit.hhs.gov). The complexity of the law and the monetary incentives associated with it require in-depth study on one's part. This chapter offers a very high-level overview, so please make it a point to expand your knowledge base and grasp the full impact that this program will have on you and those around you in the healthcare setting.

It is important to note that time-limited monetary incentives for implementation make up about $17 billion, earmarked to hospitals, critical access hospitals, and physicians and practitioners (eligible professionals [EPs]). For those that choose not to partake in the program, monetary penalties are in store. Work through the pros and cons of the program, and determine the financial implications for you. The incentives for independent physicians will more than likely not cover all of your costs associated with full acceptance of Meaningful Use regulations.

It's important to note that even though a great deal of data and information will be recorded and submitted, that doesn't mean a grassroots quality program is in place. Collecting data does not equal improving the care process and outcomes for the patient or for other medical providers. In addition, the resources that will be required for executing this program are huge and can suboptimize other clinical and business practices that don't directly relate to them. Physicians already on tight budgets will be forced to prioritize how money is spent.

Using sound scientific methods as noted in this book is essential if we are to see anything really positive come out of this massive an initiative. Also, the three-part list that follows in the quality implications section displays the first wave of compliance. The requirements will most likely increase as time goes on in regard to mandatory reporting of clinical documentation and data. Incentives and penalties will walk hand in hand with compliance.

Electronic Health Records (EHRs)

As we have discerned, the impact on ambulatory care of the Meaningful Use regulations will be significant and will provide qualified physicians utilizing a certified EHR in a "meaningful" way with additional incentive payments if they also participate in federal Medicaid and Medicare programs. A true EHR is defined as a longitudinal electronic record of patient health information generated by one or more encounters in any care delivery setting. The electronic system must have the ability to generate a complete record and include the core elements of demographics, progress notes, problems, medications, vital signs, past medical history, lab data, immunizations, and radiology reports. Employing an electronic health record is not a small feat and requires proper assessment, planning, selection of a vendor, implementing and testing, and evaluation and measure improvement. Current and future workflows involving clinical and nonclinical staff must be considered.

What are the impending benefits of an EHR? Potentially it can improve overall quality of care and decrease error rates. Rules and alerts can be built in to warn of drug interactions, allergies, or transcription errors. Advancements in electronic prescribing also allow a provider to access national data on a patient's current and past prescriptions, making the medication reconciliation process more effective. Another important benefit is using order sets that are embedded in the ERH. When coupled with integrated evidence tools as provided by organizations like Zynx Health Solutions, we are looking at the wave of the future for order sets. Provision of checklists and consistency reduces unwanted variation, and evidence-based order sets can contribute to that reduction. More information on Zynx can be found at http://zynxhealth.com/.

If you are just beginning this journey toward an EHR, one helpful road map is available from the Arkansas Foundation for Medical Care at http://www.pbrn.ahrq.gov. A word of caution is needed when implementing any electronic record program, or for ambulatory documentation in general. Spend time to make the forms, order sets, preference cards, and all aspects of clinical documentation ambulatory. Transferring inpatient documentation to an ambulatory setting is costly, inappropriate, and not in the best interests of the patient.

Meaningful Use Quality Implications

Eligible professionals must complete several clinical documentation and outcome quality initiatives when participating in the meaningful use program, which are as follows:

Implement 15 core objectives:

1. Use computerized provider order entry (CPOE) for medication orders.
2. Implement drug–drug and drug–allergy interaction checks.
3. Generate and transmit permissible prescriptions electronically.
4. Record demographics such as preferred language, gender, and race.
5. Maintain an up-to-date problem list of current and active diagnoses.
6. Maintain active medication lists.
7. Maintain an active medication allergy list.
8. Record and chart vital signs, which include height, weight, blood pressure (BP), body mass index (BMI), growth charts, and BMI for children 2 through 20 years of age.
9. Record smoking status for patients 13 years and older.
10. Implement one clinical decision support rule and the ability to track compliance with that rule.
11. Report clinical quality measures to the Centers for Medicare and Medicaid (CMS) or the state.
12. Provide patients with an electronic copy of their health information that includes diagnostic test results, a problem list, medication lists, medication allergies, a discharge summary, and procedures upon request.
13. Provide clinical summaries for each office visit.
14. Have the capability to exchange key clinical information with providers of care and other authorized entities electronically.
15. Protect EHR information through certified EHR technology.

Select five objectives out of ten from the menu set:

1. Implement drug formulary checks.
2. Incorporate clinical lab test results into certified EHR technology as structured data.
3. Generate lists of patients by specific conditions to use for quality improvement, reduction of disparities, research, or outreach.
4. Send reminders to patients per patient preference for preventive and follow-up care.
5. Provide patients with timely electronic access to their health information within four business days of the information being available to the EP.

6. Use certified EHR technology to identify patient-specific patient education resources and provide those resources to the patient, if appropriate.
7. If you are receiving a patient from another setting of care or provider of care, provide medication reconciliation.
8. Provide a summary of care record for each transition of care or referral.
9. Capability to submit electronic data to immunization registries or immunization information systems and actual submission in accordance with applicable law and practice.
10. Capability to submit electronic syndromic surveillance data to public health agencies and actual submission in accordance with applicable law and practice.

Selection and implementation of six clinical quality measures:

1. Select three measures from a core set of clinical quality measures or alternate core set clinical quality measures, such as weight assessment and counseling for children and adolescents or hypertension and BP measurement.
2. Select three out of 38 additional clinical quality measures, such as foot exams for patients with diabetes or cervical cancer screening. These data elements tie to National Committee for Quality Assurance (NCQA) or American Medical Association (AMA) current measures for the most part.

The Purpose of Clinical Documentation

Clinical documentation has five purposes: demonstrate comprehensive patient care, research, legal proceedings, accreditation, and licensing and reimbursement. Data is collected from the ambulatory setting for a variety of purposes: to track communicable diseases, immunization rates, or health prevention patterns. As the old saying goes, what is not documented is not done. It's important to accurately and objectively document patient assessments and findings and any follow-up action taken.

The accreditation process includes a review of patient care documentation, and the quality of that documentation can determine licensure status. In processing claims for reimbursement, you must show proof that services were provided as billed. The medical record is truly a record of care and must clearly delineate the care that was provided. The physician or provider of record must clearly be noted.

One particularly serious event brings to mind the importance of clear and concise documentation. An elderly woman with a history of mild congestive heart failure, occasional atrial fibrillation, and kidney stones presented to the outpatient surgery center for a routine cystoscopy and possible stent placement. Her vital signs were stable, with the only complaint of a mild urinary tract infection.

In the recovery room she developed a temperature and rapid heart rate. Her urologist had already left the procedure area and was called about a rapid heart rate, but was not told of the temperature. He consulted a cardiologist who saw the patient in the recovery area and ordered monitoring and admission to the ICU for possible administration of a cardiac drip. The patient's temperature continued to rise and she proceeded to deteriorate overnight and coded the following morning.

In a review of the postanesthesia care unit (PACU) record, orders were found to be illegible; vital signs were written on the orders and not on the proper flow sheets. Additional orders were not transcribed on blank order sheets as per policy, but instead were written in between preprinted orders. It was next to impossible to determine the physician of record for each entry. A review of contributing factors in the case showed that the critical vital sign of temperature was indicative of sepsis, yet it was not consistently recorded or communicated to the provider. Unquestionably, this case study demonstrates that accurate and legible documentation enhances communication and will help prevent adverse events for our patients. It's our responsibility to tell the patient's story so that all caregivers have the same information and knowledge to make appropriate decisions.

Authentication and Completion of Medical Records

When you think about why medical record departments are created, it brings to mind the word inspection. Most records are sent to this department incomplete. Numerous employees are hired to follow up with the person responsible for entries to complete authentication or to dictate or write notes. All in all, the cost associated with incomplete records is immense, not to mention the legal side, when an event happens, and an incomplete or erroneous record contributes significantly to the outcome of the case.

What makes sense is to have a real-time record completion process in place; that way, inspectors are not needed and these dollars can be spent on patient care instead.

Also, question the need to reorganize the medical record. Why is this done and why are additional employees needed to complete this task? Again, it contributes to unneeded expense. Order your medical records to match how care is delivered. Keep it in that order because when older records are needed, caregivers don't have to reorient themselves time and time again.

All medical record entries must be authenticated by the responsible practitioner. The definition of *authentication* is signature, date, and time. Written signatures must be legible, and the attending physician is responsible for completion of the record. All entries must be dated, timed, and completed in a timely manner by anyone who enters information into the record. In addition, the timeline for the entries must match up. If late entries are needed, then a policy and procedure that governs this process is to be followed.

Figure 9.1 displays a flow chart on the documentation process for the operating room, and Figure 9.2 offers a flow chart on discharge documentation. Using process tools such as these helps personnel know how documentation should flow for your organization. Think through how the medical record is completed, and assign categories for the flow charts—preadmission, date of visit, visit itself, discharge, follow-up care, anesthesia, admission, testing, and so on.

Medical record forms covering discharge summaries and history collection are shown in Figures 9.3, 9.4, and 9.5. These are examples, but they can be used to create your own forms. Histories and discharge planning are extremely valuable processes that contribute immensely to the quality of patient care. All caregivers should have access to complete history information for their patients. Also, patients deserve to be sent home with clearly defined discharge instructions. Both can be reviewed and analyzed for completeness using audit tools.

Table 9.2 can provide assistance when reviewing completion of history and physicals. It's a straightforward audit tool, and results can be easily analyzed, as noted in Figure 9.6. The data in this chart is broken out by physician, and standard deviations are shown. While the goal of zero defects for incomplete history and physicals is necessary, it's clear that physician J has the most incomplete records and the highest variation in practice, as the standard deviation is higher than the peer data. Appendix F also delivers a very detailed documentation audit tool that can be dissected for use. For now, it includes required documentation elements from Accreditation Association for Ambulatory Health Care (AAAHC), the Joint Commission (TJC), and Medicare's Conditions for Coverage (CfCs).

A surgical and procedural case review process is desired to determine if standards of care are met. Table 9.3 is a user-friendly tool to help do just that. Advanced directives are important for defining what the patient's needs are should an adverse event occur and the patient cannot make decisions for himself. Therefore, ensuring that proper documentation of the patient's wishes is required, and the audit tool found in Table 9.4 can be used for the review process.

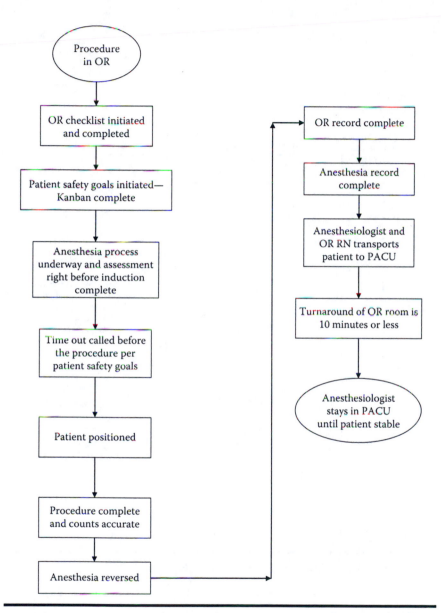

Figure 9.1 OR documentation flow chart.

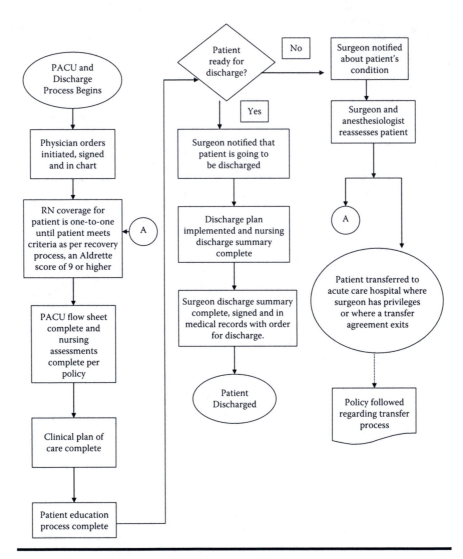

Figure 9.2   Discharge documentation flow chart.

Problem Lists

Problem lists can be best defined as a listing of clinically relevant diagnostic and physical procedures and concerns that are important to the patient's health status. Suggested items to include in a problem list are chronic conditions, allergies, diagnosis, symptoms, date on onset, and relevant changes in condition. A problem list is a key component of an ambulatory patient record for coding

| Discharge Date: _____ | | Discharge Time: _____ |

Discharged to Home via: Accompanied by: Transportation Via:
- [ ] Wheelchair
- [ ] Stretcher
- [ ] Ambulatory

- [ ] Family
- [ ] Significant Other
- [ ] Other _____

- [ ] Private Car
- [ ] Taxi
- [ ] Other _____

INSTRUCTIONS:
Diet: ☐ No Restrictions ☐ Low Fat, Low Cholesterol ☐ Other _____ ☐ Diet Instruction Sheet
Activity: ☐ No Restrictions ☐ See Instruction Sheet ☐ Other _____
Sexual Activity: ☐ No Restrictions ☐ See Instruction Sheet ☐ Other _____
Driving: ☐ No Restrictions ☐ See Instruction Sheet ☐ Other _____
Notify Doctor for: ☐ See Instruction Sheet ☐ Other _____
Other: ☐ Implant ID Card given ☐ Prescriptions Given to Patient

REFERRALS:
- [ ] Home Health _____
- [ ] Home Medical Equipment (list type) _____
- [ ] Other _____

☐ Rehab Services _____

If any problems occur or if you have any further questions, please contact your physician immediately. If you find you cannot contact him/her, but you feel that your signs and symptoms warrant physician's attention, go to the emergency room closest to you.

EDUCATIONAL MATERIAL GIVEN TO PATIENT:
- [ ] Discharge Instructions
- [ ] Medications
- [ ] Smoking
- [ ] Other

- [ ] Food and Drug Interaction Instructions
- [ ] Exercise
- [ ] Stress
- [ ] Other

- [ ] Home Care for Surgical Wounds
- [ ] Bathing
- [ ] Diet
- [ ] Other

(√ if given)		MEDICATIONS *(Do not take any additional medications without approval from your Doctor)*			
Rx	Info	Medication	Dose	Frequency (Per Day)	Doses Taken Today
				☐ Once ☐ Twice ☐ Three Times ☐ Four Times	a.m. p.m.
				☐ Once ☐ Twice ☐ Three Times ☐ Four Times	a.m. p.m.
				☐ Once ☐ Twice ☐ Three Times ☐ Four Times	a.m. p.m.
				☐ Once ☐ Twice ☐ Three Times ☐ Four Times	a.m. p.m.
				☐ Once ☐ Twice ☐ Three Times ☐ Four Times	a.m. p.m.
				☐ Once ☐ Twice ☐ Three Times ☐ Four Times	a.m. p.m.

APPOINTMENTS:
Date: _____ Time: _____ With: _____
Date: _____ Time: _____ With: _____
Patient to make his or her own appointment with: _____
- [ ] Influenza/Pneumococcal vaccine follow-up is recommended.
TESTS: Last PT result: _____ Date: _____ Time: _____
- [ ] Follow-up PT (check for PT order when pt. on Warfarin) ☐ Follow-up Ultrasound ☐ Other _____
Date of tests: _____ Location: _____ Results to: _____

I have taken all of my personal belongings. I accept, understand, and can verbalize the instructions/teaching given to me at the time of discharge. I have no further questions regarding these instructions.

_____ _____
Patient's Signature Patient Representative's Signature

_____ _____
RN Signature Relationship to Patient
- [ ] Discharge Assessment Completed

Figure 9.3 Nursing discharge summary.

documentation, accurate care, and discharge documentation. It is ongoing and added to along the way.

Allergy and Sensitivity Documentation

Allergy and sensitivity documentation are required elements in all medical records regardless of the patient setting for care. In turn, the information must be updated with each patient visit and validated along the care journey. Many adverse events are due to delivery of medication or use of a product to which the patient is sensitive

☐ OUTPATIENT H&P DICTATED OR WRITTEN ON CHART			☐ UNABLE TO OBTAIN	
HISTORY				

	PREVIOUS HOSPITALIZATIONS, TREATMENTS, SURGERIES OR CARDIAC PROCEDURES	DATES	PREVIOUS HOSPITALIZATIONS, TREATMENTS, SURGERIES OR CARDIAC PROCEDURES	DATES

FAMILY	☐ CANCER MOTHER/FATHER/SISTER/BROTHER LOCATION:_____ ☐ HEART ATTACK/CHEST PAIN (BEFORE AGE 65) MOTHER/FATHER/SISTER/BROTHER COMMENTS:_____ _____ _____ _____ ☐ NO PROBLEMS	HABITS	☐ SMOKER: CURRENT/FORMER ____ PACKS/DAY FOR ____ YEARS QUIT ____ ☐ HAS ANYONE ASKED YOU TO QUIT SMOKING? ☐ Y ☐ N ☐ CAFFEINE ____ CUPS PER DAY ☐ ALCOHOL ____ PER DAY ☐ STREET DRUGS ☐ EXERCISE AT LEAST TWO TIMES A WEEK ☐ SLEEP APNEA (STOP BREATHING WHILE SLEEPING) COMMENTS:_____ _____ ☐ NO PROBLEMS
HEAD & NECK	☐ LENS IMPLANT R/L ☐ CATARACTS R/L ☐ VISUAL CHANGES R/L ☐ GLASSES/CONTACTS ☐ GLAUCOMA ☐ HEARING LOSS R/L ☐ RINGING IN EARS ☐ DENTURES/PARTIALS UPPER/LOWER ☐ GOITER OR THYROID DISEASE COMMENTS:_____ ☐ NO PROBLEMS	NERVES	☐ PROBLEMS WITH SPEECH ☐ WEAKNESS IN ARMS OR LEGS ☐ EPILEPSY OR SEIZURES ☐ DIZZINESS ☐ FAINTING ☐ HEADACHES ☐ NUMBNESS/TINGLING IN ARMS OR LEGS ☐ STROKE COMMENTS:_____ _____ _____ ☐ NO PROBLEMS
CIRCULATION	☐ HEART ATTACK/CHEST PAIN ☐ PERIPHERAL VASCULAR DISEASE (DECREASED BLOOD SUPPLY TO LEGS) ☐ HIGH BLOOD PRESSURE ☐ BLOCKED ARTERIES OF NECK ☐ IRREGULAR HEART BEAT ☐ HEART VALVE DISEASE ☐ CONGESTIVE HEART FAILURE ☐ BLOOD CLOTS LUNGS/LEGS ☐ BLEEDING PROBLEMS ☐ PACEMAKER/DEFIBRILLATOR COMMENTS:_____ _____ _____ ☐ NO PROBLEMS	LUNGS	☐ ASTHMA/EMPHYSEMA ☐ PNEUMONIA/BRONCHITIS ☐ BLOODY SPUTUM ☐ SHORTNESS OF BREATH ☐ TUBERCULOSIS ☐ VALLEY FEVER ☐ HOME OXYGEN USE ___ LITERS PER MINUTE CONTINUOUS/AT NIGHT/AS NEEDED COMMENTS:_____ _____ _____ _____ _____ _____ ☐ NO PROBLEMS

Figure 9.4 Patient history form page one.

or allergic. The results can be catastrophic, and, if the event should go forward in the legal world, hard to defend if the records are not complete and followed.

Ambulatory Surgery Center Documentation

CMS published revised guidelines for ambulatory surgery centers effective May 18, 2009. New standards were added and revisions were made to the original CfCs that were first published on August 5, 1982. These standards apply for all ASCs having AAAHC/Medicare deemed status or other deemed status through an accrediting organization (AO). The standards that significantly impact clinical documentation are highlighted in this chapter. Failure to perform and document these required assessments can lead to survey findings, immediate jeopardy, as well as placing patients at risk.

DIGESTION	☐ NAUSEA/VOMITING ☐ HEARTBURN/INDIGESTION ☐ BLOODY VOMIT ☐ STOMACH ULCERS ☐ HIATAL HERNIA ☐ PANCREATITIS ☐ GALLSTONES ☐ LIVER PROBLEMS ☐ BLACK/BLOODY BOWEL MOVEMENTS ☐ DIARRHEA/CONSTIPATION ☐ HIGH CHOLESTEROL COMMENTS:_____ _____ _____ _____ ☐ NO PROBLEMS	URINE & GENITALS	☐ FREQUENT URINATION (PASSING WATER) ☐ DRIBBLING OF URINE ☐ PAIN WITH URINATION ☐ BLOODY URINE ☐ URINATING AT NIGHT ☐ KIDNEY PROBLEMS/FAILURE ☐ DIALYSIS HEMO/PERITONEAL _____ TIMES PER WEEK GOAL WEIGHT _____ KG DAYS (CIRCLE) S M T W T F S *MALES ONLY* ☐ PROSTATE PROBLEMS *FEMALES ONLY* ☐ VAGINAL BLEEDING/DISCHARGE ☐ PAST MENOPAUSE ☐ UTERUS AND/OR OVARIES REMOVED COMMENTS: _____ _____ ☐ NO PROBLEMS
SKIN	☐ RASHES/LESIONS ☐ ITCHING/DRYNESS ☐ OPEN SORES/ULCERS COMMENTS: _____ _____ _____ _____ _____ _____ ☐ NO PROBLEMS	MUSCLE & BONE	☐ RESTRICTED MOVEMENT ☐ DISABILITIES ☐ ARTHRITIS LOCATION: _____ COMMENTS: _____ _____ _____ _____ _____ _____ _____ ☐ NO PROBLEMS
SOCIAL	☐ ANXIETY ☐ DEPRESSION ☐ RECENT LOSS OF LOVED ONE(S) ☐ RECENT CHANGES IN LIFE ☐ DIFFICULTY COPING ☐ STRESS COMMENTS: _____ _____ ☐ NO PROBLEMS	OTHER	☐ DIABETES SINCE AGE: _____ ☐ LOW BLOOD COUNTS ☐ IMMUNE SYSTEM DISORDERS ☐ THYROID DISORDERS ☐ CANCER LOCATION: _____ ☐ CHEMOTHERAPY/RADIATION THERAPY COMMENTS: _____ NO PROBLEMS

I LEARN BEST BY: ☐ READING   ☐ WATCHING VIDEOS   ☐ TALKING   ☐ OBSERVING   ☐ HANDS ON

Figure 9.5   **Patient history form page 2.**

An admission and presurgical assessment completed by a physician or a licensed independent practitioner (LIP) is required to be documented on all patients admitted to a center. A patient's medical history and physical must be completed within the past 30 days and updated prior to the procedure, and be present on the chart before the surgical procedure.

CfC §416.42, the standard for anesthesia risk and evaluation, requires a physician to examine the patient immediately before surgery and to evaluate the risk of anesthesia and risks of the procedure to be performed. This assessment must be recorded in the patient record prior to the procedure. The risks of anesthesia must be separately identified and written in the consent process.

CfC §416.42 requires that prior to discharge from an ASC, each patient must be evaluated by a physician or by an anesthetist as defined by CfC §410.69(b) in accordance with applicable state health and safety laws, standards of practice, and ASC policies for safe recovery.

Appendix J shows how a patient education pathway can be used for surgery centers. It's a one-page form that can be altered to meet individual needs. It gives

Table 9.2   Audit Tool for History and Physical

Review Criteria	Yes	No
1. Patient identification is noted.		
2. History and physical are less than 30 days old.		
3. History and physical are updated prior to the procedure.		
4. Preprocedure diagnosis is noted.		
5. Pertinent history is noted.		
6. Current medications are listed.		
7. Allergies and sensitivities are noted.		
8. Physical exam findings are noted.		
9. All items are legible.		
10. Original H&P and updates are authenticated by physician(s).		
11. An airway assessment is present.		
12. Informed consent information is present, including how risks, benefits, and alternatives are explained.		
13. Complete history and physical are on the chart prior to medications given and procedure start.		

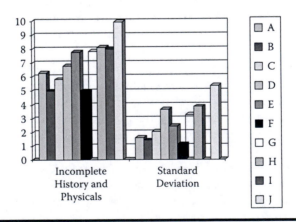

Figure 9.6   Incomplete history and physicals.

Table 9.3   Surgical/Procedure Case Review Form

Date:								
Indicator: Surgical/Procedure Case Review								
Criteria:								
1. Indications for procedure match approved medical staff criteria such as Miliman, Interqual, or a facility-based criteria.								
2. Pre-op and post-op diagnoses are the same.								
3. Patient is free of intra-op/procedure complications.								
4. Pathology matches the procedure.								
X = Met		0 = Not Met		N = Not Applicable				
Medical Record Number	Procedure	Physician	Admission Date	1	2	3	4	Comments
13453	Cataract Extraction	Kildaire	4/12/10	x	x	x	NA	No tissue

the patient a high-level overview of what to expect throughout the surgical/ procedural event.

A complete comparison of AAAHC and CMS standards is available through the Accreditation Association for Ambulatory Health Care.

Communication

The medical record, whether paper based or electronic or both, is a communication tool between providers. Consults to other providers are to be noted and copies of consult notes included in your records. Once again, timelines are

Table 9.4 Advance Directive Medical Record Review

MR# _____ Age _____ Sex m f		
Admit Date _____		
Dx _____ Surgery/Procedure _____		
MD _____ Length of Stay _____		
Criteria	*Y/N*	*Comments*
1. Advance directive initiated before the date the surgery or procedure is scheduled?		
2. Orders/implementation meet the requirements of the advance directive? process?		
3. Copy of advance directive, durable power of attorney, or living will in the medical record if noted necessary?		
4. Documentation on the advance directive form complete?		
5. Documentation in the initial nursing assessment and clinical pathway complete?		
6. Reassessment process of patient's wishes initiated if patient's condition warrants?		
7. Patient and/or significant other educated on process if requested?		
8. Other?		

important in this record and all entries should line up. When reviewing records for completeness, note the times of the entries, the times and dates of dictation and transcription, and the times and dates of the care events.

Security and Retention of Medical Records

There must be a designated person in charge of medical records. This person's responsibilities include:

■ Securing confidentiality, security, and physical safety of records
■ Timely retrieval of individual records upon request

- Supervision of the collection, processing, maintenance, storage, retrieval, and distribution of records
- Maintenance of the approved format

Each practice must have a formal plan or record retention schedule for the transfer of eligible records to inactive storage and to outline methods for subsequent retrieval of stored material.

You must retain records on a schedule based on your state's statute of limitations and Medicare conditions and accreditation guidelines. Records stored at off-site locations should be logged and readily available to authorized personnel.

Regulatory Requirements

Ambulatory care settings are subject to a number of regulatory and licensing agencies; however, the principal agencies are outlined in our accreditation chapter. Know the CMS, federal, and state requirements that are appropriate for your setting

Summary and Key Points

1. The patient's medical record is the record of care.
2. Know how Meaningful Use regulations impact your organization, center, or office. If needed, work with experts to implement the program appropriately.
3. Set a goal to complete records on the day of service, eliminating the need to hire inspectors and to chase down caregivers to complete the record.
4. Document the key requirements under the Meaningful Use regulations.
5. Include core elements for recording in the medical record.
6. Do not transfer inpatient documentation to an ambulatory setting. Spend time to make the documentation process applicable for the setting in which it's to be used.
7. Secure and protect health information.
8. Perform studies and audits to ensure completion of the medical record.

Sources

American Health Information Management Association (AHIMA), http://www.ahima.org.
Arkansas Foundation for Medical Care, http:// www.afmc.org.

Blumenthal, D., MD M.P.P., and M. Tanner, RN MHA .The "meaningful use" regulation for electronic health records. *NEJM* (July 2010): 363–366, http://www.nejm.org/doi/pdf/10.1056/NEJMp1006114.

Health Information Technology (HIT), http://www.hhs.gov/healthhit.

Healthcare Information and Management Systems Society (HIMSSEHRA), http://www.himss.org/ASP/index.asp.

Quality Insights. 2009. *The meaningful use of health care data: The electronic health record in the ambulatory care and physician office setting*, http://qipa.org/shared/content/Meaningful%20Use%20of%20Data%20CNE%20Packet%20FINAL.pdf.

Chapter 10

Risk Management and Safety

If we did all things we are capable of, we would astound ourselves.

—Thomas Edison

Introduction

Medical errors can occur in all settings, and there are many definitions of the term *error*. For the purposes of this chapter, ambulatory settings include office-based surgical practices, ambulatory surgical centers, diagnostic imaging centers, urgent care centers, and dental and medical offices. There is much debate in the literature about what constitutes an error. James Reason's research defines a medical error as "the failure of planned actions to achieve their desired goal." He concludes that there are three areas that influence how providers define error, and they are: (1) the process that occurred versus the outcome that occurred, (2) rare versus common occurrences, and (3) system versus responsibility at the individual level. He identifies three additional elements to consider when defining if an error has occurred: (1) What was the outcome and did harm occur? (2) Was the event rare or a common occurrence? (3) Does the responsibility fall primarily on human or system error?

Errors that almost occur are defined as a *near miss* or *close call*. In a near miss, a process variation occurred that, if repeated, could indeed cause a serious adverse outcome. A *sentinel event* is defined as an unexpected occurrence involving death or serious psychological or physical injury.

Challenges and Opportunity in the Ambulatory Setting

The challenges in ambulatory care are different from those in the inpatient setting, and it is important to recognize the differences as you develop a safety plan. The human factor differences include varied staff skill mix, fewer resources and support staff, multitasking, and responsibility for a broader range of areas. Staff may be less experienced and have a differing knowledge base. Patients are responsible for coordination of their own care, and can create their own safety risk due to compliance or health literacy issues.

The environmental challenges include distractions such as phones, time constraints, and overbooked appointment schedules. There may be limited equipment available for emergency situations and infrequent drills or opportunities for staff education. Use of off-site laboratory and pharmacy makes it difficult to ensure continuity of care.

According to E. M. Lapetina and E. M. Armstrong's article "Preventing Errors in the Outpatient Setting: A Tale of Three States," there are two potential sources of error that differ in the ambulatory environment—the setting and the actors. The setting refers to separate office practices or outpatient centers and the actors are the solo practitioners. In these settings there is often a lack of peer review and insufficient training, especially for crisis response and resuscitation. Operations or procedures with minimal or no anesthesia assistance can set up a routine office practice for disaster. Taking into consideration the nuances of the ambulatory setting, this chapter will identify the common causes of errors and strategies to keep patients safe, and will introduce tools to monitor safe practices and evaluate processes when a safety event does occur.

Common Causes of Errors in the Ambulatory Setting

Patient Care Errors

A *diagnostic error* is defined as a diagnosis that is missed, wrong, or delayed as detected by some subsequent test or finding. Missed or delayed diagnoses result from failures to order the appropriate tests, incorrect interpretation of tests, or failed follow-up appointments or tests. Another common cause of a missed or delayed diagnosis is filing system errors, an error highlighted by Sue Sheridan, an advocate for patient safety. Her husband's misfiled pathology report kept secret a malignant tumor that ultimately claimed his life because of delayed treatment for his condition. Laboratory testing errors, including implementing the appropriate lab test, misidentification of specimens, lost test results, and slow response to abnormal lab test results can lead to a delayed or missed diagnosis.

Errors in diagnosis can be linked to poor history recording and communication breakdowns.

Common solutions for preventing future diagnostic errors are as follows:

- Implement a reliable process for diagnosis to address timely reporting of abnormal or critical test results. Examples of this are designed in electronic medical records (EMR), use of a mailbox for alerts, and task alerts to office staff to check for lab results.
- Utilize computer-assisted clinical decision support tools for certain departments like lab and pathology.
- Identify how communication processes can result in missing information or incorrect information. What is the office's current practice for receiving information—fax, phone call, or computerized alert directly to the provider?
- Include in daily tasks for staff a review of outstanding reports, log lab tests to be completed, and ensure all specimens are processed.
- Track errors as part of occurrence screens. Review for patterns and origins of error.

Communication Errors

The Joint Commission has reported that the most common cause of medical error is ineffective communication. Caregivers and providers are often unaware that patients misinterpret or misunderstand their health information. The failure to provide patients with information about a diagnosis, new medication, or relevant laboratory test is often related to communication error.

The Joint Commission reports that communication problems are at the core of many sentinel events. The breakdown occurs at patient handoffs as patients enter and leave different healthcare settings, within the team of caregivers in a particular setting (such as an outpatient surgery center or a doctor's office), and between the provider and patient, patient and caregiver, or two different providers. A technique that can assist in communicating critical information that requires immediate attention and action concerning a patient's condition is SBAR, which stands for situation, background, assessment, recommendation and request.

- Situation: What is going on with the patient?
- Background: What is the clinical background or context?
- Assessment: What do I think the problem is?
- Recommendation and Request: What would I do to correct it?

Human factors affect good communication, and it's important to recognize that people communicate differently. A culture that is blame-free and promotes safety helps bridge the gaps in communication. The foundation for safety is based on shared experiences and beliefs. Examine high-performing teams to understand how shared knowledge can create a safe environment.

Let's examine the airline industry and the interactions of the team in the cockpit. There are clear expectations delineated by checklists to avoid human error that are built into the preflight routine. Everyone in the cockpit knows the mission and has a shared mental model of what is to be accomplished and how. This can be easily translated to an outpatient operating room (OR) or procedure room using a surgical/procedural checklist prior to the start of every procedure. The World Health Organization (WHO) surgical checklist is an example of such a tool. Included in Table 10.1 is an example checklist that one facility has adopted to meet their needs. We encourage the use of checklists for all procedures such as computerized tomography (CT) scans, magnetic resonance imaging (MRI) scans, endoscopy procedures in the office, or any invasive procedure performed in any setting.

Communication error can also be attributed to system failures as they relate to filing, transition of care, and telephone and verbal orders. Some simple steps to avoid these errors are end-of-day checklists for office staff, set times for debriefing among team members throughout the day in a busy office setting, policies and procedures, and staff training that is clearly delineated for new and existing staff.

An essential part of communication between the provider and patient is informed consent. Medicare, licensing and accrediting agencies, and the law are very specific on how consent is to be given and documented.

Medication Errors

Medication errors can occur in the form of ordering, dispensing, and administering. These errors have multiple causes, such as inappropriate drug interactions, ineffective patient education with respect to correct dosage quantities, and scheduling errors. A *medication error* is defined as an error that may cause or lead to inappropriate medication use or patient harm while the medication is in the control of a healthcare professional, patient, or consumer.

In ambulatory care, there are particular areas to focus on, including high-alert medications, contrast imaging agents, injection safety, multiuse medication

Table 10.1 Surgical and Procedural Checklist

Before Induction of Anesthesia	*Before Skin Incision or Procedure Start*	*Before Patient Leaves the Procedure Area or Operating Room*
☐ Have you confirmed patient identity, site, procedure, and consent?	☐ Confirm that all teams members are introduced by name and role.	☐ Nurse verbally confirms name of procedure.
☐ H&P within 30 days?	☐ Everyone *freeze* for timeout.	☐ Counts are correct?
☐ Is site marked?	☐ Confirm patient's name, DOB, procedure, position.	☐ Specimens labeled correctly (read back and verify aloud).
☐ Is the pulse oximeter on and working?	☐ Antibiotic given within last 60 minutes?	☐ Equipment issues that need to be addressed.
☐ Does patient have allergies? ☐ Is patient at risk for difficult intubation or aspiration? ☐ Risk of >500 cc blood loss?	☐ Safety Zone: Is there any critical information to establish? Any anesthesia concerns? Any equipment concerns? Any flammables?	☐ Any issues to address?

vials, look-alike sound-alike (LASA) medications, modified medication reconciliation, and safe prescription practices. Error reducing strategies are detailed in Chapter 7.

Ambulatory Surgical Errors

Surgical errors have increased with the expansion of procedures performed in physician offices. Office physicians may be performing procedures outside of their specialty, or the lack of rescue equipment may increase the risk of an adverse event. Staff not trained to respond in the critical first ten minutes of a patient showing distress can lead to serious failures.

Table 10.2   Moderate Sedation Review Form

Number	Performance Measure	Mark All That Apply
1	Loss of appropriate response to stimulation or command during or after procedure	
2	Hypoxemia <92% SaO$_2$ (or <3 percentage points below baseline >5 minutes	
3	Wrong medication or dose given — medication error	
4	Narcan/Flumazanil requirement	
5	Equipment failure	
6	IV problem	
7	Utilization of drugs not recommended for moderate sedation	
8	Utilization of doses that exceed guidelines	
9	Utilization of route not recommended	
10	Failure to document preprocedure assessment to include mental status, airway exam, cardiac exam, respiratory exam, ASA class	
11	Failure to document postprocedure assessment	
12	Unplanned admission due to moderate sedation	
13	Drug reaction	
14	**Hyper**tension >20% pre-op >10 minutes	
15	**Hypo**tension < 20% pre-op >10 minutes	
16	Angina or ECG changes	
17	Ophthalmic or dental injury	
18	Difficult to arouse	
19	MI within 24 hours of procedure	
20	Stroke or major peripheral nerve injury within 24 hours of procedure	

Table 10.2   Moderate Sedation Review Form (Continued)

Number	Performance Measure	Mark All That Apply
21	Respiratory failure or arrest	
22	Unplanned intubation	
23	Aspiration	
24	NPO violation	
25	Death within 24 hours of procedure	
26	Oxygen saturation <90% for 5 minutes or more	
27	Total number of sedation procedures this month	

Care Transition Errors

Care transition errors can also fall under communication error, and they occur when patients transition from one type of healthcare setting or from one practitioner to another. Medical information may be kept in electronic and paper records and not travel with the patient as they navigate our complex health systems. Medication reconciliation at admission, discharge, and care transfer does not always occur in the ambulatory settings as it is required in the inpatient world.

The Health Information Technology for Economic and Clinical Health (HITECH) Act will place incentives for healthcare organizations to adopt electronic health records. One of the key objectives of this meaningful use legislation is to provide patients with timely electronic access to their health information (including laboratory tests, medication lists, medication allergies, and problem lists). There is hope for the future; perhaps care transition will be seamless and patient safety and quality improved.

Teamwork has a direct reflection on communication and is a strategy for how information builds consistency and reduces variation. One of these strategies for handoff designed to enhance information exchange during transition in care is called "I Pass the Baton." This tool is taught through a patient safety program by the Agency for Healthcare Research and Quality (AHRQ) called Team STEPPS, which stands for Strategies and Tools to Enhance Performance and Patient Safety. AHRQ and the Department of Defense completed research on high-stress work settings and complex systems, including healthcare settings. With this research they have compiled a tool kit to improve teamwork and communication. You can find more information about these strategies at http://www.ahrq.gov.

Building Your Safety Program

The overarching message from the accrediting organizations like the Accreditation Association for Ambulatory Health Care (AAAHC) and the Joint Commission is that you must have a safety program that meets or exceeds local, state, and federal requirements. There simply needs to be a written program and someone (who is qualified) must be responsible for it. Everyone participates in the safety program and can demonstrate safe practices, and there is a process for reporting safety concerns. Small practices can deputize an office manager or charge nurse to be responsible for the safety program. Within the program, you need a process to report and manage safety events. Keep the common cause errors seen in ambulatory settings in mind and include strategies for prevention of these errors. A patient safety plan can be incorporated into an overall safety or quality plan, but should include the following elements:

- Program goals (consider the organization's mission and vision)
- Scope of the program
- Participating sites and facilities
- Structure (committee structure, responsible parties, interdisciplinary approach, and who is ultimately overseeing the plan)
- Mechanism for coordination
- Communication (to patients and families, employees, and visitors)
- Staff education (including education and training)
- Safety improvement activities, including the following:
  - Priority of improvement activities
  - Routine data collection and analysis (errors, incident reports, infection-related incidents, and perception of safety among providers, staff, patient, and families)
  - Assessment of safety culture
- Sentinel event reporting
- Proactive risk assessment
- A sample safety management plan is included in Appendix G

Patient Safety Culture

Patient safety is not a fad or the latest program of the month; it must be lived every day and become a core of value for your staff. The value that you can bring by assessing the culture is to enable better and safer care; reduce risk and liability exposure and you open up the lines of communication between physicians and the staff. Dialogue is never a bad thing. The data is also aggregated and can be benchmarked with other like practices. One tool available for the physician office setting is the Physician Practice Safety Assessment developed by the Institute for Safe Medication Practices, Health Research and Education Trust, and Medical Group Management Association. The tool can be found at http://www.physiciansafetytool.org.

Another excellent resource is the AHRQ Patient Safety Culture survey (http://www.ahrq.org).

National Patient Safety Goals

The Joint Commission has published National Patient Safety Goals (NPSGs) for ambulatory care. You can use these as a framework for establishing safe practices and error prevention in the ambulatory setting.

Goal: Patient Identification

Use of patient identifiers seems simple and standard, but traditionally outpatients do not wear arm bands, so you must rely on patients and families to provide appropriate identification. Develop a process that includes acceptable identifiers like birth date or patient name. Proper identification includes labeling of containers used for blood and specimens in the presence of the patient.

An instance of improper labeling of specimens led to unnecessary procedures when a patient presented to his primary care physician with a swollen and reddened knee. He was referred to a local orthopedic surgeon, who proceeded to aspirate his knee and send the specimen to the lab for review. When the lab result was returned, it indicated a *vancomycin-resistant enterococcus* (VRE) infection, which at the time seemed unusual for a knee bug, but the patient proceeded to surgery and a hospital stay that included IV antibiotics. The unlabeled cloudy fluid submitted to the lab was inadvertently switched with another patient's urinalysis. An astute physician reviewing the case quickly called the surgeon, since VRE was not typically found in synovial fluid. The patient was notified and antibiotics stopped.

Goal: Communication

The Joint Commission recognizes one of the most common causes of medical error as ineffective communication. Procedures performed in ambulatory surgery centers require advanced communication and scheduling, including information about the patient, medical record number, pertinent allergies and sensitivities, name of the procedure, surgeon or provider, type of anesthesia, special type of equipment needed, or blood or blood products all prior to the patient being seen.

Once the procedure has been completed, there are post-op care, medications, and clinical findings and follow-up care that must be communicated to the patient, family, and next level provider. There can be paper tools, automatic messaging through an EMR, or just old-fashioned phone communication that must be done.

Goal: Improve Safety in the Use of High-Alert Medications and Medication Safety

Medication reconciliation at every step of a patient care transition, including the outpatient pharmacy, is critical. Medications and pharmacy oversight is not always as controlled in the ambulatory setting. The oversight is often done by the physician in this setting, and safety, security, and distribution of medications falls on office nurses. Administration of moderate sedation requires policy and strict adherence to administration of only medications applicable for that level of sedation. Deep sedation medications can only be administered by an anesthesiologist and, with supervision, certified nurse anesthetists. Develop a process for monitoring the outcomes of moderate and deep sedation. See 210.4 for an example of a moderate sedation audit tool. The administration and disposal of pain medications such as fentanyl patches also must be taken into consideration.

Goal: Reduce the Risk of Healthcare-Associated Infection

The expectations of this goal are that staff must be educated on infection prevention, including the hand hygiene guidelines recommended by the World Health Organization or the Centers for Disease Control (CDC). Patients and their families are to be educated on risk-reducing strategies. Your practice or facility must have a risk assessment and a surveillance mechanism. The surgical care and improvement requirements for the National Quality Measures Surgical Care Improvement Project (SCIP) are to be followed and include appropriate and timely use of antibiotics and appropriate hair removal.

Goal: Medication Reconciliation

Strategies to reduce medication errors must be in place and must include reconciling medications by comparing current and newly ordered medications and communicating medication changes to the next level provider. Patients must receive a list or have access to a list of their medications.

Universal Protocol

The Universal Protocol (UP) for preventing wrong person, wrong site, wrong side, wrong procedure, or wrong implant surgery is required in all settings that perform invasive or surgical procedures.

Use of a perioperative checklist, such as the WHO checklists, can also help reduce error. Included in the WHO Universal Protocol requirement is the marking of the operative site. The procedure site is required to be marked by a licensed independent practitioner or other provider who is privileged by the organization.

The most important aspect of the UP requirements is performing effective *timeouts*. The timeout requires active communication among all members of the surgical team as a final check that the correct patient, site, position, procedure, and all relevant information and equipment is available prior to the initiation of the procedure. Visual reminders and checklists posted for staff provide clues to critical steps to be followed. One unique process shared by a large healthcare system is the practice of placing a metal tent marked "timeout" on the sharps. The tent cannot be removed by anyone, including the surgeon, until the time out has been completed.

Surgical and Anesthesia Safety

If you are a center that performs outpatient surgeries (ASC) you need to pay close attention to specific aspects of care. Ambulatory surgery is defined as a planned surgical episode where the patient requires less than a 24-hour hospital stay.

Nineteen safety violations closed a Florida endoscopy center in May 2009. These violations were for standard state and Centers for Medicare and Medicaid (CMS) requirements including:

- Medical equipment and routine maintenance checks
- Emergency generators tested and maintained
- Informing patients of their rights and responsibilities
- Training staff
- Appropriate supervision of nursing and anesthesia staff
- Following moderate sedation policy on patient monitoring and documentation of outcomes and adverse events

Airway Maintenance

Pay close attention to intraprocedural monitoring and staffing requirements for sedation and pain assessment. Include the following in your plan:

- Annual assessment of all nursing and support staff for competency for procedures performed
- Staff education on new drugs and procedures
- Staffing effectiveness requirements included in department review of staffing as it relates to serious and sentinel events

Malignant Hyperthermia

Malignant hyperthermia is a rare reaction to anesthesia in which anesthesia medications cause the body to overheat. If not corrected immediately, death can ensue. A recommended checklist and staff training can assist preparedness. See Chapter 12 for details on how to prepare for this rare but potentially devastating event.

Postanesthesia Monitoring

Many accrediting and licensing agencies require best practices to prevent surgical site infections. Practice requirements include the following:

- Appropriate use of antibiotics, appropriate hair removal, perioperative normothermia
- These are the three classifications of surgical site infections (SSI):
  - Superficial incision infections
  - Deep incision infections
  - Infection of the organ or space
- Following infection in the ASC setting requires that letters be sent to surgeons to find out if an event has occurred. This tracking is part of the quality and infection prevention program for that ASC.
- Refer to the Centers for Disease Control and Prevention (CDC) for more information on infections in the ambulatory setting.

Environmental Safety

The Joint commission, for example, defines environmental safety requirements based on whether an ambulatory center is a *healthcare occupancy* or *business occupancy*. A *healthcare occupancy* is defined as a building or part of a building used to provide treatment to four or more patients on an outpatient basis at the same time that meets one of the following criteria:

- Facilities that provide treatment for patients incapable of taking action for self-preservation in an emergency condition without assistance
- Facilities that provide surgical treatment requiring general anesthesia

All other settings are considered business healthcare occupancy.

When writing your environment safety plans you must include the following elements:

- Safety and security for staff, patients, and visitors (i.e., policies on slips, trips, and falls)
- Hazardous materials and waste management (sharps disposal)
- Emergency preparedness (i.e., pan flu epidemic plan)
- Life safety (i.e., exit lighting)
- Management of medical equipment (i.e., recall management)
- Utilities management (i.e., generator testing, emergency outlets)

MRI Safety

The Joint Commission issued a sentinel event alert in 2008 highlighting the risks of using MRIs. This alert outlined the types of injuries that can occur when working with patients and strong magnetic fields. These risks include:

- Injury related to equipment or device malfunction caused by the magnetic field (pace makers, infusion pumps)
- Injury due to attend to patient support systems such as metal oxygen tanks or patient medication pumps
- Hearing injury due to the noise of the scanner
- Injury or anaphylaxis from injection of contrast media
- Adverse events due to the handling, storage

Quick tips for risk reduction in MRI suites include the following:

- Appoint a staff member as the safety coordinator for the area
- Implement checklists and written protocols to support safe practices
- Ongoing staff education on MRI safety
- Do not bring any devices or equipment into the MRI environment

Radiation Safety

Preventing excessive radiation exposure and potential computed tomography scan malfunction are the top two considerations for radiation safety. Quick tips for reducing risk for these areas are as follows:

- Scan only when necessary and only the indicated area.
- Be judicious when using radiation in children (refer to the Society for Pediatric Radiology for specific guidelines).
- Take accurate patient histories regarding implanted devices.

Surgical Fires

In 2009 a patient was awarded $1.3 million in damages after suffering third-degree burns to the face and neck during surgery. Include safety measures for handling potential fire fuel sources, such as oxygen under drapes, in staff education for any operating and licensed independent practitioners and anesthesia providers. Know what flammables are in use, such as the prep solutions, as vapors are highly flammable. In addition, when using lasers or bovies, initiate safety protocols to ensure that safety procedures are in place.

Work Flow Analysis and Redesign

Safety cannot always be achieved through policies and procedures. You must consider the underlying work flows and proactively look for opportunities for error. Safety rounds by the staff can be a good method for identifying gaps in process. Other techniques you can use are critical-to-quality tools that identify critical processes, partial processes, and unnecessary processes. This gives you the opportunity to reduce steps and potentially prevent variations in care. Other visual cues, such as the use of just-in-time or Kanban, can signal when a critical supply is low or when items are out of order. *Kanban* is Japanese for "signal card," and it can be placed on a bin to signal that new stock needs to be ordered.

Safety Program Training

As Sue tells in her story, she had faith and trust in a system that failed to communicate important information. There is less staff (actors) in the ambulatory setting to set up checks and balances and no safety net if an office staff has only two members. Staff is often multitasking, the receptionist may also be responsible for medical records, and the scope of their responsibilities is broad. Continuity of care can be a challenge when labs are often off-site and patients must communicate to office staff when results are not received. Patients often coordinate their own care and bring inherent risks with them such as chronic conditions managed by multiple physicians and the trend toward polypharmacy. This is important to keep in mind as you train your staff and develop education for patients. A safety training program should include the following:

- Competency is initial and ongoing, including consideration of skill mix. Competency may include demonstrated skill such as point of care lab testing.
- Staff orientation
  - Current policy and patient safety initiatives (such as the NPSG and how they apply to the practice)
  - Basis of the safety practice (hand hygiene practices prevent infections)
  - How to report errors and near misses
  - How data is tracked and reported
- Specific strategies for error prevention (I Pass the Baton for handoff reports)

What to Do If You Experience a Safety Event

Establish a clear process for staff in a policy for reporting and analyzing the root cause of an event. To build transparency and accountability for safety in any setting, it's important to promptly obtain the facts and details of circumstances surrounding an event. What constitutes a safety event is any occurrence that is outside the routine care or operation of your center and has potential for harm. There are recommended events to track and there are also unexpected events. Routine surveillance for common occurrence screens for an outpatient surgery center and a radiology suite are included in Tables 10.3 and 10.4.

Use of RCA and FMEA Tools

If you experience an event, whether or not it resulted in harm, root cause analysis (RCA) is an excellent tool to use to identify prevention strategies. The process for completing an RCA should be multidisciplinary, openly identifying the process that needs to change and factors that contributed to the error. Included in the analysis is a determination of human and other factors, related processes and system issues, underlying causation, and potential contributing factors. A sample RCA tool is included in Appendix H. Failure Mode Effects Analysis (FMEA) is a tool used to proactively analyze potential failures in a system or process. This is an excellent tool to use for high-risk settings such as chemo infusion.

Table 10.3   Pre-Op/Holding Occurrences

Number	Pre-Op/Holding Occurrence	Mark All That Apply
1	Laboratory/radiology results reported incorrectly	
2	Delay in performing test/procedure	
3	Pre-op lab missing/not done	
4	MD not notified/delayed/no MD response	
5	Orders delayed/error	
6	Patient dissatisfied with care	
7	Patient required assisted ventilation after moderate sedation or experienced significant deviation from outcome (see Moderate Sedation outcome measures)	
8	Complication of procedure	
9	Patient presents with complaint, personal injury, claim	
10	Any other anticipated occurrence—list below	
10a		
10b		
10c		
10d		
10e		

In summary, safety and risk management is complex in the ambulatory setting. There are many other resources and organizations, and a few that we recommend are listed below.

Accreditation Association for Ambulatory Health Care (AAAHC), http://www.aaahc.org

AHRQ, http://www.ahrq.gov

Table 10.4   Radiology Occurrences

Number	Radiology Occurrence	Mark All That Apply
1	MRI burns	
2	Misidentification of patient resulting in wrong or unnecessary treatment	
3	Missed treatment or procedure	
4	Delay in treatment or procedure orders resulting in delay in performing test or procedure	
5	Medication error	
6	Patient injury due to complication of procedure	
7	Equipment failure—requires explanation	
8	Patient or visitor fall or injury	
9	Pregnant patient radiated without consent	
10	Any other anticipated occurrence—list below	
10a		
10b		
10c		
10d		
10e		

American Society of Anesthesiologists, http://www.asahq.org
Federal Ambulatory Surgery Association, http://www.fasa.org
Institute for Healthcare Improvement, http://www.ihi.org
National Committee on Quality Assurance, http://www.ncqa.org
National Patient Safety Foundation, http://www.npsf.org
National Quality Forum, http://www.qualityforum.org
World Health Organization, http://www.who.int/en/

Summary and Key Points

1. Deputize a safety officer and be sure that person is trained in patient safety processes.
2. Medical error can occur in the ambulatory setting.
3. Top risk areas include medication safety, communication, care transition error, and surgical and anesthesia safety for surgery centers.
4. Have a written safety plan.
5. Identify key stakeholders who are responsible for safety in your setting.
6. Track and trend occurrences specific to your setting.
7. Orient and train your staff.
8. Use tools to encourage teamwork.
9. Encourage transparency and a culture of safety.

Sources

Agency for Healthcare Research and Quality (AHRQ) and U.S. Department of Defense (DOD). 2009. *TeamSTEPPS Tools and Materials*, http://teamstepps.ahrq.gov/abouttoolsmaterials.htm.

Graber M. 2006. Diagnostic errors in medicine: A case of neglect. In Schiff G. D. (ed.), *Getting results: Reliability communicating and acting on critical test results*. Oak Brook, IL: Joint Commission Resources, pp. 24–133.

Joint Commission Resources. 2009. *A patient safety handbook for ambulatory care providers*. Oak Brook, IL: Joint Commission Resources, pp. 1–149.

Lapetina, E., and E. Armstrong. 2002. Preventing errors in the outpatient setting: A tale of three states. *Quality of Care* (July/August): 26–39.

Reason, J. 2001. Understanding adverse events: The human factor. In London V. C. (ed.), *Clinical risk management: Enhancing patient safety*. London: BMJ Publications.

Chapter 11

Licensing, Deemed Status, Accreditation, and Certification

Excellence is doing ordinary things extraordinarily well.

—**John W. Gardner**

Defining Licensing, Deemed Status, Accreditation, and Certification

In order for most outpatient programs to receive payment from Medicare and Medicaid programs, they must be certified as complying fully with the Conditions for Coverage (CfCs) for ambulatory surgery centers (ASCs), the Conditions of Participation (CoPs), or other appropriate conditions or regulations as found on the Centers for Medicare and Medicaid Services (CMS) website. The certification survey is conducted by a selected state agency on behalf of CMS. Deemed status can also be awarded to an outpatient program via private accrediting organizations (AO) such as the Accreditation Association for Ambulatory Health Care (AAAHC) or the Joint Commission (TJC) if deemed status has been granted to this AO by CMS.

CMS conducts random validation surveys and compliance investigations of organizations with deemed status through the state agency or the AO or both.

AOs are required to give CMS detailed information about the organization they survey for deemed status, including all findings and outcomes. Deemed status surveys are unannounced, so keeping an organization survey-ready is desirable so that unfortunate outcomes or involuntary relinquishment of deemed status does not occur.

Accreditation is optional for the most part. Sometimes insurance companies require accreditation before paying for patient care. However, state licensing and agency surveys easily provide the needed outcomes for payment and operations. What you need to keep in mind is that three different sets of standards exist when seeking accreditation, licensing, and deemed status.

Here is how we determine importance. Knowing and complying with the appropriate ambulatory state licensing standards is required in order to hang a shingle on your door. If a license is suspended or taken away, you are out of business. If you want to receive Medicare and Medicaid funding, compliance with the appropriate CMS conditions is absolute, as violations can put your organization in immediate jeopardy and funding can immediately stop. Never let your adherence to these standards slip. Remember that any organization that comes in to survey you has the right to report you to others. So if a bad outcome is being investigated, you could have the state, Medicare, the AO, and other state and federal agencies in to investigate. The third set of standards is the AO's, and AO's are as different as night and day. Knowing AAAHC standards does not mean you know the standards for TJC or the American Association for Accreditation of Ambulatory Surgery Facilities (AAAASF).

The state, CMS, and AOs refer to organizations such as the Centers for Disease Control and Prevention (CDC), the Occupational Safety and Health Administration (OSHA), the Drug Enforcement Agency (DEA), the Food and Drug Administration (FDA), and the Environmental Protection Agency (EPA), for example. Specifics are not given in the state, CMS, and AO standards, so it's up to the outpatient leaders to know where to look to obtain this information and to comply as well. Multiple state, CMS, and federal standards may relate to your facility. Any and all references to other organizations have to be followed up on and adhered to in detail.

If you administer or dispense medications, then you may need a pharmacy license, depending on the state standards. Also, monthly reports from a consulting pharmacist that are sent to the state may be required (as in South Carolina) for ASCs. Radiology and nuclear medicine requirements are different from state to state as well. Risk management (RM) state requirements are more detailed in some states. For example, Kansas has a rigorous RM program, and failure to report and act on risk events as noted by the licensing agency can result in a misdemeanor for one or more caregivers, leaders, contract workers, vendors, or employees.

If a physician offers endoscopy procedures or plastic surgery procedures in the office setting, going through the full licensing, deemed status, and accreditation process is not always required. In some states, very little oversight exists for these types of programs. It doesn't mean that investigations cannot arise should a grievance, complaint, or bad outcome occur.

Getting in trouble with any of these agencies can be devastating, because criminal charges can also be levied. Reports are shared through healthcare news channels regarding egregious acts committed by ambulatory caregivers and leaders. Not only is the quality of care compromised, but our tax dollars pay for the investigations that have to take place when these acts occur. For example, patients exposed to hepatitis from the use of dirty needles, instruments, or equipment is bad enough, but those who contracted the disease have had their lives changed forever. Tracking down these patients takes time and money, and then caring for them for life puts an added drain on the healthcare system. Caregivers are indicted for these acts, and imprisonment is oftentimes in the pipeline, as it should be.

Get to know your state requirements and attend all training programs that are offered. Texas does a nice job with orientation programs for new facilities. If programs do not exist, ask to meet with the appropriate experts at the state agencies so you can receive guidance. If you have the resources, hire an expert, either as a consultant or employee, or retain a lawyer who understands licensing, accreditation, and deemed status.

Why Become Accredited?

Inviting accrediting agencies to survey your program provides a yardstick against which to measure your facility. It takes away the guessing game as to whether or not your program is top notch in its field. It demonstrates that there is a desire to elevate the standards of care offered to to patients and their family members or significant others. Our patients deserve the best that we can offer, and accreditation is a step in the right direction.

Staying survey-ready is one way to keep everyone on their toes and in excellent form. When we know someone else is looking at us from the outside, our competitive spirit kicks in, and we want to be on our best behavior.

It is also important to be aware that states have cut way back in funding for surveyors and surveys; so much so that years can go by before a full state or CMS survey reoccurs. Therefore, mediocrity can set in, as turnover of staff and other factors chip away at the importance of standards conformity. Having an AO come in at least every three years helps maintain high standards of care.

It's important to offer a word of caution when choosing the AO route. AOs are at times not as tough regarding Medicare, federal, and state regulations, so organizations don't always get the gist of what it could be like should a full state, federal, or Medicare survey occur. When we invite an AO in to survey, we pay deeply for this survey, as it's not cheap. We become a customer, so to speak. AOs know we have a choice with accrediting options. This is not to say they aren't tough, because they are, but in a different way. But they are not nearly as grueling or threatening as a full state, Medicare, or federal agency survey, especially in response to a complaint, safety event, or other concern.

When covering fifty states, it's tough to keep up to speed on all state requirements. Therefore, the AO standards can take precedence during the accreditation survey. Employees, leaders, and physicians get a false sense of security as they believe they have fully complied with all regulatory requirements and standards, and at times that is not the case. But inviting an AO in to your facility is still a very good idea.

Accreditation makes us focus on the ordinary and extraordinary. The ordinary tasks can become routine. If left to chance, the opportunity for risks and errors increases, thus eroding the excellence that we strive to achieve. Shortcuts to care due to familiarity and boredom are too common in healthcare. Also, we don't know what we don't know, and it's impossible to create a culture of safety when there's knowledge out there that has not been tapped.

If you are still on the fence about accreditation for your outpatient program, consider the following attributes:

1. The self-analysis and peer review inherent in the process helps an organization improve its care, services, and outcomes.
2. Accreditation can assist in streamlining the facility's processes and programs.
3. Helps to maintain strict standards of care within the facility—anesthesia, lab, pathology, biomedical, engineering, and other ancillary services.
4. Ensures that all healthcare professionals are vetted and properly credentialed and privileged.
5. Encourages and enforces safe medication and equipment practices.
6. Defines what constitutes appropriate and complete medical documentation.
7. Improves overall safety, thus decreasing risk and unnecessary costs associated with risk occurrences.
8. To become accredited dispels myths and encourages scientific thinking.
9. Oftentimes builds in benchmark programs, demonstrating that the facility meets and exceeds national standards.
10. It's the right thing to do.

Tools exist in the marketplace to help with assessment and ongoing readiness for outpatient and ambulatory surveys at the state, federal, or niche level. For example, the AAAHC provides excellent checklists and assessment products. The AAAHC makes it easy to comply, as they really strive to help in the preparation timeline with these effective tools. This organization is a favorite in the ambulatory accreditation world.

If the outpatient program(s) is affiliated with an inpatient system, there may be a tendency to go the route of the Joint Commission. That isn't a problem if the ambulatory standards are selected for use for a freestanding ambulatory program. Try not to make the inpatient standards fit the freestanding environment. Selections made might be easier for the hospital and acute care side, but it may not be the best choice of action for ambulatory settings.

Overcoming fear of selecting an accrediting organization such as AAAHC has to occur, and there may be misinformation about these organizations, such as lower quality standards or issues. That is not true, so ensure that you look at all information carefully and select the best accrediting agency for your program.

Certification of Programs

These programs exist to certify clinical services across the country. Many are disease or procedure specific, while others are in the form of Centers of Excellence (COE). Certification takes quality to another level, as evidence-based care processes specific to the disease are used to evaluate programs around the country.

Some insurance companies also enforce the use of COE or certification programs. Participation in those programs requires complete adherence to their guidelines. Frustrations abound, however, because differences exist among the programs. Bariatric certification is a great example of complexity and competing requirements. The American College of Surgeons and the Surgical Review Corporation (SRC) each provide COEs for bariatric programs. To receive insurance funding, an outpatient program must have COE status from one or the other. At times, to receive funding from all necessary insurance agencies, adhering to the requirements of both COEs is required. In addition, bariatric COEs are embedded in a variety of insurance programs. Navigating through all of the paperwork, required databases, and patient requirements can be a nightmare, leading to the addition of staff that specializes in all of the different requirements.

A cost is involved with any certification or COE. TJC has extensive certification programs available for a variety of diseases. The National Committee for Quality Assurance (NCQA) also offers an array of certification programs. If the organization has the money to participate, it's recommended.

Ambulatory Accreditation and Certification Programs

Choosing an accreditation or certification program requires research on your part. Take time to learn what's available, listing the pros and cons of each that are of interest. Some of the criteria to use when selecting your program can be based on application to your mission, vision, and values, the cost of the program, the reputation of the program, deemed status opportunity, and the resources needed to comply, including staff, software, and hardware.

Organization names and websites for many of the accreditation and certification programs have been compiled for your use. In addition, Appendix I presents state contacts for ambulatory licensing and standards.

Familiarize yourself with the state practice acts for the employees who work in your outpatient facility. States have different requirements for nurses, Certified Registered Nurse Anesthetists (CRNAs), physician assistants, radiology technicians, pharmacists, medical assistants, and all other caregivers. Also, medical boards define specific requirements relating to outpatient services. Work within the standards of practice and care and the law. A good rule of thumb here is to not ask your employees to perform a task or service that is outside their scope of care and practice.

Survey Preparation

Medicare published surveyor guidelines on their website for the Conditions for Coverage. Tables 11.1, 11.2, and 11.3 display three examples of this tool. This does not take the place of the actual CfC conditions and interpretive guidelines; it's another tool that can be used to assess readiness, as there are sections that define what the surveyor looks for in regards to compliance.

Accreditation Listing

- Centers for Medicare and Medicaid Services (CMS), http://www.cms.gov/CFCsAndCoPs/.
- Accreditation Association for Ambulatory Health Care (AAAHC), http://www.aaahc.org/eweb/StartPage.aspx.
- The Joint Commission Ambulatory Care Accreditation (TJC), http://www.jointcommission.org/accreditation/ahc_seeking_ambulatory_health_care.aspx.
- American Association for Accreditation of Ambulatory Surgery Facilities, Inc., http://www.aaaasf.org/consumers.php.

Table 11.1   CMS Conditions for Coverage Survey Prep Example

§416.2 Definitions
As used in this part; "Ambulatory surgical center" or "ASC" means any distinct entity that operates exclusively for the purpose of providing surgical services to patients not requiring hospitalization, has an agreement with CMS under Medicare to participate as an ASC, and meets the conditions set forth in Subpart B and C of this part.
Interpretive Guidelines §416.2
The ASC must use its space for ambulatory surgery exclusively. Record keeping must be exclusive to the ASC, and the staff must be responsible to the ASC. For example, a nurse could not provide coverage in the ASC and in an adjacent clinic (or hospital) at the same time. The ASC is not required to be in a building separate from other health care activities (e.g., hospital, clinic, physician's office). It must be separated physically by at least semi-permanent walls and doors.
The regulatory definition of an ASC does not allow the ASC and another entity to mix functions and operations in a common space during concurrent or overlapping hours of operation. Another entity may share common space only if the space is never used during the scheduled hours of ASC operation. However, the operating and recovery rooms must be used exclusively for surgical procedures.
The ASC may not perform a surgical procedure on a Medicare patient when, before surgery, an overnight hospital stay is anticipated. There may, however, arise unanticipated medical circumstances that warrant a Medicare patient's hospitalization after an ASC surgical procedure. The ASC must have procedures for the immediate transfer of these patients to a hospital (42 CFR §416.41). Such situations should be infrequent.
ASC covered procedures (see 42 CFR §416.65) are those that generally do not exceed 90 minutes in length and do not require more than four hours recovery or convalescent time. Thus, ASC patients generally do not require extended care as a result of ASC procedures. An unanticipated medical circumstance may arise that would require an ASC patient to stay in an overnight healthcare setting. Such situations should be infrequent. When extended care in a non-hospital healthcare setting is anticipated as a result of a particular procedure, that procedure would not be a covered ASC procedure for Medicare beneficiaries.

Table 11.2   CMS Conditions for Coverage Survey Prep Example

§416.40 Condition for Coverage: Compliance with Licensure Law
The ASC must comply with State licensure requirements.
Interpretive Guidelines §416.40
In States where licensure is required for a facility providing ambulatory surgical services, ask to see the facility's current license. If the State license is revoked, the ASC is out of compliance with this condition. This may result in its termination from participation in Medicare. Where a State has no applicable licensure requirements, or where ambulatory surgical services may be provided without licensure, a facility will be eligible if it meets the definition in §416.2 and all other applicable Medicare requirements.
Failure of the facility to meet State licensure law may be cited when the authority having jurisdiction (AHJ) has made a determination of noncompliance and has also taken a final adverse action as a result. If the surveyor identifies a situation that indicates the provider may not be in compliance with State licensure law, the information may be referred to the AHJ for follow-up. If the facility is not in compliance with State licensure law, the facility could be found out of compliance with §416.40.
§416.41 Condition for Coverage: Governing Body and Management
The ASC must have a governing body that assumes full legal responsibility for determining, implementing, and monitoring policies governing the ASC's total operation and for ensuring that these policies are administered so as to provide quality health care in a safe environment. When services are provided through a contract with an outside resource, the ASC must assure that these services are provided in a safe and effective manner.
Interpretive Guidelines §416.41
The ASC must have a designated governing body that demonstrates its oversight of ASC activities intended to protect the health and safety of patients. <ul><li>An individual may act as the governing body in the case of sole-ownership, absentee ownership, or in other special cases.</li><li>Responsibilities may be formally delegated to administrative, medical, or other personnel for carrying out various activities. However, the governing body must retain ultimate responsibility.</li></ul>
The ASC must establish and carry out activities that will ensure that contracted services are provided in a safe manner.

Table 11.2   CMS Conditions for Coverage Survey Prep Example (Continued)

Survey Procedures and Probes §416.41
Review chapter or titles of incorporation, bylaws, and partnership agreements. Annotate on the survey report form if full legal responsibilities have been established.

- National Committee for Quality Assurance (NCQA). http://www.ncqa.org/.
- Institute for Medical Quality, http://www.imq.org/programs/ambulatory-care/accreditation/.
- Healthcare Facilities Accreditation Program, http://www.hfap.org/AccreditationPrograms/amb_care.aspx.
- Ambulatory Surgery Center Association, http://www.ascassociation.org/businessdirectory/accreditationorganizations/.
- American College of Surgeons—Bariatric Surgery Center Network, http://www.acsbscn.org/Public/AboutBSCN.aspx.
- National Accreditation Program for Breast Centers (administered by the American College of Surgeons), http://accreditedbreastcenters.org/standards/standards.html.
- Surgical Review Corporation COE for freestanding outpatient bariatric programs, http://www.surgicalreview.org/coeprograms/asmbs/overview.aspx
- Urgent Care Association of America, http://www.ucaoa.org/.
- Urgent Care Center Accreditation (UCCA) through the American Academy of Urgent Care Medicine, www.aaucm.org.
- Community Health Accreditation Program, http://www.chapinc.org/.
- American Academy of Sleep Medicine, http://www.aasmnet.org/.
- American Commission for Health Care, http://www.achc.org/.
- Physician Office Laboratory Accreditation (COLA), http://www.cola.org/pol.html.
- American College of Radiology, http://www.acr.org/.
- The Joint Commission Disease Certification Programs, http://www.jointcommission.org/certification/certification_main.aspx.

Summary and Key Points

1. Adhere to state, CMS, and federal requirements at all times.
2. Know what other state and federal requirements pertain to your facility, such as DEA, FDA, CDC, and OSHA.

Table 11.3   CMS Conditions for Coverage Survey Prep Example

§416.41 Standard: Hospitalization
The ASC must have an effective procedure for the immediate transfer to a hospital of patients requiring emergency medical care beyond the capabilities of the ASC. This hospital must be a local, Medicare participating hospital or a local, nonparticipating hospital that meets the requirements for payment under §482.2 of this chapter. The ASC must have a written transfer agreement with such a hospital, or all physicians performing surgery in the ASC must have admitting privileges at such a hospital.
Interpretive Guidelines §416.41
An "effective procedure" encompasses: • Written guidelines (e.g., policies and/or procedures); • Arrangement for ambulance services; and • Transfer of medical information.
Survey Procedures and Probes §416.41
Request documentation of a transfer agreement or evidence of admitting privileges. • Policies and procedures must be established for transferring patients requiring emergency care. • Appropriate personnel should be aware of transfer procedures.
§416.42 Condition for Coverage: Surgical Services
Surgical procedures must be performed in a safe manner by qualified physicians who have been granted clinical privileges by the governing body of the ASC in accordance with approved policies and procedures of the ASC.
Interpretive Guidelines §416.42
"In a safe manner" means that: • The equipment and supplies are sufficient so that the type of surgery conducted can be performed in a manner that will not endanger the health and safety of the patient; • Access to operative and recovery areas is limited; • All individuals in the surgical area are to conform to aseptic techniques;

Table 11.3 CMS Conditions for Coverage Survey Prep Example (Continued)

- Appropriate cleaning is completed between surgical cases;
- Suitable equipment is available for rapid and routine sterilization of operating room materials;
- Sterilized materials are packaged, labeled, and stored in a manner to ensure sterility and that each item is marked with the expiration date; and
- Operating room attire is suitable for the kind of surgical cases performed. (Persons working in the operating suite must wear clean surgical costumes in lieu of their ordinary clothing. Surgical costumes are to be designed for maximum skin and hair coverage.)

Survey Procedures and Probes §416.42

Policies and procedures should contain at a minimum:

- Resuscitative techniques;
- Aseptic technique and scrub procedures;
- Care of surgical specimens;
- Appropriate protocols for all surgical procedures, specific or general in nature, and include a list of equipment, materials, and supplies necessary to properly carry out job assignments;
- Procedures addressing the cleaning of operating room after each use;
- Sterilization and disinfection procedures;
- Acceptable operating room attire;
- Care of anesthesia equipment; and
- Special provision for infected or contaminated patients.

3. Assign responsibility for oversight of all programs, and communicate the status at least monthly through staff meetings. Keep compliance topics top of mind for everyone.
4. Hold mock surveys at least twice a year. Invite an outside resource to perform these mock programs for your facility. Build in accountability.
5. Accreditation may or may not be voluntary. For example, in North Carolina, the state requires ambulatory surgery facilities to be accredited within two years of completion of the facility.
6. Take time to select the appropriate accrediting body.

7. If resources allow, determine if certification or center of excellence programs are beneficial for your facility.
8. Do not allow your employees, physicians, contract workers, or vendors to perform duties outside their scope of care and practice as defined by their boards, certification programs, or other mandatory oversight group.

Chapter 12

Practice Makes Perfect

Healthcare should adopt the safety culture of the aviation industry. They must stop thinking of accidents as inevitable and start thinking about them as unimaginable. We in aviation have learned a lot, and we're anxious to share it with you.

—Captain Chesley "Sully" Sullenberger

Why Practice?

Outpatient employees must be at the top of their game. They do not have hospital code teams that arrive to take over during an emergency event. In many cases there are fewer than a half dozen employees on site. Therefore, practicing for the worst possible outcome is clearly one way to ensure that patients receive the best care possible in this setting. Creating and using well-defined checklists that walk a user through the steps should things go wrong are needed across the board. Augment that with exercises and drills to practice and role play life-threatening and safety disaster response.

PDPC and FMEA

Why do things fail? That is the million dollar question and the premise for error-free healthcare services. Using methodologies to analyze and discover all potential failure modes of a system along with the effects these failures have on the system are critical as they help to determine how to fix and/or lessen the failures or effects on the system.

Obviously, we don't want to induce failure in our real-time processes because we are caring for people and they could get hurt. Instead, do the exercises through simulation and role playing, and define it on paper. Start with this question: If we wanted this process/service/deliverable to fail, how could we make that happen?

An effective tool to identify potential problems is the Process Decision Program Chart (PDPC). Traced back to the post–World War II era, this tool has been around for quite some time. It's one of the seven management and planning tools. Other tools in this bucket are the affinity diagram, interrelationship diagraph, tree diagram, prioritization matrix, matrix diagram, and the activity network diagram.

A useful way of planning is to break down tasks into a pecking order, using a tree diagram. The PDPC extends the tree diagram a couple of levels to identify risks and countermeasures for the bottom-level responsibilities. Rectangle-shaped boxes are used to emphasize risks and cloud shapes draw attention to possible countermeasures for those risks. Figure 12.1 shows an abbreviated patient safety PDPC chart. Potential problems are identified (rectangles) and the clouds demonstrate the countermeasures to take to alleviate the risks and problems.

The PDPC is similar to failure modes and effects analysis (FMEA) in that both identify risks, the potential penalties of failure, and contingency actions; the FMEA also rates relative risk levels for each potential failure point. The FMEA is used frequently in healthcare for risk management oversight and intervention, but few have heard of the PDPC. If you enter Healthcare FMEA into an Internet search engine, numerous examples will come up for review and study. Of particular interest are the NASA examples, as FMEA and PDPC are used without fail in space and aeronautics programs.

Doing either correctly relies on the right people giving the right information, covering all bases. It's an interactive exercise, and best done with everyone in the same room building on one another's knowledge base. You don't need a fancy computer program for these tools; use Post-It® notes and flip chart paper, or a drawing board. Keep it going and don't give up until all potential failures and possible fixes are identified.

The questions to ask the team relate to inputs and outputs, both of which we have covered in previous chapters. What inputs (x's) exist and which are absolute? What is value added versus nonvalue added? Are there any adverse inputs that are related to the good inputs? Adverse inputs in some cases are required due to regulations or other mandatory needs, and they need to be included in the process steps. What can be done to lighten the adverse effect is to brainstorm the actions that can be taken to smooth away the potential rough edges and negative

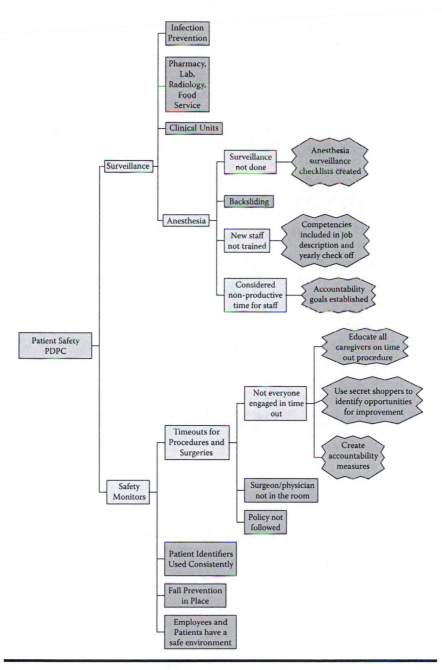

Figure 12.1 Patient safety PDPC.

impact. What outputs (*y*'s) are we expecting and wanting? Why are they needed and how should they behave? What are these outputs meant to accomplish?

For both inputs and outputs, are there alternatives that would work? Think about how inputs and outputs depend on actions, conditions, or events. What is controllable and what is out of your control? Which variables are inflexible? Which assumptions need to be surfaced and vetted? Which myths require debunking? How can historical events help sort through the problem, offering valuable lessons learned? How is this different from before?

5 Whys: Why, Why, Why, Why, Why

This is an effective tool and it's so simple when you think about it. The 5 Whys is a constructive way to investigate the cause of a problem that occurs in a workflow. It's a uniform method that probes the real causes of a problem instead of focusing on artificial reasons. It keeps the users and owners from making quick decisions or assumptions based on surface information.

The method involves asking the question "Why?" five times. The 5 Whys exercise can be partnered with brainstorming, nominal group, force field analysis, and cause-and-effect diagrams to get to the root cause of a concern. The information gathered from the questions will allow your organization to take necessary corrective action so that problems and issues are abolished or mitigated.

Two examples using the 5 Whys follow: medication error for a patient and a delay in cancer diagnosis. Both could and do contribute to devastating outcomes.

Medication Error

1. A patient received the wrong dose of antibiotic. Why?
2. Two different doses were stored together. Why?
3. A policy does not exist for separating doses of the same medicine. Why?
4. A check is not in place to ensure that the right dosage is given. Why?
5. Because it's an outpatient program, a defined medication safety program is not in place. Why?

Cancer Diagnosis Delay

1. The patient's diagnosis of breast cancer was delayed. Why?
2. The mammography report was not sent to the referring physician. Why?
3. The report was filed in the wrong patient's file. Why?
4. The wrong patient's label was on the report. Why?
5. The radiology tech was distracted and put the wrong label on the report. Why?

The 5 Whys help identify why things are happening, but structure is needed to take it to the next level. It's a good time to complete a root cause analysis (RCA) if an event actually happened, or a FMEA or PDPC if it's preventive. Then use PDCA or another scientific method to continually improve the process. Brainstorming the reasons why something broke down does not help with implementation of solutions. Scientific methodology will do that for you.

Using Checklists to Improve Safety and Quality

Checklists are used to decrease errors in many industries, and healthcare is one of them. However, our checklists and the processes associated with them are rather meager when compared to aviation, the military, and NASA. Case in point—look at how hard it's been to implement the World Health Organization checklist in surgery.

Coming from an extensive background with clinical pathways, checklists, order set creation, and implementation, it's easy to say that the road in many cases was difficult to navigate. Roadblocks and excuses are too numerous to name, but here are a few:

- I don't have the time to spend to create these documents.
- My patients are sicker.
- My specialty is different.
- I won't practice cookbook medicine.
- This would be too expensive and we can't afford it.
- No one tells me what to do.

We work in a complex environment that is fast paced, with more variables than we can count. Distractions exist and are due, in part, to patient volume, process irregularities, errors in handoffs, physician rounding or requiring information, and staffing shortages or cuts. We work with families, significant others, a variety of hospitals, and other care delivery programs, and technology and medicine changes just about every day. It's overwhelming to say the least. Decreasing human error under stressful conditions is the rationale for creating checklists in healthcare.

Currently, checklists exist to help nurses be successful. Preoperative checklists ensure that the patient is completely ready for the procedure. We have a valuables checklist so that patients don't lose their dentures, jewelry, money, and other items while receiving care. Checklists are part of crash carts and are used for documenting codes, the contents of the cart, and defibrillator checks.

Anesthesiologists use a checklist for equipment safety prior to any procedure. Environmental surveillance rounds are in the form of a checklist. Medicare surveyors use checklists when visiting healthcare facilities; for example, the infection prevention checklist for ambulatory surgery centers.

Checklists aren't foreign to us, but there aren't enough in place. With all of the distractions that we experience in the workplace, checklists could be used as memory aids. Especially in critical and emergency situations, they can mean the difference between life and death. Think about creating checklists for these processes and then attach mock drills to each to determine compliance:

1. Time out before a procedure or surgery
2. Checking patient identification
3. Verbal order and read back checklist
4. Abnormal labs or other tests
5. IV starts and therapy
6. Anything having to do with medications
7. How to process a patient checking in
8. How to collect billing and insurance information
9. How to follow wait times of patients
10. How to check for complete medical records at the end of each business day
11. Facility checks such as generator, warmers, refrigerators, humidity, and electrical
12. How to collect co-pays
13. How to answer the phone
14. How to complete an assessment
15. What to do when a patient or visitor falls
16. What to do if an emergency happens
17. What to do when an unwanted intruder enters the facility
18. What to do if a caregiver suffers a heart attack or other health problem during a procedure or surgery
19. How to contact the police
20. How to keep employees safe: walking out to the car, keeping doors locked, identifying potentially harmful situations
21. How to discharge a patient
22. Disaster and bioterrorism responses and preparation
23. Linen, waste products, biohazard materials, bloodborne pathogen checklists
24. Food and kitchen safety checklists
25. What to do to prevent a needlestick

26. Checking medical gases for accuracy and volume
27. Single-use items versus multiple-use items
28. Sentinel event checklist

Figure 12.2 is a checklist that can be used to enhance life safety. Evaluating how personnel and equipment hold up in case of a potential fire helps to save lives should a real fire ever occur. How often do these drills happen in your facility? Knowing how to evacuate, how to use a fire extinguisher, and how to call for help are basic security measures, and practice does make perfect. Hold these drills quarterly, and if new staff are hired, make sure they are oriented and checked off as well.

If you are using a generator, as required if you are doing surgeries and have Medicare deemed status or Accreditation Association for Ambulatory Health Care (AAAHC) or the Joint Commission (TJC) accreditation status, then proper checks for the generator are needed. Table 12.1 is an example that was shared by a state fire marshal. Make it a rule of thumb to check the generator first thing on Monday if closed over the weekend. If the building's electricity went out, tripping the generator on, you may find it empty of diesel fuel.

The hyperlink at the end of this paragraph takes you to the malignant hyperthermia (MH) site, where you will find checklists and mock drill kits for physicians and staff to use. This site is sponsored by the Malignant Hyperthermia Association of the United States. Checklists and mock drills help save lives when an event such as malignant hyperthermia occurs in the outpatient setting. If surgeries and procedures are performed in your facility that are trigger agents for MH, then it's important to follow the checklists for stocking a cart, checking the cart, supplies, and equipment, and administering care. Malignant Hyperthermia Association of the United States: http://medical.mhaus.org/index.cfm/fuseaction/Content.Display/PagePK/MockDrillKit.cfm.

Codes and Drills

Hurricane Katrina was a wake-up call for the healthcare industry, as the disaster was of epic proportion and lessons learned abounded after this tragic disaster. Disaster drills have become much more specific. The Agency for Healthcare Research and Quality (AHRQ; http://www.ahrq.gov), publishes detailed drill protocols and checklists for hospitals. Pull them up and learn from them; adapt the checklists to your environment. Know what it takes to be a part of the community should a disaster occur. Natural disasters are covered, along with bioterrorism. Unfortunately, the latter is ingrained in our society today.

Date of Fire Drill	Time Drill Conducted	Location of Fire:		Shift(s) Involved: (check all that apply)		1st □	2nd □	3rd □
				Location of Fire:				

ALARM PERFORMANCE

How/why was the fire alarm sounded: □ Manual Pull   □ Sprinkler System   □ Actual Fire   □ Power Outage

How was the drill initiated: □ Fire alarm pull station   □ Smoke alarm

List specific location of the fire alarm pull station/smoke alarm used:

If a drill, what technique was used to represent/indicate fire (eg red cloth, sign, etc.)?

Drill type: □ Audible Alarm   □ Coded/Silent Alarm

Note: If alarm not audibly tested during drill, the alarm must be sounded at another time during the drill

Date Alarm Audibly tested (if not tested during drill): ___ / ___ / ___   Did all staff hear the alarm: □ Yes   □ No

Did all fire emergency equipment function properly (fire doors, smoke dampers, etc.)   □ Yes   □ No

Did auto dispatch notification function correctly: □ Yes   □ No   What time did the dispatch receive alarm:

PERSONNEL PERFORMANCE (R.A.C.E)

RESCUE

Were all the residents and visitors evacuated from the fire zone (ie were all areas secured):   □ Yes   □ No

Was there a proper/systematic search conducted: □ Yes   □ No

Did staff account for all residents: □ Yes   □ No

ALARM

Who activated the alarm: Name:

Was the alarm properly activated: □ Yes   □ No

Did staff call the fire department: □ Yes   □ No   □ N/A   Drill Only

Was the fire alarm reset: □ Yes   □ No   □ N/A   Coded Alarm   OR CODED ANNOUNCEMENT

CONTAINMENT

Did staff close resident room doors: □ Yes   □ No

Were corridor doors unobstructed: □ Yes   □ No

Did all corridor doors latch properly: □ Yes   □ No

EXTINGUISHMENT/EVACUATION

Were proper fire extinguishers taken to fire area: □ Yes   □ No

Did staff simulate using a fire extinguisher: □ Yes   □ No

Did staff stay with evacuated residents: □ Yes   □ No   □ NA   Residents not evacuated

If a "large" fire, were evacuation plans as outlined in "Fire evacuation Procedure" Followed   □ Yes   □ No   □ NA

How long did it take to secure/evacuate all areas _____ Minutes

COMMENTS/SCENARIO

SIGNATURE OF PERSON SUPERVISING DRILL:		TITLE:	

Figure 12.2 Fire drill critique example.

Table 12.1   Generator Log Example

Month or Week	Operator	Start Time	Stop Time	Elapsed Run Time	Oil Pressure/ Temperature	Fuel Oil Pressure	Jacket Water Temperature	Battery Amperes	Phase 1—amps	Phase 1—volts	Phase 2—amps	Phase 2—volts	Phase 3—amps	Phase 3—volts	Frequency

Have the following codes and drills in place for all ambulatory programs:

- Fire drill
- Disaster drill
- Unwanted intruder drill
- Impaired practitioner drill
- Bioterrorism drill
- Malignant hyperthermia drill (if using the trigger medications)
- Allergic reaction to medications or ingestible drill
- Violence in the workplace drill

Emergency Carts or Boxes for Outpatient Settings

When stocking emergency carts or boxes, it's important to know your population of patients, the competencies of the staff, as well as the overall scope and services provided by your organization. The following is by no means all inclusive. It's a list to get you started and to get you thinking.

- Dantrolene (only if trigger agents are used) and all medications and supplies that support intervention. A malignant hyperthermia cart is separate from a crash cart and is stocked appropriately, as noted on the malignant hyperthermia website mentioned earlier.
- Crash cart contents should follow advanced cardiac life support (ACLS) and pediatric advanced life support (PALS) guidelines and should be stocked separately for adults and children.
- All equipment, medications, and supplies are to be appropriate for the age of the patient.
- Medications to consider in an emergency box or cart are as follows:
  - Medications to treat anesthetic toxicity
  - Medications to treat hypertension and arrhythmias
  - Medications to treat anaphylactic reactions
  - Reversal agents, including naloxone hydrochloride and flumazenil
- Equipment to consider:
  - Oxygen, suction, Ambu bag, appropriately sized airway masks, oral or nasal airways, and tongue blades
  - EKG oscilloscope
  - Defibrillator/monitor or automated external defibrillator that is also powered by a battery pack
  - Glucometer
  - Blood drawing equipment
  - Stethoscope, sphygmomanometer
  - Pulse oximeter
  - Emergency power source
  - Suction machine that is also battery powered
- For ASCs, a tracheotomy set

Scenario Training

Scenario training is a process by which a mock patient is brought into the organization and is taken through the system in order to test policies, equipment, supply availability, resource utilization, staff education levels, communication, and building structure. The purpose of scenario training should be well communicated to employees, physicians, and to their staff. It is important for them to act and function in the manner that they would if these were real patients. They must take scenario training seriously.

Staff must be available in the facility to provide care for the mock patient and family. Volunteers will be needed to play the role of the patient, family member(s), or physician. Employees from all ancillary services are invited to participate to allow for full competency with contract staff. Personnel are also needed to critique each scenario (two people per scenario).

Product and vendor representatives will be on-site during scenario training to handle any problems or issues that arise with their product, equipment, and instruments. Between scenarios they are to provide immediate training and updates for employees, physicians, and contract workers.

The primary responsibility for coordinating scenario training rests with the clinical leader of the facility. This leader is responsible for setting the scenario schedule, keeping it on time, and running the debriefing meetings. The clinical leader is responsible for assigning people to play the roles of the patient and family members, assigning two people to critique each scenario, and for assigning a physician to be involved in many of the scenarios. If a physician is not available, assign a staff member to play the role of the physician.

The employees in the scenario are those who actually perform the tasks or roles on a day-to-day work schedule basis. The employee may be prompted that they will be receiving a patient. However, they should not have access to the scenario ahead of time so that real-life occurrences will play out.

The person assigned to play the patient is given a copy of their assigned scenario. They are responsible for memorizing the patient information they are given, such as the signs and symptoms they are to verbalize, reactions or emotions they should be showing, and past medical history they are to provide. The person may need to ad-lib if asked questions or to increase the reality of the scenario. They may also ask questions of the staff and physicians to test other systems or processes they think might occur; for example, a patient scheduled for a procedure might ask for procedure information and education if it is not offered to them.

The person assigned to play the family member is given a copy of their scenario. They are responsible for memorizing the information about the patient as well as their own part. They may also need to ad-lib if asked questions and can ask questions of the caregivers as well.

Physician involvement is important to the success of the scenarios. The physician is given the scenario to read so that he or she will know what the patient's symptoms are and what procedures will be done on the patient. Physicians may ad-lib as needed but should not alter the general theme of the scenario.

Two people are needed to critique each scenario. Using the critique form provided, they will watch the scenario as it unfolds and document the issues that arise. They are instructed to write down the positive things that occur as well as the negative. The appraisers will be prepared to help facilitate the scenario if the actors or the caregivers get stuck and don't know what to do or where to go next. The appraisers should not, however, participate in the scenario. The best individuals to assist with critiquing are those familiar with the facility processes or individuals from other facilities that have been through the process.

Before the day's scenarios begin, the team meets for scenario prep. During this meeting the scenarios for the day are discussed and the participants announced. Any modifications to the scenario schedule are made at this time. Occasionally, the scenario order must be rearranged at the last minute due to a physician's scheduling conflict, or an entire scenario needs to be switched. Be prepared with extra scenarios to substitute in their place.

After each scenario, the team meets with the appraisers to evaluate the scenario. The appraisers report on the opportunities for improvement that they noted during the scenarios. The improvement opportunities are categorized under nine headings: communication, process, supplies, equipment, structure, information management, education, forms, and leadership. It's important to note that positive feedback is also recorded and shared. See Table 12.2 for an example of a scenario critique form.

Each of the categories is assigned to an employee or leader to fix or attempt to fix before the next scenario. If the issue cannot be resolved before the next scenario, it should be resolved before patients are cared for, and definitively before any regulatory or licensing survey occurs. Scenario training can be set up and documented as a quality improvement effort.

Team norms to consider when rolling out scenarios:

1. Everyone participates.
2. There are no side conversations.
3. There is no finger pointing or blame; stick to the process for improvement.
4. Keep cell phone interruption to a minimum.
5. Take it seriously.
6. Some problems may take time and resources to fix, so alternate plans must be in place to accommodate problems that would interrupt care or business practices.

If interested, the information shared on scenarios can be applied to the following endoscopy example. Use this format to create scenarios that are pertinent to your outpatient setting.

Table 12.2 Scenarios Critique Form

Scenario Number and Name: Date: Appraiser Number 1: Appraiser Number 2: Instructions:	Enter an Overall Score for Each Section: *1 Poor* *2 Less Than Expected* *3 Met Expectations* *4 Above Average* *5 Excellent*
ENTER COMMENTS IN THIS SECTION	**ENTER EACH SCORE IN THIS SECTION**
Communication	
Process	
Supply	
Equipment	
Structure	
Information Management	
Education	
Forms	
Leadership	

Scenario Example for Endoscopy

Bea Smith is a 31-year-old lady who had a hernia repair 37 days ago. She began experiencing pain in the upper gastric region a couple of days ago. She said the pain was a level 5 on a scale of 1 to 10.

Ms. Smith is single, has never been married, and lives by herself. She does not have family in the area. Her friend Kathy will take her home after the procedure. She has private insurance and does not have allergies to any medication or food.

Processes for the Scenario: Sedation protocol and policy; narcotic and medication management during the procedure; ensuring a safe discharge for the patient; patient education prior to medications given; endoscopy equipment usage and cleaning of equipment; insurance verification for the procedure; gastric specimen to pathology; verification that physician has endoscopy privileges at the

ASC; follow-up appointment regarding biopsy; sending a copy of the test results to her primary care physician; and sending the patient home with a prescription for Pepcid.

The form of anesthesia used is called moderate sedation. The sedation policy is to be followed for this process. Inform Ms. Smith that she will notice several monitoring devices placed on her body prior to the procedure. Safety during the sedation is of utmost importance.

Equipment devices are: Blood pressure cuff (measures her blood pressure at frequent intervals during anesthesia); pulse oximeter (a device placed on her finger, toe, or earlobe that measures the amount of oxygen in her body at all times and displays her pulse rate); and ECG (electrocardiogram; a constant picture of a heart tracing is displayed on a monitor screen for the care delivery staff to see).

Before the procedure: Do a pregnancy test and review the patient's history. Patient informed the nurse that she took her medications for high blood pressure and her thyroid condition this morning with a small sip of water. Other than the medication, the patient has been NPO since 10:00 p.m. last night. It is now 11:00 a.m.

A responsible adult did accompany her to the center. It was emphasized that she should not drive or operate machinery for at least 8 hours after the procedure. The sedation given during the procedure causes drowsiness, dizziness, and will impair her judgment, making it unsafe for her to drive or operate machinery.

The physician explains the procedure in detail, including possible complications and side effects.

The procedure is performed by an experienced physician who has clinical privileges to perform endoscopy. Ms. Smith was asked to wear a patient gown and to remove her eyeglasses. She does not have dentures or other removable dental work. The endoscopy tech has set up the room with the endoscopy equipment. The circulating nurse monitors the patient.

A local anesthetic (pain-relieving medication) is applied at the back of her throat.

She is given Demerol (100 mg) and Versed (4 mg) intravenously when the doctor is in the room. It's important for the nurse to note that an ASA level and anesthesia evaluation is completed by the doctor and that it's in the medical record prior to sedation.

The patient is then positioned on her left side for the procedure. A mouthpiece is placed in her mouth. She is breathing on her own without any problem. The physician inserts an endoscope into her mouth, through the esophagus and into the stomach. The procedure lasts 20 minutes. The patient has mild gastritis and a specimen was taken to be sent to the lab to see if H. Pylori is present. The patient will be treated medically with Pepcid (40 mg) twice a day to reduce the stomach acid in the stomach and will be seen in one week at the doctor's office.

After the procedure the patient was brought to the postanesthesia care unit (PACU). The procedure nurse let Ms. Smith's friend Kathy know that the procedure was complete. Patient education includes the treatment of temporary soreness in her throat. Lozenges may help.

The physician who performs the endoscopy will also send the test results to Ms. Smith's primary or referring physician. After about 45 minutes, Ms. Smith was awake and responding to questions. The physician came in to discuss the results with her at that time.

Once again, a responsible adult must accompany Ms. Smith home. She is not to drive or operate machinery for at least 8 hours after the procedure. Ms. Smith was told that if she has severe abdominal pain, a continuous cough, fever, chills, chest pain, nausea, or vomiting within 72 hours after the procedure, to please call the doctor who performed the procedure. The patient was discharged in Kathy's care 2 hours postprocedure.

Operative Report

Patient Name: Bea Smith

Date of Surgery:

Date of Discharge:

Surgeon: Dr. Scope

Anesthesiologist: None—moderate sedation

Preoperative Diagnosis: Morbid Obesity, Dyspepsia

Postoperative Diagnosis: Morbid Obesity, Dyspepsia, Mild Gastritis

Procedure: Upper Endoscopy

Estimated Blood Loss: Zero

Drains: None

Place of Surgery: Surgery Center

Findings: Mild bile reflux gastritis

Indications for Procedure: The patient is a 31-year-old woman who has been suffering morbid obesity for many years and who had a hernia repair 37 days before this procedure. She has now come in with a complaint of dyspepsia and abdominal pain. I advised the patient to undergo upper endoscopy. The risks, benefits, and alternatives were discussed with the patient, who understood and agreed and wished to go ahead with this procedure.

Description of the Procedure: The patient was led to the procedure suite in the surgical center.

The patient was administered intravenous sedation medications. A bite block was placed, and an Olympus endoscope was introduced into the oropharynx without difficulty. The endoscope was advanced into the esophagus and advanced into the stomach without difficulty and with no identification of abnormality. However, it was determined that the patient would be checked for H. Pylori, so a specimen was taken.

The proximal stomach appeared normal. There was no evidence of esophagitis, no evidence of gastroesophageal reflux, and no evidence of band erosion. The distal stomach appeared to have mild enteral gastritis from bile reflux. The pyloris appeared normal and the proximal duodenum was normal with no evidence of any ulcers. The endoscopy was retroflexed and proximally there again was no evidence of any abnormalities. There was no gastric erosion. The endoscope was withdrawn without difficulty, and the patient was taken to recovery in good condition.

Summary and Key Points

1. Checklists are helpful memory aides.
2. Be proactive and think through everything that could fail in your organization. Come up with countermeasures and actions to take should processes fail.
3. Use FMEA, PDPC, and the 5 Whys to identify potential failures and to react to real-time failures. Create mock scenarios and drills from the findings.
4. Create a culture of safety for your staff, patients, visitors, and physicians.
5. Practice makes perfect; have regular drills and mock codes.
6. Create scenarios that use real examples to help employees and physicians practice and to help identify potential and existing problems.
7. Keep emergency boxes or carts stocked and check them daily for expirations and missing items. Check equipment daily per manufacturing guidelines, ensuring that all equipment is in working order.
8. We have a long way to go in our industry. Use aviation, NASA, the nuclear energy industry, and the military as muses. Checklists are inherent in everything they do.

Sources

Bens, Ingrid. 1999. *Facilitation at a glance: A pocket guide of tools and techniques for effective meeting facilitation.* Salem, NH: Goal/QPC and AQP.

Boehringer, Robert D., Amanda Dietz, Paul King, and Ralph Smith. 2008. *The process management memory jogger: Building cross-functional excellence.* Salem, NH: Goal/QPC.

Gawande, Atul. 2009. *The checklist manifesto: How to get things right*. New York: Metropolitan Books.

Goal/QPC. 1995. *The team memory jogger: A pocket guide for team members*. Salem, NH: Goal/QPC and Oriel, Inc.

Goal/QPC. 2000. *The problem-solving memory jogger: Seven steps to improved processes*. Salem, NH: Goal/QPC.

Gosbee, John, and Lauran Lin Gosbee. 2010. *Human factors engineering to improve patient safety*. Oakbrook Terrace, IL: Joint Commission.

Harman, Willis, and Howard Rheingold. 1984. *Higher creativity: Liberating the unconscious for breakthrough insights*. New York: G. P. Putnam's Sons.

Joint Commission. 2009. *A patient safety handbook for ambulatory providers*. Oakbrook Terrace, IL: Joint Commission.

Joint Commission. 2010. *FMEA in health care: Proactive risk reduction*. Oakbrook Terrace, IL: Joint Commission.

Nance, John. J. 2008. *Why hospitals should fly*. Bozemann, MT: Second River Healthcare Press.

Reason, James. 1990. *Human reason*. Cambridge, U.K.: Press Syndicate of the University of Cambridge.

Wachter, Robert M., and Kaveh G. Shojania. 2005. *Internal bleeding: The truth behind America's terrifying epidemic of medical mistakes*. New York: Rugged Land, LLC.

Appendix A: Checklist on Policies, Procedures, and Plans for an Outpatient Setting

CATEGORY	DOCUMENT	ACTIONS TO TAKE
Administration and Leadership	Appointment of: Quality and Patient Safety Officer, Compliance Officer, Infection Prevention Officer, Risk Manager	
	Chain of Command	
	Communication	
	Compliance Plan	
	Conflict of Interest	
	Federal Employer Identification Number (FEIN)	
	Governance document (Bylaws or Policy)	
	Health Insurance Portability and Accountability Act (HIPAA)	

CATEGORY	DOCUMENT	ACTIONS TO TAKE
	Licenses: state, city, business	
	Minutes for committee and staff meetings	
	National Provider Identifier (NPI) Numbers	
	Organizational charts: medical staff, leadership, committee, investor, links to others, such as a corporate structure	
	Satisfaction surveys and reports: patients, staff, physicians, referring resources	
	Staff meetings	
Anesthesia	Anesthesia Machine Preventive Maintenance	
	Anesthesia Scope of Practice (including criteria for what defines an outpatient)	
	Assessments and evaluations for preanesthesia, perioperative anesthesia, and postanesthesia	
	Call Schedules	
	Clinical Documentation	
	Daily safety checks	
	Discharge Criteria from Postanesthesia Care Unit (PACU) I and II	
	Malignant Hyperthermia	
	Medical clearances for patients	
	Plan of Care	
	Pregnancy Tests	

CATEGORY	DOCUMENT	ACTIONS TO TAKE
	Safety Per Case	
	Sedation Policy	
Care of the Patient	Advance Directive	
	Allergies and Sensitivities	
	Assessment and Reassessment	
	Blood and Blood Products	
	Clinical Laboratory Improvement Amendments (CLIA) Waived and Nonwaived Testing	
	Communication Needs of Patients and Families	
	Confidentiality	
	Latex Allergy	
	Management of Acute and Chronic Pain	
	Organ Donation	
	Patient and Family Abuse and Neglect	
	Patient and Family Education	
	Patient and Family Grievance and Complaints	
	Patient Safety	
	Patients Rights and Responsibilities	
	Point of Care Testing	
	Preventing Falls and Gait Belts	
	Restraints and Seclusion	
	Scope of Care and Service and Plan of Care	

CATEGORY	DOCUMENT	ACTIONS TO TAKE
Clinical Documentation	Admission Database	
	Ancillary Care Plans	
	Anesthesia Perioperative Record	
	Anesthesia Preadmission Assessment	
	Anesthesia Preoperative Assessment	
	Clinical Pathways	
	Diagnostic Summary/Problem List	
	Discharge Summary	
	History and Physical	
	Nursing Discharge Summary	
	Operative/Procedure Note	
	Patient Education	
	Patient Plan of Care	
	Perioperative/Procedure Nursing Plan of Care	
	Physician Order Sets	
	Physician Progress Notes	
	Preoperative/Procedure Checklist	
	Vital Signs Flowsheet	
Codes and Emergency	After Hours Emergencies	
	Calling 911	
	Codes Critique Process	
	Cardiopulmonary Resuscitation (CPR) Record	

CATEGORY	DOCUMENT	ACTIONS TO TAKE
	Crash Cart Contents and Checks	
Environment of Care	Hazardous Materials and Waste Management Plan	
	Pharmacy Waste Management Plan	
	Fire Safety Plan	
	Utility Management Plan	
	Security Management Plan	
	No Smoking	
	Surveillance Rounds	
	Facility Safety Plan	
	Safety Officer	
	Equipment Management Plan	
Financial Management	Access and Use of the Safe	
	Accounting	
	Accounts Payable and Receivable	
	Bad Debt	
	Budgets	
	Capital Budget—Three-Year Plan	
	Charge Master	
	Consent to Treat and Financial Responsibilities for the Patient	
	Contractual Allowance	
	Copay Collections	
	Equipment and Instrument Inventory	

CATEGORY	DOCUMENT	ACTIONS TO TAKE
	External Financial/Accounting Audits of the Business	
	Financial Reports	
	Medicare and Medicaid	
	Month-end Closing	
	One Level of Care Audits	
	Profit and loss (P&L) Reporting	
	Patient Valuables	
	Payer Contracts	
	Payroll/Salary/Wages/Benefits	
	Petty Cash	
	Supply Chain Management	
	Supply Formulary	
	Volume, Census, and Key Statistics Reports	
Human Resources	Annual Mandatory Training	
	Cancellation of Staff	
	Continuing Education	
	Contract Workers and Contracts	
	Employee and Practitioner Health	
	Employee, Contract, Volunteer, Student Files, and Checklists: education, employee health, and human resources (HR)	
	Employee Handbook	
	Float and PRN (as needed) Pool	

CATEGORY	DOCUMENT	ACTIONS TO TAKE
	Job Descriptions	
	Management Orientation	
	Managing the Media and Press	
	Nursing Hours Based on Volume (clinical productivity)	
	Pay Increases and Market Adjustments	
	Physician/Practitioner Orientation	
	Relocation	
	Sexual Harassment	
	Skills and Competencies for Staff	
	Staff Orientation	
	Staffing Plan	
	Substance Prevention and Abuse Policy	
	Tracking of Licensure, Certifications, and Board Renewals	
	Vacation, Sick Time, and Holidays	
	Vendors	
	Visitors and Observers	
	Volunteers	
	Zero Tolerance with Violence in the Workplace	
Infection Prevention	Cleaning, Sterilization, and Disinfecting	
	Endoscopes	
	Flash Sterilization	

CATEGORY	DOCUMENT	ACTIONS TO TAKE
	Infection Prevention Plan and Authority Statement	
	Infection Prevention Surveillance	
	Infection Prevention Training and Education	
	Isolation	
	Occupational Safety and Health Administration (OSHA) Bloodborne Pathogens Exposure Plan	
	OSHA Logs	
	Patient Care: Hygiene, IV Therapy, Injections, Ice Machines/Chests, Pest Control, Collecting/Handling Specimens, Toy Sanitation, Thermometers, Hygrometers, Temperature Monitoring, Catheters, Linen, Vending Areas/Break Rooms.	
	Reporting to the Health Department	
	Standard Precautions	
	Terminal Cleaning	
Information Management	Approved Abbreviations	
	Chart Deletion, Amendment, and Correction	
	Clinical Record Documentation and Forms	
	Dangerous and Unapproved Abbreviations	
	Downtime Process and Forms	

CATEGORY	DOCUMENT	ACTIONS TO TAKE
	Electronic Medical Record and Electronic Signatures	
	Health Information Plan	
	Information Systems (IS) Annual Evaluation	
	IS Security	
	Medical Record Order and Organization	
	Retention, Preservation, and Destruction of Records	
	System Logical Map	
Medical Staff and Allied Health Practitioners	Allied Health Professional Credentialing Policy	
	Clinical Privileging Profiles	
	Credentialing File Format and Order	
	Credentialing File Forms	
	Medical Staff Bylaws	
	Medical Staff Health and Impaired Practitioner Policy	
	Medical Staff Rules and Regulations	
	Practitioner Peer Review	
	Practitioner Quality File Format and Order	
	Practitioner Quality Profiles for Reappointment	
Medications	Contract Pharmacist Oversight	
	Controlled Substance Administration	

CATEGORY	DOCUMENT	ACTIONS TO TAKE
	Drug Enforcement Agency (DEA) Certificate	
	Formulary	
	Inventory and Counts	
	Medication Administration Record	
	Medication Dispensing System	
	Medication Management and Administration	
	Medication Samples	
	Reconciliation of Medications	
	State Regulations and Reporting	
Patient Discharge and Transfer	911 and emergency medical services (EMS) Process	
	Against Medical Advice Discharge and Documentation	
	Emergency Medical Treatment and Active Labor Act (EMTALA) Policy	
	Patient Discharge and Instructions	
	Refusal of Treatment Documentation	
	Transfer Clinical Form	
	Transfer Consent Form	
	Transfer Documents for Receiving Facility	
Quality: Clinical and Operational Improvement	Annual Evaluation of Quality Program	
	Center of Excellence Programs	

CATEGORY	DOCUMENT	ACTIONS TO TAKE
	Certification Programs	
	Glossary	
	Logs: medication refrigerator, nutrition refrigerator, warmers, hygrometers, biologicals, expired medications and supplies, crash carts, malignant hyperthermia, medication emergency boxes, operating room (OR)/procedure room.	
	Metrics and Scorecard	
	Material Safety and Data Sheets	
	Pay For Performance Studies/Measures	
	Quality Plan	
	Scientific Methodology Worksheet (i.e., plan, do, check, act [PDCA])	
Risk Management And Prevention	Action Plan for Risk Reduction	
	Correct Site, Patient, and Verification Process—Per World Health Organization Standards	
	Drug Reaction Report	
	Failure mode and effects analysis (FMEA) Format and Plan	
	Informed Consent	
	Internal Review Community Board Process for Off-Label Procedures/Medications/Treatment and Consent Forms and Reporting	
	Medication Error Form	

CATEGORY	DOCUMENT	*ACTIONS TO TAKE*
	Occurrence Form	
	Risk Management Annual Evaluation	
	Risk Management Assessment and Surveillance	
	Risk Management Plan	
	Root Cause Analysis	
	Self-Reported Sentinel Event	
	Sentinel Event	

Appendix B:
Quality Glossary

accountable care organization (ACO): Part of the healthcare reform initiative 2010. A local network of healthcare providers that can manage the full continuum of care of patients, with the goal of improving health quality outcomes and reducing healthcare costs. It is believed by some that an ACO could change the healthcare system because ACO healthcare provider participants would receive payment for improving the quality of healthcare and reducing costs.

ADR: Adverse drug reaction.

aggregate: Pertaining to an entire number or quantity of something; the total amount or complete whole. An aggregate data indicator is a performance measure based on collection and aggregation of data about many events or phenomena. The events or phenomena may be desirable or undesirable, and the data may be reported as a continuous variable or a discrete variable. The two major types of aggregate data indicators are rate-based indicators (also called discrete variable indicators) and continuous variable indicators.

algorithm: A step-by-step problem-solving procedure; especially an established recursive computational procedure. Trustworthy clinical care pathways are algorithms designed using geometry and applied statistical methods. An algorithm can be graphed as a flow diagram.

Ambulatory Surgery Center (ASC): Any distinct entity that operates exclusively for the purpose of providing surgical services to patients not requiring hospitalization and in which the expected duration of services would not exceed 24 hours following an admission.

ANOVA: Analysis of variance. A basic statistical technique for analyzing experimental data. It subdivides the total variation of a data set into meaningful component parts associated with specific component parts associated with specific sources of variation in order to test a hypothesis on the parameters of the model or to estimate variance components. There are three models of ANOVA—fixed, random, and mixed. Can be Excel based through a single-factor experiment with two levels of the factor, where the factor is mortar formulation and the two levels are the two different formulation methods. P values are used in regression analysis studies.

ARRA: American Recovery and Reinvestment Act of 2009.

attribute data: Includes percents, number of departments, affects, counts, or counts per department, for example. It is yes/no or go/no-go data.

benchmark: A point of reference or standard by which something can be measured, compared, or judged, as in benchmarks of performance. It is a standard unit for the basis of comparisons; that is, a universal unit that is identified with sufficient details so that other similar classifications can be compared as being above, below, or comparable to the benchmark.

brainstorming: A technique that generates a great deal of ideas in a short period of time.

causal (causation): The relating of causes to the effects they produce.

cause-and-effect diagram: Also known as the Ishikawa diagram or fishbone diagram. This tool helps to identify the x variables that contribute to the outcome, or Y variable. Can have defined categories, or one can affinitize the information received into like categories. Defined categories are typically people, methods, machines, materials, and environment.

clinical pathway: A course followed by a process. Clinical pathways establish high standards through the use of algorithms, recursion, computation, and graphed statistical pictures that confirm or refute the wisdom of intervention decisions.

common cause variation: Causes of variation that are inherent in a process over time. The effect of every outcome of the process and everyone working in the process. Also known as random patterns or chance variation.

computerized provider order entry (CPOE): CPOE is the process of providers inputting orders directly into an electronic medical record.

cost of poor quality: This goes along with cost of quality (COQ). It is the cost of failing to produce and deliver 100% quality to customers based on their expectations.

control chart: A chart that has upper and lower control limits containing values of some statistical measure for a time series of sample data or subgroup data. The data is plotted. The chart usually shows a central line, such as a mean or median, to help detect trends and variation patterns.

correlation coefficient: Determines the degree of association between two variables.

- R = –1.0 strong negative; when *X* increases, *Y* decreases
- R = –0.5 slight negative; when *X* increases, *Y* generally decreases
- R = 0 no correlation; the two variables are independent
- R = +.5 slight positive; when *X* increases, *Y* generally increases
- R = + 1.0 strong positive; when *X* increases, *Y* increases

CRUD: Complexity, rework, unnecessary steps, and delays.

crystal ball: A user-friendly, graphically oriented forecasting and risk analysis program that takes the uncertainty out of decision making.

culture: Culture is based on a family of employees who are connected by a web of common beliefs, shared commitments, and collective memories. It is a covenantal community rather than an organization.

cube: An analysis cube is produced when three or more factors, each set at two levels, are arranged orthogonally. A square is produced when two factors, each set at two levels, are arranged orthogonally.

customer: One who regularly, customarily, or repeatedly makes purchases of, or has business dealings with, a provider of a product or services. A receiver or beneficiary of an output of a process (service or product), either internal or external to an organization, such as a hospital.

data: Factual information. In science, facts are represented as numbers. Values derived from experiments are the foundation for reasoned analysis. Because all data vary, numbers must always be evaluated using an applied probability reference time.

data mining: To harvest data. To obtain core data elements that provide the highest level of value to the organization.

deduction: A method of mathematical reasoning that goes from the general to the specific or from a premise to a conclusion. Geometry provides the reliable line of logic for deduction.

dimension: Attributes of organizational performance that are related to organizations "doing the right things" (that is, appropriateness, availability, and efficacy) and "doing things well" (that is, continuity, effectiveness, efficiency, respect and caring, safety, and timeliness). Performance dimensions are definable, measurable, and improvable.

DMAIC: The methodology used for Six Sigma: Define, Measure, Analyze, Improve, and Control.

EHR: Electronic health record.

FMEA: Failure modes and effects analysis. This is a systematic method for documenting potential failure modes, determining effects, identifying causes of failures, developing a plan, and then taking action based on team decisions. This is used in all safety programs for healthcare and in the world of business and industry.

force field analysis: Analyzes the driving and restraining forces in a situation.

Gemba: The actual or real place. It's where work gets done and value is created for the customer.

HAC: Healthcare-acquired condition.

Healthcare Quality Improvement Act of 1986 (HCQIA): Protects the public from incompetent physicians by allowing those physicians on peer review committees to communicate in an open and honest environment and thus weed out incompetent physicians, without the specter of a retaliatory lawsuit by the reviewed physician. The Health Care Quality Improvement Act of 1986 was enacted to reduce medical errors. However, it has backfired and been used as a sword by privileging/credentialing committees of hospitals and other organizations to restrict or deny medical staff membership and privileges. Many times these actions are taken based on economic or political reasons, not quality of care decisions.

histogram: Graphical display of tabular frequency distribution for a sample or population of data.

HITECH: The Health Information Technology for Economic and Clinical Health Act.

induction: A method of mathematical reasoning in which a conclusion is reached about all members of a given set by examining just a few members of that set. Induction remains the only process by which essentially new knowledge comes into the world. Specifically, this form of reasoning is now known as statistical thinking. For example, a case in which a physician reaches a conclusion by observing a patient's reaction to a therapeutic maneuver.

I pass the baton: Hand-off communication tool that stands for Introduce, Patient, Assessment, Situation, Safety, the Background, Actions, Timing, Ownership, and Next.

sentinel event: Unanticipated event in a healthcare setting resulting in death or serious physical or psychological injury.

kanban: Japanese word for a method of inventory control.

Kano Model: A methodology to analyze customer needs by reviewing what displeases customers, what satisfies, and what delivers the *Wow* factor, the true delighters.

LASA: Acronym for *look-alike sound-alike*; refers to common medications that can be interchanged in error.

MDRO: Multidrug-resistant organism.

mean: The arithmetic average of a set of data.

median: The value falling in the middle of a data set once the data is sorted in order from ascending to descending.

N: Sample size.

nominal group technique: A decision-making tool that is an alternative to brainstorming as it takes everyone's ideas and opinions into account.

normal distribution: In probability theory and statistics, the normal distribution, or Gaussian distribution, is an absolutely continuous probability distribution. It is often described as variables that cluster around the mean. It is characterized by two parameters, the mean and the standard deviation sigma. It is a bell-shaped curve with a single peak, symmetrical about the center line, the mean, defined by a data set or a population.

occurrence screen: A list of triggering events that are reportable for quality review.

Pareto chart: Pareto analysis is the application of the principle of determining which few steps in a process are vital or most important and taking action to alter or reinforce those steps rather than the many other incidental steps in the process. A Pareto chart is a special form of vertical bar graph that displays the relative importance of all the data and is used to direct efforts to the largest improvement opportunity by highlighting the vital few in contrast to the many others.

PDCA: The plan, do, check, act cycle. A planning and improvement methodology in which improvements are planned and tested for feasibility.

performance improvement: The study and adaptation of functions and processes to increase the probability of achieving desired outcomes; the third segment of a performance measurement, assessment, and improvement system. Performance Improvement is the language of the Joint Commission.

PI: Process improvement or process identification. The Joint Commission uses PI for performance improvement. The common term used in healthcare is quality, or quality improvement.

Picker Institute: The Picker/Commonwealth Program for Patient-Centered Care was established in 1987 at Boston's Beth Israel Hospital and the Harvard Medical School to promote an approach to hospital, ambulatory, and health services focusing on the patient's needs and concerns, as the patient defines them, and to explore models of care that make the experience of the care process more humane. The program defines seven dimensions of patient-centered care in the inpatient and ambulatory setting: respect for patients' values, preferences, and expressed needs; coordination and integration of care; information, communication, and education; physical comfort; emotional support and alleviation of fear and anxiety; involvement of family and friends; and transition and continuity.

poka-yoke: The first step to mistake proofing a process or a system (Japanese term).

PQRI: Physician Quality Reporting Initiative quality data set collected in an ambulatory care environment.

probability: A number that expresses the likelihood of an event occurring or not occurring. Zero is the number used to describe an impossible event. One is the number used to symbolize a certain event. Binary numbers, 0 and 1, are the foundation for computing as well as probability.

process: A series of actions, changes, or functions that bring about a result. Flow diagrams are the indispensable tool for describing process flows. Probabilities summarized with control charts and analysis of variance cubes define process qualities.

quality assurance: All planned or systematic actions necessary to provide adequate confidence that a service or product will satisfy given requirements for quality. Medicare standards refer to quality assurance instead of performance improvement or other quality terms.

quality control: The process through which actual performance is measured; the performance is compared with goals, and the difference is acted on. The use of operational techniques and statistical methods to measure and predict quality.

quality function deployment: A method of evaluating a process or a system, and how it impacts the customer's expectations.

queue: Time that a product or service waits to get worked on. Associated with waiting.

range: Difference between the largest data value and the smallest data value in a data set.

RCA: Root cause analysis is a problem-solving technique used to identify underlying causes and contributing factors.

SBAR: A hand-off communication technique; stands for situation, background, assessment, and recommendation or request.

scientific methods: The principles and empirical processes of discovery and demonstration considered characteristic of or necessary for scientific investigation, generally involving the observation of phenomena, the formulation of a hypothesis concerning the phenomena, experimentation to demonstrate the truth or falseness of the hypothesis, and a conclusion that validates or modifies the hypothesis.

shift: A change in the process; for example, a shift in the process average for length of stay would mean the average changed direction, either up or down.

sigma: A Greek letter that represents the standard deviation: σ.

simulation studies: A process-engineering tool for improving business practices. Process Model is an example of a product that is available that combines simple flowcharting technology with powerful simulation capability to bring flowcharts to life through graphical animation.

SIPOC: A Six Sigma tool used to identify a high-level picture of a process that depicts how a specific process services customers.

Six Sigma (6σ): A two-character summary of an international method that uses statistics to compare products and services differing in complexity and nature. Also known as world-class quality—3.4 defects per million opportunities.

special cause variation: The output of a process that is not stable or random. *See* common cause variation.

stability: The absence of special causes of variation. Can refer to being in statistical control.

statistical process control: Statistical charts based on numerical measurements that become a picture of a process over time.

standard deviation: Positive square root of the variance—a measure of the dispersion about the mean of a data set.

subject knowledge: Information not readily quantified or measured, such as personal opinions, values, concepts, and social relationships.

System: Composed of the interacting, interrelated, or interdependent elements that form a complex whole. Work processes form a work system. A system is a network of structures or channels for communication. Any system can be best described and analyzed with geometry.

TeamSTEPPS®: Evidence-based teamwork system to improve teamwork and communication skills among healthcare professionals.

upper control limit (UCL): The UCL of a control chart calculated based on the average range (within subgroup) and the grand mean (between subgroups) of the data.

Value Added (VA): VA is a lean term that denotes an action or process steps that add value to a service, product, or process, in terms of what the customer values.

variable: Any item, such as a quantity, attribute, phenomenon, or event that can have different values. Examples are length in millimeters, time in minutes, and temperature in degrees. They vary as in a variable number of factors. It is referred to as x values or independent variables.

variance: Describes the spread or dispersion of the probability associated with a data set: σ^2. One can add variances, but you cannot add standard deviations.

voice of the customer: Refers to Noriaki Kano's model of the three levels of customer knowledge.

World Class Quality: Refers to 3.4 defects per million opportunities. It is quality based on the measure of goodness and the ability to exceed customer expectations. A World Class Quality company can say they spend less than 10 percent of their profit on rework, waste, nonvalue-added steps, and delays. This company would be competitive, a leader in their field.

XmR (Individual and Moving Range or IR) Control Chart: A graphic display of data in the order that they occur with statistically determined upper and lower limits of expected common-cause variation. A control chart is used to indicate special causes of variation, to monitor a process for maintenance, and to determine if process changes have had the desired effect.

Sources

Certified Six Sigma Black Belt Primer. West Terre Haute, IN: Quality Council of Indiana, 2001. http://www.qualitycouncil.com.

Gerteis, Margaret, et al. *Through the Patient's Eyes: Understanding and Promoting Patient-Centered Care.* San Francisco, CA: Jossey-Bass Inc., 1993.

Graban, Mark. *Lean Hospitals: Improving Quality, Patient Safety, and Employee Satisfaction.* New York: CRC Press. Taylor and Francis Group. A Productivity Press Book, 2009.

LSS Primer. West Terre Haute, IN: Quality Council of Indiana, April 2, 2007. http://www.qualitycouncil.com.

Montgomery, Douglas G. *Design and Analysis of Experiments.* New York: John Wiley and Sons, 1997.

O'Leary, Margaret, et al. *Lexicon Dictionary of Health Care Terms, Organizations, and Acronyms for the Era of Reform.* Oakbrook Terrace, IL: Joint Commission on the Accreditation of Healthcare Organizations (JCAHO), 1994.

Sloan, Daniel, and Guinane, Carole S. *Analyzing Clinical Care Pathways: 3-Dimensional Tools for Quality Outcomes Measurement and Improvement.* Chicago: McGraw-Hill, 1999.

Appendix C: Quality Reporting Measures

Reporting Process	Source	Assignment	J	F	M	A	M	J	J	A	S	O	N	D
Report Card Overall														
Quality Control														
Lab—include waived testing														
Respiratory Therapy—medication boxes														
Pharmacy														
Radiology—crash carts, medication boxes														
Nuclear Medicine—waste, use, keys														
All Patient Refrigerator Temps														
All Warmer Temps														
All Crash Cart and drug box Checks														
All Procedure Cart Logs														
Malignant Hyperthermia cart/supply logs														

Latex Allergy Logs—if have a cart or kit							
Trach Set, C-Section Set, and other required sets mandated by some state standards							
Tissue and Patient Logs—state and Medicare mandated for some programs							
Tissue Storage and Issuance: daily temperature logs, alarms, emergency backup and incoming tissue log							
If called in for off-hour cases—carts, med boxes, etc. checked							
Patient Rights / Organizational Ethics							
Patient Satisfaction							
Informed Consent—includes sterilization consent for Medicaid							
Advance Directives							

Reporting Process	Source	Assignment	J	F	M	A	M	J	J	A	S	O	N	D
Pain Management, Assessment, Reassessment														
Patient/Family Complaint Resolution														
Abuse—know your state standards regarding compliance														
Procurement / Donation of Organs / Tissue														
Effectiveness of the organ procurement program														
Ethics Report—could be minutes that go forward														
Research—audits or medical record reviews														
Care of Patient														
Anesthesia (adverse events)														

Adverse events or patterns of adverse events during moderated or deep sedation and anesthesia use. Analysis performed.					
Operative & Invasive Procedures—Milliman and/or Interqual Appropriateness Reviews					
All major discrepancies between preoperative and postoperative (including pathologic) diagnoses. Analysis performed					
Patient selection, preparation, education					
Procedure performance and postprocedure monitoring					
Tissue Review (to include normal organ removal)					
Adverse reactions to tissue or donor infections					

Reporting Process	Source	Assignment	J	F	M	A	M	J	J	A	S	O	N	D
Blood and Blood Product Administration Reviews														
Ordering, distributing/ dispensing, administering, monitoring, transfusion reactions														
All confirmed transfusion reactions, if applicable to the hospital. Analysis performed.														
Restraint and Seclusion														
Timeliness Studies—Reports, testing, TAT (turnaround time)														
Contract Services quality— Dialysis, Chaplain, Social Services, PT, OT, RT, Speech, Stress Testing, Infection Prevention, Nutrition, etc.														
Interqual and Milliman— Appropriateness of admission														
Avoidable Days and Denials														

AMA or Transfer						
Clinical Pathway/Care Plan Review/Revisions/Data						
Leadership						
One Level of Care: Patients with comparable needs receive the same standard of care, treatment, and services.						
Implementation of the budget and, as appropriate, the long-term capital expenditure plan is monitored.						
Clinical Practice Guidelines—Required if approved to use in organization						
Specific flow process indicators: available supply of patient beds, space; efficiency of patient care, treatment, and service areas; safety of patient care, treatment, and service areas; support service areas that impact patient flow.						

Reporting Process	Source	Assignment	J	F	M	A	M	J	J	A	S	O	N	D
Medication Management														
Medication Use Standards; patient info at point of ordering; selection, procurement and storage; QC on storage, security/accessibility of emergency meds														
All serious adverse drug events.														
All significant medication errors, if applicable and as defined by the hospital. Analysis performed.														
Ordering, distributing/ dispensing, administering, monitoring, medication errors, adverse drug reactions, DUE, narcotic waste and witnessing														
Credentialing: Physicians and AHP														
Expired licenses, certification, and mandatory requirements														

Timeliness of appointment/ reappointment										
Allied Health Peer Review										
Contracted Medical Staff Peer Review										
Medical Staff Peer Review										
Physician Proctoring Studies										
TB Screen										
Quality Profiles for Reappointment										
Human Resources/Education—employees/contract/volunteers/agency/medical staff										
Staffing Effectiveness and Staffing Effectiveness Issues. Analysis Performed.										
Request to not participate in care										
Competency assessments, skills checklist, report to the governing body										

Reporting Process	Source	Assignment	J	F	M	A	M	J	J	A	S	O	N	D
Orientation for: employees, contract workers, registry staff, volunteers, physicians, AHP														
Employee Satisfaction														
Physician Satisfaction														
Staffing and acuity levels assessed														
Completion/currency of: licenses, certificates, registrations, and evaluations														
Needs assessment for: Employees														
Medical Staff														
Patients														
Families														
CME Education based on PI findings														
Registry evaluations														

Education : Patient/Family

Appropriate consultation timely—i.e., dietary, diabetes, cardiovascular disease											
Patient Education											

Environment of Care

Mandatory Education—employee, physicians, contract, allied health											
Quality Measures											
Surveillance rounds—integrates infection control and patient safety											
Hazardous Conditions—Analysis Performed											
Statement of Conditions or other Documents											

Infection Prevention

USP—NF 797 infection control											

Reporting Process	Source	Assignment	J	F	M	A	M	J	J	A	S	O	N	D
Infection prevention measures and surveillance results														
Comparative Performance														
Pay for Performance Measures														
Medicare Suggested measures														
State PRO data														
Benchmarking Studies														
Risk Management: High-Risk Population														
Deaths and Autopsies														
Arrests and Resuscitation Process/Outcomes														
Litigation														
Sentinel Event Alert and Response to Alert														
Sentinel Event/RCA														
High-Risk Populations/Activities														

Against Medical Advice Discharge													
Return to ED 24 hr after Discharge													
Readmits within 31 days													
Unplanned return to OR													
Unplanned admission from outpatient to inpatient setting													
Renal failure secondary to contrast utilization													
Unexpected increase in patient acuity assignment													
Adverse reaction to tissue or donor infections													
Transfer to another facility													
Information Management													
Needs assessment													
Knowledge-based assessments as per IM plan													

Reporting Process	Source	Assignment	J	F	M	A	M	J	J	A	S	O	N	D
Medical Records Management														
Medical Record Review: clinical pertinence, timeliness, compliance with policies on: signature/date/time, legibility, completion														
Delinquencies														
Medicare record completion items														
Accreditation/Medicare/State/CAP Survey														
Findings from surveys														
Patient Safety														
Patient Satisfaction Survey question about safety														
Patient Safety Goals and Measures														
Patient Safety Issues, Root Cause Analysis, Common-Cause Analysis, Sentinel Events														

Plans, Appraisals, Approvals									
Quality Plan Yearly Update and Goals									
Quality Plan Annual Appraisal									
Information Management Plan Yearly Update									
Information Management Plan Annual Appraisal									
Patient Safety Yearly Update									
Patient Safety Annual Appraisal									
Environment of Care Plans Yearly Update									
Environment of Care Plans Effectiveness Evaluation									
Risk Management Plan Yearly Update									

Reportinwwg Process	Source	Assignment	J	F	M	A	M	J	J	A	S	O	N	D
Risk Management Annual Appraisal														
UR and Case Management Plan Update														
UR and Case Management Yearly Appraisal														
Infection Prevention Plan Update														
Infection Prevention Plan Yearly Appraisal														
Strategic Plan Approval														
Scope of Care and Service/Plan for Patient Care—annual review and approval														

Appendix D: Infection Prevention Plan Example

(Insert Year Plan is Effective)
(Insert Name of Facility and Scope of Services)
(Include Risk Assessment with Plan)

The Infection Control and Prevention Program is a multifaceted program that complies with current Medicare, licensing and accreditation standards, Occupational Safety and Health Administration (OSHA) regulations, other regulatory agency requirements, (insert name of FACILITY and the STATE in which facility is located).

Vision

To promote disease prevention and the reduction of healthcare-associated infections through the implementation of infection prevention principles throughout the continuum of care.

Mission

1. Provide quality patient care delivery free of infectious outcomes.
2. Make a contribution to the organization by ensuring safety, health, and welfare for all clients and healthcare workers in an economically sound, effective manner.
3. Foster increased participation, knowledge, and responsibility of each healthcare worker and patient in the Infection Control and Prevention Program.

Goals

1. Limiting unprotected exposure to pathogens.
2. Limiting the transmission of infections associated with procedures.
3. Limiting the transmission of infections associated with the use of medical equipment, devices, and supplies.
4. Improving compliance with hand hygiene guidelines.
5. Conduct surveillance for items with a mitigated score of 12 or higher or that are mandated by law.

Mitigated Score	Event and Risk	Goals	Strategies	Rationale for Strategy	Case Finding and Surveillance Methodology	Risk Adjustment	Types of Rates Generated	Method of Analysis	Reporting Body and Frequency
	Hand hygiene	100% compliance in all areas		CDC, WHO, CMS	Observation and Secret Shoppers		% compliance = # of observed compliance/# of opportunities * 100	Compared to goal and historical data	Infection Prevention and Governing Body committees at least quarterly
	Critical Instrument (high-level disinfectant)	Prevent lapses in high-level disinfection of semicritical instruments	Process surveillance at least quarterly in all areas; high-level disinfecting (HLD) probes or scopes	CDC, WHO, CMS	Visit each area using HLD for scopes/probes at least quarterly to observe HLD		Compliance: # of steps successfully completed/# of total steps * 100	Compare each unit to past performance	Infection Prevention and Governing Body committees at least quarterly
	MRSA	Maintain rate below 0.20					# of patients with MRSA/ patient visits * 100		Infection Prevention and Governing Body committees at least quarterly

Mitigated Score	Event and Risk	Goals	Strategies	Rationale for Strategy	Case Finding and Surveillance Methodology	Risk Adjustment	Types of Rates Generated	Method of Analysis	Reporting Body and Frequency
	Instrument Sterilization	Ensure instruments are safe for use on patients. Decrease the number of false positive Biological Indicators in CSS.	Report all positive biological indicators. Explore possible causes with manager follow up to ensure all mitigation completed.	CDC, WHO, CMS	Monthly sterilizer reports			Database	Infection Prevention and Governing Body committees at least quarterly
	Outbreaks	Identify, investigate, and mitigate outbreaks 100% of the time.	Investigate occurrences that are greater than expected.	CDC, WHO, CMS				Track by incident and analyze and trend over time	Infection Prevention and Governing Body committees at least quarterly

Influenza Deaths	Indentify, investigate, and report deaths due to influenza to the Health Department 100% of the time	Per state law, report all deaths to local Health Department.					Infection Prevention and Governing Body committees at least quarterly
MRSA	Identify all health care facility–acquired MRSA infections in outpatients.	Best practice to reduce					Infection Prevention and Governing Body committees at least quarterly
BBP exposures	To reduce occupational exposures to blood/body fluids	Employee Health, manager, or responsible staff member	OSHA Law	Employee Health reports all occupational injuries.	Track all exposures by type and job class.	Compare to historical data	Infection Prevention and Governing Body committees at least quarterly

Mitigated Score	Event and Risk	Goals	Strategies	Rationale for Strategy	Case Finding and Surveillance Methodology	Risk Adjustment	Types of Rates Generated	Method of Analysis	Reporting Body and Frequency
	Employee exposure to TB	Prevent employee exposures to TB patients 100% of the time.	Educate staff on signs and symptoms and precautions.	CDC, CMS	Staff or manager notifies IP or EH of potential exposure to TB patients.			Case-by-case basis	Infection Prevention and Governing Body committees at least quarterly
	Pandemic influenza	Follow/ revise pandemic plan as needed.	Continue to update pandemic plan as needed.	CDC, CMS	NA	NA	NA	NA	Infection Prevention and Governing Body committees at least quarterly

Appendix E:
Risk Assessment

EVENT & Rationale A-History B-Geographic Risk C-Literature Based	PROBABILITY 0 = NA 1 = LOW 2 = MED	IMPACT 0 = NA 1 = LOW 2 = MED	Current Quality Initative 15-National 10-Facility	RISK SCORE Probability + Impact + QI	MITIGATION 1-Policy/ Procedure 1-Surveillance/ Feedback 2-Targeted Initiatives	Mitigated Score Risk- Mitigation	Required	Indicator for Plan Year Yes No UC - Under
TJC National Patient Safety Goals								
Example: Hand Hygiene/ A, C	1	2	15	18	4	14	✓	Yes
Surgical Site Infections								
Complete if applicable								
Device-Related Infections								
High-level disinfection of endoscopes and probes								

Epidemiologically Significant Organisms									
Outbreaks									
Influenza deaths/ B, C									
Employee Exposures to Communicable Diseases									
BBP exposures / A, C									
Emerging Pathogens									
Pandemic Influenza/ C									
Environmental Condition									
TBA									
Specialty Services									
Flash sterilization / A									

Appendix F: Medical Record Review Criteria Audit

FOR ALL AMBULATORY SURGERY PATIENTS
☐ Patient identification, including name, birth date on record
☐ Patient arrival mode and time of arrival
☐ All entries legible
☐ All entries dated and timed
☐ Informed consent signed
☐ Documentation of consent risk and benefits noted on record as applicable
☐ Consent includes patient ID, patient name, procedure description, name of licensed, signature of patient or legal guardian, date and time the consent was obtained, signature and professional designee witnessing the consent
☐ Signed admission consent is in the chart
☐ All physician orders dated, timed, and signed
☐ Correlation between diagnosis and procedure and postprocedure findings documented
☐ Pain assessment documented for both acute and chronic initial and follow-up

☐	All entries dated and authenticated according to policy
☐	Verbal orders are dated and authenticated within defined time frame. Read back and verification noted.
☐	Time out is observed and documented prior to all procedures
☐	For applicable procedures, site marking conducted prior to procedure according to policy
☐	Allergies, intolerance, and drug adverse reactions documented
☐	Patient release of information signed
☐	Patient rights and advance directive given
☐	Advanced directive information is completed prior to informed consent signature
☐	Documentation of advance directive on chart or option to complete advance directive
☐	Evidence of advance directive in plan of care
☐	Fall risk documented
☐	Blood and blood products administered are clearly documented as per policy
PRIOR TO DAY of SURGERY	
☐	Complete nursing assessment (Plan of Care) in patient chart
☐	Patients identified as high risk for anesthesia, preadmission visit completed and on chart
☐	Documentation of bill of rights and advance directive options given to patient prior to day of surgery
☐	Translation policy followed and documentation of consent as applicable
ANESTHESIA	
☐	A signed anesthesia consent on chart
☐	Preanesthesia assessment is documented. Must be performed and documented 48 hours prior to surgery.
☐	Documentation of ASA classification prior to anesthesia

▢	Preop plan for anesthesia is recorded
▢	Prior to induction, patient is reevaluated for anesthesia
▢	Patient's physiological status is measured and assessed during anesthesia
▢	Post-op anesthesia assessment documented in medical record, including cardiac function, BP and pulse rate, respiratory rate, airway patency, oxygen saturation, mental status, temperature, pain, nausea and vomiting, and postoperative hydrations
▢	Patient discharged by LIP from recovery area and documentation of discharge criteria being met
▢	Anesthesia operative orders, including medications, are signed, timed, and dated
▢	Intraoperative anesthesia record is complete.
▢	Intraoperative anesthesia record is complete and all pertinent events noted.
▢	The medication record conforms to practitioner's orders.
▢	Discharge medication education documentation
SURGEON or PHYSICIAN	
▢	History and Physical signed, dated, and timed, and completed within 30 days prior to surgery/procedure date
▢	Presurgical assessment completed upon admission according to state health and safety laws and facility policy
▢	Statement of impression since last H&P or admission
▢	The reasons for treatment are documented
▢	Surgical admission orders are signed, timed, and dated
▢	Operative report is documented immediately post-op and must include:
▢	Findings
▢	Procedures
▢	Specimen(s) removed
▢	Post-op diagnosis

☐	Name of surgeon/assistant
☐	Immediate postoperative note
☐	Clearance for surgery, procedure, or treatment
☐	All diagnostic and therapeutic procedures and test results such as pathology and lab, radiology
☐	Findings and techniques of the operation, including a pathologist's report on all tissues removed during surgery, except those exempted by the governing body
☐	Postoperative orders are signed, timed, and dated
☐	Discharge orders are written no earlier than 30 minutes prior to leaving
☐	Respiratory care is ordered by a physician as needed for the patient

NURSING

☐	Prior to the procedure, individualized nursing care plan
☐	The preprocedure flow sheet is completed and in the chart
☐	Perioperative/procedural plan
☐	Postoperative assessment process at a minimum
☐	Postoperative/procedural monitoring and documentation includes:
☐	Physiological status
☐	Mental status
☐	IV fluids administered
☐	Medications administered
☐	Impairments and functional status
☐	Pain and intensity and quality
☐	Blood and blood components
☐	Hand-off communication
☐	Drugs and biologicals documented
☐	Reassessment and patient response

☐	Allergies and ADRs documented
☐	Assessment for suspected abuse and neglect

PATIENT EDUCATION

☐	Education needs assessed and individualized
☐	Education documented
☐	Education as appropriate for pain, medical equipment use, medications, nutrition, community resources

PATIENT DISCHARGE

☐	Final disposition, condition, and follow-up instructions
☐	Discharge instructions for patients and families
☐	Discharge plan in place and signed
☐	Signed discharge order
☐	Patient discharged in company of responsible adult
☐	Documentation if emergency transfer, reason for transfer, patient stability, and acceptance by receiving facility

PEDIATRIC CARE

☐	As appropriate, assessment by age group
☐	Developmental age
☐	Length/height
☐	Head circumference
☐	Weight
☐	Immunization status
☐	Family guardian expectations

AMBULATORY CARE

☐	For continuing ambulatory care procedures:
☐	Known significant diagnosis and conditions

☐	Known significant operative and invasive procedures
☐	Known adverse and allergic drug reactions
☐	Medications known to be prescribed for and used by patients
PATIENT CALL BACK	
☐	Process to call patients 24 hours postdischarge

Appendix G: Safety Management Program

Purpose

The purpose of this plan is to establish, support, and maintain a safety program that is based on monitoring and evaluation of organizational experience, applicable state and federal regulations, and accepted practice within the healthcare industry.

Goal

The safety management plan goal is to provide a physical environment free of hazards and to manage staff activities to reduce the risk of injuries that could affect patients, employees, visitors, or other guests.

Objectives

This plan is based on the following objectives:

- Maintain and supervise all grounds, buildings, and equipment, including all activity areas used by patients.
- Ensure that emergency service areas are clearly marked and easily accessible.
- Establish a risk-assessment program that proactively evaluates the impact on patient and public safety of the buildings, grounds, equipment, occupants, and internal physical plant and systems.
- Provide a safety officer or designee, appointed by the leadership, who is qualified by experience or education; responsible for developing, implementing, and monitoring the facility or practices safety program; and responsible for

intervening whenever conditions exist that either pose an immediate threat to life or health or pose a threat of damage to equipment or buildings.

- Establish a safety committee to include representatives deemed appropriate per leadership. For small practices or centers this can consist of key personnel.
- Report and investigate all incidents that involve occupational illness and patient, employee, or visitor injury and property damage.
- Require facility safety policies and procedures that are distributed, practiced, and enforced.
- Review facility safety policies and procedures as frequently as necessary, but no less than annually.
- Promote an ongoing hazard surveillance program, including response to product safety recalls.
- Use safety training in the orientation of new employees and continuing education of employees.
- Require an annual plan and evaluation of the objectives, scope, performance, and effectiveness of the documented safety management plan.

Scope

This plan applies to outpatient surgery centers, ambulatory clinics, and physician offices and employees.

Policy Elements

Safety Management Policy Statement

The administration of the facility and its governing body believe in a strong commitment to the maintenance of a safe and sanitary environment for all patients, employees, and visitors. This commitment is evidenced by the development and support of the safety steering committee, composed of members that represent a cross section of the departments and services within the facilities (if appropriate and depending on the size of your facility and staff). This committee continues to lead us in the development of policies and programs that affect all areas and provide guidance in the safe performance of our duties.

Each employee is required to comply with safety and health standards and with the policies and procedures that apply to their specific job responsibilities in an effort to maintain a safe work environment. Any violation of policy may result in disciplinary action.

The safety committee is authorized, through the chair or the safety officer, to take action when a hazardous condition exists that could result in personal injury to individuals or damage to equipment or buildings.

Maintenance and Supervision of Grounds and Equipment

The safety committee or its designee will develop written policies and procedures to enhance safety within the facility and on the campus, monitor equipment and utility preventive maintenance and inspection procedures, and monitor the education and training of users to protect against failure or user error.

An environment tour will be made of the buildings and grounds of the facility to ensure maintenance, supervision, and safe use of these buildings and grounds by patients, staff, and visitors. Patient areas will be assessed a minimum of twice yearly, nonpatient areas a minimum of annually. All buildings shall comply with the appropriate provisions of the National Fire Protection Association's Life Safety Code, 2000. Consideration will be given to parking lots/structures and the security and safety needs of these facilities, activity and waiting areas, and special environmental conditions. Plans and policies will be developed and implemented to cover security, safety, and the functional needs of patients, visitors, and employees.

Risk Assessment

The safety management program, which proactively evaluates the impact of buildings, grounds, equipment, occupants, and internal physical systems on patient and public safety, is conducted by using incident reports, accident investigation, and reports from various agencies, such as insurance companies, state or county health agencies, and local fire and police departments.

Hazard Surveillance

An ongoing hazard surveillance program, including response to product safety recalls, shall be maintained and reported through the safety steering committee.

Examination of Safety Issues

All safety-related issues shall be examined by the safety committee. The safety committee will include representation from those areas deemed appropriate. Nonsupervisory employees will participate in activities of the safety program.

All members of the safety committee are appointed by the administration/safety officer or designee. The committee shall evaluate the safety management program compliance by evaluation at least annually.

Incident/Injury/Illness Reporting and Investigation

The safety committee/risk management committee or designee shall review all reports of accidents or injuries to patients, visitors, and other personnel. Summary reports of incidents shall include description of the incident, root cause, corrective actions taken, and preventive measures taken. Refer to the appropriate policies and procedures. The safety committee will establish an incident reporting system for investigating and evaluating all incidents reported and for documenting review of all such reports and actions taken.

Safety Officer/Designee

The safety officer and the safety committee are appointed by the leadership of the facility or clinic. Administration has delegated to the safety committee or officer the authority to take action when hazardous conditions or potential hazardous conditions exist that could result in personal injury, damage to equipment or damage to buildings. This delegated authority has been approved by the administration and is responsible for the following:

- Orientation and education of new and existing employees
- New employee orientation and continuing education to include general processes, area-specific safety, and job-related hazards
- Maintain patient and family involvement with safety
- Coordinate patient and employee educational activities
- Recommend purchases of safety equipment and suggestions for any necessary physical changes to improve safety conditions

Performance Improvement

The safety committee or designee shall meet quarterly or when necessary and record the activities. A review of the safety program's performance shall be conducted at least annually.

Performance indicators

The following indicators shall be utilized in evaluating the performance of the safety management program:

- Environmental health and safety
- Life safety management
- Emergency preparedness
- Security
- Hazardous wastes
- Infection prevention
- Equipment management
- Utilities management

Equipment Inspection, Preventive Maintenance, and Testing

Monitor equipment and utilities for preventive maintenance and inspection procedures and monitor education and training of users to protect against failure or user error. Log all safety recalls and action taken to correct defects.

Safety Policies and Procedures

The safety committee or responsible designee will develop written policies and procedures to enhance safety within the facility. All safety policies will be reviewed annually in accordance with facility policy. Any revisions, updates, or changes shall be submitted to the appropriate leader for approval. The ultimate responsibility for development and maintenance of current safety policies shall lie with the safety officer or designee for the facility.

Annual Evaluation

The effectiveness of the safety management program will be evaluated annually. Evaluation shall include all areas of safety management.

Responsibilities

Executive Leadership

To meet general and specific safety goals of the safety management plan, executive leadership shall appoint a safety officer(s) (chair of the safety steering committee) who is qualified to oversee the safety management program.

Safety Officer

- Provides oversight for the health and safety program at the facility

Management

- Enforces facility safety rules and regulations and documents all violations.
- Takes prompt corrective action when unsafe acts or conditions are observed.
- Ensures that the work environment is safe.
- Ensures that safety has been considered prior to the commencement of each task or function.
- Ensures, through instruction and surveillance, that each employee is aware that he or she is expected to work safely and that willful violations of safety rules will be cause for disciplinary actions, up to and including termination.
- Cooperates fully with safety officer/the safety steering committee in the promotion of safety activities. Seeks assistance from the safety officer relative to safe practices and procedures.
- Ensures that employees receive all required safety training and education. Assists in conducting training as needed.
- Instructs employees on emergency situations and expected actions.
- Complies with safety equipment and protective devices.
- Reports all injuries and accidents and evaluates causation.

All Employees

- Learn the safe and correct way to perform their assigned duties and shall ask their supervisor anything about which they are in doubt
- Perform their jobs in a safe and responsible manner
- Use required safety devices and use personal protective equipment
- Report any accident, personal injury, or patient complaint regarding the health or safety practices, no matter how slight, to their supervisor immediately
- Report any safety hazard
- Practice good housekeeping at all times; keep equipment, tools, materials, instruments, and work areas clean and orderly
- Attend all required safety-related training
- Know what actions to take in case of fire or other emergency situation in their work area(s)
- Comply with tobacco-free campus

Appendix H: Root Cause Analysis and Corrective Action Plan

Submitted by:
Date of event:
Day of week:
Time of day:
Date of submission:
(Completion is required within 45 days of the event.)

Location of event:

Staffing detail (include the skill mix, the staffing patterns, permanent versus contract staff):

Please describe what happened. Include job titles of involved personnel; no proper names. Include relevant events in a sequential timeline.

Flowchart of Event

Using the following key, draw a flowchart depicting what occurred. (Example tool: Microsoft Visio)

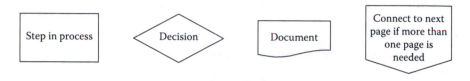

Figure H.1   Ambulatory surgery infection scorecard.

Arrow directs to the next symbol.

Contributing Factors and Root Cause

Include in each of following categories any factors or conditions that you feel contributed to the event.

Category	Contributing Factor	Explain
Staffing		
Policy		
Environment		
Human factors		
Current competence and training		
Equipment		
Availability of information		
Communication		
Culture/attitude		

Of the contributing factors, at what point did the event first perpetuate? Can this be affected by a process redesign or corrective plan of action? (What is the root cause?)

For each category, including factors that could have contributed to the event, what could have been done differently to account for the contributing factors? In other words, for each category, how can this be prevented in the future? (What are the proximate causes and how can they be corrected?)

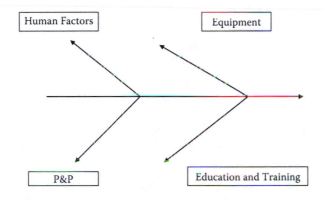

Figure H.2   Fishbone diagram—Illustration of contributing causes

Patient Outcome and Event Impact

What was the patient outcome? Did the patient suffer a permanent loss of function or death? (Review sentinel event policy.)

Were there controllable factors that contributed to the severity? If so, explain.

If this was a near miss, what prevented the event from occurring?

What is the action plan to prevent this from recurring?

Note: Follow your organization and state requirements for Peer Protection. Report safety events to leadership, regulatory, and governing bodies as outlined per policy and per organization Patient Safety Plan.

Appendix I: State Contacts for Ambulatory Licensing and Standards

Alabama

Alabama Association of Ambulatory Surgery Centers
1440 Highway Drive
Oxford, AL 36203
Phone: 256-241-2234
Fax: 256-241-2236
Website: http://www.aaasc.net/about-us/
Alabama Department of Public Health
The RSA Tower
201 Monroe Street
Montgomery, AL 36104
Phone: 334-206-5175
Website: http://www.adph.org/providers/Default.asp?id

Alaska

Department of Health and Social Services
Section of Certification and Licensing Administration
350 Main Street, Room 404
P.O. Box 110601
Juneau, AK 99811-0601
Phone: 907-269-3640
Website: http://www.hss.state.ak.us/dph/cl/default.htm

Arizona

Arizona Department of Health Services
Division of Licensing Services
150 N. 18th Avenue, 4th Floor
Phoenix, AZ 85007
Phone: 602-364-3030
Fax: 602-364-4764
Website: http://www.azdhs.gov/als/index.htm
Rules and Regulations: http://www.azsos.gov/public_services/Title_09/9-10.htm

Arkansas

Arkansas Department of Health
4815 West Markham Street
Little Rock, AR 72205
Phone: 501-661-2000 or 800-462-0599
Website: http://www.healthy.arkansas.gov/Pages/default.aspx

California

California Department of Public Health
Licensing and Certification
P.O. Box 997377, MS 3000
Sacramento, CA 95899-7377
Phone: 916-552-8700
Website: http://www.cdph.ca.gov/programs/LnC/Pages/LnC.aspx

Colorado

Colorado Department of Public Health and Environment
4300 Cherry Creek Drive
South Denver, CO 80222-1530
Phone: 303-692-2000
Website: http://www.cdphe.state.co.us/
Rules and Regulations: http://www.cdphe.state.co.us/regulations/healthfacilities/
10110120ambulatorysurgicalcenters.pdf

Connecticut

Connecticut Department of Public Health
Facility License and Investigations Section
410 Capitol Avenue, MS #12HFL
P.O. Box 340308
Hartford, CT 06134
Phone: 860-509-7444
Website: http://www.ct.gov/dph/taxonomy/ct_taxonomy.asp?DLN=46939&dph
Nav=|46939|

Delaware

Delaware Health and Social Services—Division of Public Health
Office of Health Facilities Licensing and Certification
417 Federal Street
Jesse Cooper Building
Dover, DE 19901
Phone: 302-744-4700
Fax: 302-739-6659
Website: http://dhss.delaware.gov/dhss/dph/hsp/hflc.html

Florida

Bureau of Health Facility Regulation
Hospital and Outpatient Services Unit
2727 Mahan Drive, Mail Stop #31
Tallahassee, FL 32308
Phone: 850-412-4549
Fax: 850-922-4351
Website:
http://www.fdhc.state.fl.us/mchq/Health_Facility_Regulation/Hospital_
Outpatient/ambulatory.shtml

Georgia

Georgia Department of Community Health
2 Peachtree Street, NW
Atlanta, GA 30303
Phone: 404-656-4507
Website: http://dch.georgia.gov/02/dch/home/0,2467,31446711,00.html

Hawaii

Hawaii State Department of Health
1250 Punchbowl Street
Honolulu, HI 96813
Website: http://hawaii.gov/health/permits/hospital/index.html
Rules and Regulations: http://gen.doh.hawaii.gov/sites/har/AdmRules1/11-95.pdf

Idaho

Department of Health and Administration
650 W. State St., Room 100
P.O. Box 83720
Boise, ID 83720-0003
Phone: 208-332-1824
Fax: 208-334-2307
Website: http://adm.idaho.gov/adminrules/rules/idapa16/16index.htm

Illinois

Illinois General Assembly
705 Stratton Building
Springfield, IL 62706
Phone: 217-782-3944
Website: http://www.ilga.gov/commission/jcar/admincode/077/07700205sections.html

Indiana

Indiana State Department of Health
Division of Acute Care
2 North Meridian Street, 4A
Indianapolis, IN 46204
Phone: 317-233-7474 (Acute Care Receptionist) or 317-233-1325 (ISDH Main Switchboard)
Website: http://www.in.gov/isdh/20132.htm

Iowa

Iowa Department of Public Health
Lucas State Office Building
321 E. 12th Street
Des Moines, IA 50319-0075
Phone: 515-281-4344
Fax: 515-281-4958
Website: http://www.idph.state.ia.us/adper/admin_review.asp

Kansas

Kansas Department of Health and Environment
1000 S.W. Jackson, Suite 200
Topeka, KS 66612-1365
Phone: 785-296-1240
Fax: 785-296-3075
Email: healthfacilities@kdheks.gov
Website: http://www.kdheks.gov/bhfr/regs/index.html
Rules and Regulations: http://www.kdheks.gov/bhfr/download/amb_sug_ctr_regs_04202001.pdf

Kentucky

Kentucky Cabinet for Health and Family Services
Office of Inspector General
275 East Main Street 5E-A
Frankfort, KY 40621
Phone: 502-564-2888
Fax: 502-564-6546
Website: http://chfs.ky.gov/os/oig/default.htm
Rules and Regulations: http://www.lrc.state.ky.us/kar/902/020/101.htm

Louisiana

Louisiana Department of Health and Hospitals
628 N. 4th Street
P.O. Box 629
Baton Rouge, LA 70821-0629
Phone: 225-342-9500
Fax: 225-342-5568
Website: http://www.dhh.louisiana.gov/
Rules and Regulations: http://www.dhh.louisiana.gov/offices/publications/pubs-112/asc_st_regs.pdf

Maine

Department of Health and Human Services
Licensing and Regulatory Services
State House Station
41 Anthony Avenue
Augusta, ME 04333
Phone: 207-287-9300 or 800-791-408
Website: http://www.maine.gov/dhhs/index.shtml
Rules and Regulations: http://www.maine.gov/dhhs/dlrs/licensing-rules.html

Maryland

Office of Health Care Quality
Department of Health and Mental Hygiene
Spring Grove Hospital Center
Bland Bryant Building
55 Wade Avenue
Catonsville, MD 21228
Phone: 410-402-8040 or 800-492-6005
Fax: 410-402-8277
Email: ohcqweb@dhmh.state.md.us
Website: http://dhmh.maryland.gov/ohcq/regulated_programs/ambulatory_care.htm

Massachusetts

Massachusetts Office of Health and Human Services
Division of Health Care Finance and Policy
2 Boylston St.
Boston, MA 02116
Phone: 617-988-3100
Website: http://www.mass.gov/?pageID=eohhs2agencylanding&L=4&L0= Home&L1=Government&L2=Departments+and+Divisions&L3=Division+of+ Health+Care+Finance+%26+Policy&sid=Eeohhs2
Rules and Regulations: http://www.mass.gov/?pageID=eohhs2modulechunk& L= 4&L0= Home&L1=Government&L2=Departments+and+Divisions&L3= Division+of+Health+Care+Finance+%26+Policy&sid=Eeohhs2&b=terminalco ntent&f=dhcfp_government_regs_related_pubs&csid=Eeohhs2#114_3_47

Michigan

Michigan Department of Community Health
Capitol View Building
201 Townsend Street
Lansing, MI 48913
Phone: 517-373-3740
Website: http://www.michigan.gov/mdch/0,1607,7-132-2946_5093---,00.html

Minnesota

Minnesota Office of the Revisor of Statutes
700 State Office Building
100 Rev. Dr. Martin Luther King Jr. Blvd.
St. Paul, MN 55155
Phone: 651-296-2868
TTY: 1-800-627-3529
Fax: 651-296-0569
Website: https://www.revisor.mn.gov/index.php
Rules and Regulations: https://www.revisor.mn.gov/rules/?id=4675

Mississippi

Mississippi State Department of Health
570 East Woodrow Wilson Drive
Jackson, MS 39216
Website: http://msdh.ms.gov/msdhsite/_static/30.html
Rules and Regulations: http://www.msdh.state.ms.us/msdhsite/_static/resources/109.pdf

Missouri

Missouri Department of Health and Senior Services
P.O. Box 570
Jefferson City, MO 65102
Phone: 573-751-6400
Fax: 573-751-6010
Website: http://www.dhss.mo.gov/Health/index.html
Rules and Regulations: http://www.sos.mo.gov/adrules/csr/current/19csr/9c30-30.pdf

Montana

Department of Public Health and Human Services
Quality Assurance Division
Licensure Bureau
2401 Colonial Drive, 2nd Floor
P.O. Box 202953
Helena, MT 59620-2953
Phone: 406-444-2676
Fax: 406-444-1742
Website: http://www.dphhs.mt.gov/qad/assistedliving/contactus.shtml

Nebraska

Nebraska Department of Health and Human Services
301 Centennial Mall South
Lincoln, NE 68509
Phone: 402-471-3121
Website: http://www.hhs.state.ne.us/licensing.htm

Nevada

Nevada Department of Health and Human Services
4126 Technology Way, Room 100
Carson City, NV 89706-2009
Phone: 775-684-4000
Website: http://dhhs.nv.gov/

New Hampshire

New Hampshire Department of Health and Human Services
Bureau of Health Facilities Administration
129 Pleasant St.
Concord, NH 03301-3852
Phone: 603-271-4592
Fax: 603-271-4968
Website: http://www.dhhs.state.nh.us/DHHS/BHFA/default.htm

New Jersey

New Jersey Department of Health and Senior Services
Division of Health Facilities Evaluation and Licensing
P.O. Box 360
Trenton, NJ 08625-0360
Phone: 609-292-7837
Toll-free in NJ: 1-800-367-6543
Website: http://www.state.nj.us/health/
Rules and Regulations: http://www.state.nj.us/health/healthfacilities/rules.shtml

New Mexico

New Mexico Department of Health
Division of Health Improvement
1190 S. St. Francis Dr.
Santa Fe, NM 87502
Phone: 505-827-2613 (main)
Phone: 505-476-9025 (Health Facility Licensing and Certification Bureau)
Website: http://dhi.health.state.nm.us/HFLC/hflc_regindex.php

New York

New York State Department of Health
Corning Tower
Empire State Plaza
Albany, NY 12237
Website: http://www.health.state.ny.us/

North Carolina

North Carolina Division of Health Service Regulation
2712 Mail Service Center
Raleigh, NC 27699-2712
Phone: 919-855-4620
Website: http://www.ncdhhs.gov/dhsr/index.html
Rules and Regulations: http://www.ncdhhs.gov/dhsr/testrules.htm

North Dakota

North Dakota Department of Health
Division of Health Facilities
600 East Boulevard Ave., Dept. 301
Bismarck, ND 58505-0200
Phone: 701-328-2352
Fax: 701-328-1890
Website: http://www.ndhealth.gov/HF//
Rules and Regulations: http://www.ndhealth.gov/HF/North_Dakota_Ambulatory_Surgical_Centers.htm

Ohio

Ohio Department of Health
Community Health Care Facilities and Services
246 N. High St.
Columbus, OH 43215
Phone: 614-995-7466
Website: http://www.odh.ohio.gov/
Rules and Regulations: http://www.odh.ohio.gov/rules/final/f3701-83.aspx

Oklahoma

Oklahoma State Department of Health
Medical Facilities Service—Facility Services Division
1000 N.E. 10th Street
Oklahoma City, OK 73117-1299
Phone: 405-271-6576
Fax: 405-271-1308
Email: medicalfacilities@health.ok.gov
Website:http://www.ok.gov/health/Protective_Health/Medical_Facilities_Service/Facility_Services_Division/index.html
Rules and Regulations: http://www.ok.gov/health/documents/MF%20Title%2063-2657%20ASC%20statutes%20through%202000.pdf

Oregon

Department of Human Services
Health Care Licensure and Certification
800 N.E. Oregon Street, Suite 305
Portland, OR 97232
Phone: 971-673-0540
Fax: 971-673-0556
Website: http://oregon.gov/DHS/ph/hclc/index.shtml
Rules and Regulations: http://arcweb.sos.state.or.us/rules/OARs_300/OAR_333/333_076.html

Pennsylvania

Pennsylvania Department of Health
Health and Welfare Building
8th Floor West
625 Forster Street
Harrisburg, PA 17120
Website: http://www.portal.state.pa.us/portal/server.pt/community/department_of_health_home/17457
Rules and Regulations: http://www.pacode.com/secure/data/028/subpartIVFtoc.html

Rhode Island

State of Rhode Island Department of Health
Office of Facilities Regulation
3 Capitol Hill
Providence, RI 02908
Website: http://www.health.ri.gov/programs/facilityregulation/

South Carolina

South Carolina Department of Health and Environmental Control
2600 Bull Street
Columbia, SC 29201
Phone: 803-898-DHEC (3432)
Website: http://www.scdhec.gov/regulatory.htm

South Dakota

South Dakota Department of Health
600 East Capitol Avenue
Pierre, SD 57501
Phone: 606-773-3361
Website: http://doh.sd.gov/Resources/Statute.aspx

Tennessee

Tennessee Department of Health
Health Care Facilities
220 Athens Way, Plaza 1 Metrocenter
Nashville, TN 37243
Phone: 615-741-7221 or 800-778-4504
Website: http://health.state.tn.us/HCF/applications.htm

Texas

Texas Department of State Health Services
Health Facility Licensing Program
1100 West 49th Street
Austin, TX 78756
Phone: 512-834-6646
Website: http://www.dshs.state.tx.us/HFP/rules.shtm#asc
Rules and Regulations: http://www.dshs.state.tx.us/HFP/PDF/Abulatory
Surgical/AmbulatorySurgicalCntRuleChpt135.pdf

Utah

Utah Department of Health
Bureau of Health Facility Licensing, Certification and Resident Assessment
P.O. Box 144103
Salt Lake City, UT 84114-4103
Phone: 801-538-6158 or 800-662-4157
Website: http://health.utah.gov/hflcra/rules.php
Rules and Regulations: http://www.rules.utah.gov/publicat/code/r432/r432-
500.htm

Vermont

Vermont Department of Health
108 Cherry Street
Burlington, VT 05402
Phone: 800-464-4343
Fax: 802-865-7754
Website: http://healthvermont.gov/regs/index.aspx

Virginia

Virginia Department of Health
The Office of Licensure and Certification
9960 Mayland Dr., Ste. 401
Richmond, VA 23233-1463
Website: http://www.vdh.virginia.gov/olc/

Washington

Washington State Department of Health
Facility Services Licensing
P.O. Box 47852
Olympia, WA 98504-7852
Phone: 360-236-2905
Fax: 360-236-2901
Website: http://www.doh.wa.gov/hsqa/fsl/HHHACS_AmbSurgCent.htm

West Virginia

Office of Health Facility Licensure and Certification
408 Leon Sullivan
Charleston, WV 25301
Phone: 304-558-0050
Website: http://www.wvdhhr.org/ohflac/Rules.aspx

Wisconsin

Wisconsin Department of Regulation and Licensing
P.O. Box 8935
Madison, WI 53708-8935
Phone: 877-617-1565
Website: http://drl.wi.gov/

Wyoming

Wyoming Department of Health
The Office of Health Care Licensing and Surveys
400 Qwest Bldg.
6101 Yellowstone Rd.
Cheyenne, WY 82002
Phone: 307-777-7123
Website: http://wdh.state.wy.us/ohls/ruleslist.html
Rules and Regulations: http://soswy.state.wy.us/Rules/RULES/5074.pdf

Appendix J: Patient Education Pathway Example

	General Information	Tests	Activity	Medications and Treatments	Diet	Discharge Planning
Pre-op	You are scheduled to have a _____ procedure today. You will be taken to the operating room and a nurse will be there to care for of you during the procedure. Your surgeon and an anesthesiologist will be present, with the surgeon performing the procedure and the anesthesiologist giving you medications and fluids during the procedure.	If you are a female, a urine pregnancy test will be completed prior to surgery.	Up as needed prior to surgery. Please inform the staff if you have a history of falling.	You will be weighed and the orders that your physician has written will be implemented. The anesthesiologist will complete an assessment.	You will not be allowed to eat or drink anything prior to surgery. An IV will be started.	You can ask for help with your discharge needs at any time. Please let your nurse know if you will need some information resources that are available to help you with your healing journey.

In Recovery	Family members are encouraged to participate in your care. It is important that you rest. Be sure to notify your nurse if you are experiencing pain.	Blood may be drawn if ordered.	When you are ready, your nurse will get you up and into a chair. You will also go for a short walk.	Medications will continue as needed. Oxygen will continue until your recovery process is complete. Your IV will be discontinued after your recovery process has progressed. You will need to urinate prior to going home.	If you do not vomit or have nausea, then you will be given water. Other fluids will be given as ordered by your physician.	Before you can go home, you will have gotten out of bed, into a chair, and walked. You will not have any nausea or vomiting. You will have urinated. Your discharge instructions will include diet, medications, activity, and follow-up appointments with your doctor.
Postoperative Long Term	It is important to keep all of your physician appointments. Follow your physician's plan of care.	Your physician may order lab tests or other tests.	Please follow all physician instructions for activity. Notify your physician immediately if you have pain, bleeding, or uncontrolled nausea and vomiting.	Your physician will determine what medications to send home with you and what medications should be continued as you progress.	You should continue on the prescribed diet at home.	Your physician is your caregiver for continuing care. Follow the instructions given to you.

Index